Financial Freedom for Women

Peter J. Prato Ph.D.
Rita Lynne Ph.D.

STRESS RESOURCE NETWORK PUBLISHING
PLEASANTON, CALIFORNIA

FINANCIAL FREEDOM FOR WOMEN

Text Copyright © 1999
Stress Resource Network, Inc.

All rights reserved. No part of this book may be reproduced or transmitted in any form or by any means, electronic or mechanical, including photocopying, recording or by any information storage and retrieval system, without permission in writing from the publishers. Inquiries should be addressed to the publishers:

Stress Resource Network, 699 Peters Avenue, Pleasanton, CA 94566
(925) 484-2330

Library of Congress Catalog Car Number: 99-97574

Publisher's Cataloging-in-Publication
(Provided by Quality Books, Inc.)

Prato, Peter J.
   Financial freedom for women / Peter J. Prato, Rita Lynne. – 1st ed.
   p. cm.
   Includes index.
   ISBN : 0-9676695-0-2

   1 . Women--Financial, Personal. 2. Women--Scholarships, fellowships, etc.--Directories.
   3. Scholarships--United States--Directories.
   I. Lynne, Rita. II. Title.

HG179.P73 2000   332.024'042
                                         QB199-1822

Printed in the United States of America by *Morris Publishing*
3212 East Highway 30 • Kearney, Nebraska 68847 • 800-650-7888

CONTENTS

Introduction 1
EDUCATION 9
   Ways to Increase Financial Aid 11
   Scholarships 17
   Grants 91
   Fellowships 161
   Awards 201
   Loans 215

BUSINESS 229
   How to Apply for a Loan 230
   Preparing a Business Loan 241
   Business Resources 251
   SBA Demonstration Programs 269
   National Association of Women Business Advocates 275
   National Score Women's Business Ownership
   Coordinators 281
   Venture Capital Clubs/
   Venture Capital Funders/ SBA 285
   SBA Office of Women's Business Ownership 293
   Small Business Development Centers 315

GENERAL WELFARE 327
   General Resources 329

ARTS AND CULTURE 357
   General Resources 359

OTHER RESOURCES 381
   Mutual Funds 383
   Retirement Accounts 389
   Stock Market/Bond Investments 401

REQUEST FOR FUNDING 437
INDEX 441
BIBLIOGRAPHY 450

Introduction

Whatever you can do or dream....do it!
Boldness has genius, power and magic in it.

Recent psychological surveys have found stressful financial conditions are among the leading causes of emotional stress for women. The Working Woman Count Survey, a study conducted by the Women's Bureau, U.S. Department of Labor (1994), surveyed a sample of over 250,000 working women. These women were from all sections of America. The survey found "that a staggering 99% of all women will work for pay sometime in their lives" and that "nearly every woman has a stake in what happens in America's work force."

This national survey found concern and apprehension related to job insecurities, personal financial problems and multiple roles contributed to working women's emotional and psychological stress. Sixty five percent of the women responding noted a need for improving pay scales and 61% indicated (without further education or training) they had little or no opportunity to advance. Considering nearly half of the U.S. workforce is made up of women – and they account for 62% of the increase in the labor force by the year 2005 – these findings are critical.

A regional study on 298 working mothers in Denver, Colorado, also addressed working mothers' stress. This study obtained results closely matching the Working Mothers Count Survey (Prato 1994). It showed financial related stressors such as "working in an inferior job just to survive," "the problem of greater effort for advancement when related to males," "late mortgage payments," "rent increase," "too many bills and too little money," "fear of job loss by a spouse" and the "cost of day care" were significant sources of emotional stress in working women. Many of these reflected financial strain.

These findings are supported by other studies. Freedman and Bisesi (1986) isolated similar stressors for working women. These included salary and career problems and discriminatory employment policies. Other research (Verbrugge, 1984, Pearlin and Radabaugh, 1976) shows much of the stress noted can be reduced through increased income. That in turn, results from advanced education and enhanced job skills.

The question becomes how to help women take the next step to relieve financial strain. Information provided in this directory, *Financial Freedom for Women,* has been compiled to meet this need. *Financial Freedom for Women* contains over 1,000 resources including loans, grants, scholarships, fellowships and awards. These sources offer help to advance education, improve job skills, move ahead in a chosen career, obtain support during emergencies and locate resources for starting or expanding a business.

In today's society women are transforming various arenas of the world in which they live. They are making a difference as entrepreneurs, business executives, managers, researchers, political and spiritual leaders, scholars and athletes. They are also making a difference as mothers, wives and family members.

One of the fastest growing segments of the U.S. economy is businesses owned by women. According to the Small Business Administration there are over 5 million women owned businesses in the US today. This agency predicts women will own 40 to 50 percent of all small businesses by the year 2000. In fact, the record number of women not only own their own businesses, they also employ as many people as all the Fortune 500 companies combined! Additionally, *Working Mother Magazine* cited a recent study of Fortune 500 companies by Catalyst, a research organization. It revealed more profitable companies are likely to have women on their boards. Specifically, 95% of the companies ranking in the top 100 for earnings had at least one female director, while only 68 of the bottom 100 had at least one. In addition, a growing number of Fortune 500 companies — 81% - have at least one woman director. This is up from 69% in 1993.

Working Mother Magazine also publishes *The Working Mother 100*, an annual list of companies responsive to the needs of working women. This list includes a number of major corporations (Aetna, Allstate, Amoco, Xerox) who are offering working women child care benefits, flexible work schedules, equal pay for equal work and other programs important to women. Women are creating new business opportunities for women. Working women have expanded needs for day care services, personal assistance, live-in family aids, financial services, consulting and advisory services.

Yet, many women are not aware millions of dollars in financial support are available exclusively for them. There are financial resources to assist women with personal, living and medical expenses. Education support for secondary, undergraduate, graduate or postgraduate study as well as for research is available. There are larger sums of money available today for women than ever before.

There are funds available to assist women's organizations. These funds are ear-marked for educational advances, career development, athletic training, the arts, research and travel opportunities as well as political and religious-spiritual development.

Unlike other directories, *Financial Freedom for Women* has been *developed exclusively for women*. Advisors, educators, researchers, business counselors, bankers and women seeking financial aid can now locate sources in one directory. The directory is divided into five general categories:

- **Support for Educational needs**
- **Support in the arts and culture arenas**
- **Support for general welfare needs**
- **Support for business development**
- **Support for investments and retirement**

The education section of the directory provides information within five categories. The five categories are Scholarships, Grants, Fellowships, Awards and Loans. Resources within the Business, General Welfare and Arts and Culture sections also may refer to scholarships, grants, awards, etc. To help clarify what each program is, the authors have provided this information:

Scholarships: Programs which primarily support studies at the undergraduate level within the United States. Usually no return of service or repayment is required.

Grants: Programs that provide funds to support women's efforts, travel, projects, creative activities or research on any level. Usually no repayment is required.

Fellowships: Programs that support studies at the graduate or postgraduate level within the United States. Usually no return of service of repayment is required.

Awards: Competitions, prizes and honors granted in recognition of women's personal accomplishments, professional contributions or public service. Usually no repayment is required.

Loans: Programs providing money that eventually must be repaid, with or without interest.

To be included in the *Financial Freedom for Women* directory, the referenced program must meet the following criteria:

- *The program must be open to women residing in the United States*
- *The program must be open to women at any level of education: high school through postdoctoral and professional levels.*
- *The program must accept applications from individuals directly or through an intermediary*

Entries appear within one of five categories and listed alphabetically by program title. Within each program the authors provide a basic profile including title of funding organization, organization address and telephone number (when available), title of program (when available), purpose, limitations or restrictions for applications and number of awards given each year showing dollar amounts. Please note the absence of certain information indicates the information was not available. To receive detailed information on a program, contact the institution for packets, applications, etc.

When using this directory, look for programs offering your particular need or interest for financial aid. A scholarship for undergraduate courses, a grant for independent study, emergency funds for personal, living or medical expenses, etc. Keep in mind, more than one section may offer funding leads for your needs. For instance, if you are a graduate student looking for money to pay education and research costs, you may want to search through fellowships, loans, grants and awards. Program titles can be misleading. For example, The American Business Women's Association Founder's Scholarship is available only to graduate women, thus it is listed under fellowships, not scholarships. The index in the back of the book can also help you locate sources. The bibliography may also direct you to other resources if you want to expand your search.

If, after you have contacted sources and they may not be able to help you, ask them to offer suggestion about similar sources. Asking can result in receiving valuable suggestions about other sources.

If you do not have time to research for funding programs, The Stress Resource Network will do an extensive custom reach for you using this directory and several other resources. SRN will locate resources specific to your inquiry, including research of any local, county and/or state programs which may be available for your needs. The receive this service, complete the Request For Funding application in the back of this directory. Mail the completed form and appropriate research fee to the address located on the form. Please allow three weeks to complete the search and mail the information to you.

Excluded from the directory are funds administered by academic institutions, foundations or corporations solely for the benefit of their city, county or state resident. Write directly to these funding programs for more information on funds available.

At publication of this directory, all information on sources for financial assistance was up-to-date. Since then, some program may have changed addresses, telephone numbers or may have rewritten their requirements. If there is a source in this directory that cannot be reached, please contact the Stress Resource Network. This information has been compiled and prepared with expressed intention of enhancing and advancing the quality of women's lives, and in turn, the lives of their loved ones. If the information in this directory contributed to this enhancement and the reduction of financial stress, then the principals of the Stress Resource Network will also have been rewarded in the process.

We wish you success and good fortune in your search!

Peter J. Prato, Ph.D.   Rita Lynne, Ph.D.
Pleasanton, California

EDUCATION

The key to reducing financial strain many women experience is to advance their careers and job opportunities through further education. This section helps find financial resources for secondary, undergraduate, graduate or postgraduate study. For many women, obtaining that financial aid means the difference between advancement and not moving ahead.

To make it easy to find entries, they have been arranged alphabetically by sponsoring foundation or program title. Each listing includes the purpose of the financial assistance and criteria eligibility. For detailed information on the amounts available, exact program description, application deadlines and other information, contact each lending institution directly.

Ways To Increase Financial Aid

If you are college-bound you most likely are focusing your financial attention on every-rising tuition. For instance, costs are up another 7.3% for the 1998-99 academic year, to an average of $10,333 at private schools and $2,780 at public schools. Due to the 13.5% decline in America's college population since 1975, student-hungry schools are more willing than ever to negotiate financial aid packages. At some colleges that could mean a savings of up to 50% or more in financial aid, college tuition, room, board and fee packages.

Recently, an outstanding student from Phoenix was offered aid packages for Brown and Harvard Universities equal to $22,000 of her roughly $30,000 total yearly costs. That meant she still had to come up with $8,000 to study at either school. But after she notified both schools of more generous aid offers from nine other schools, Brown cut her costs to $4,000 and Harvard reduced it to $6,000.

Another top applicant from Iowa City had initially decided to enroll at Stanford University. Stanford had offered him $1,700 toward the $30,000 total annual costs. He had rejected five other schools that offered about the same amount. However, one school wouldn't take no for an answer. It increased its offer to a full-tuition scholarship of $17,000 a year! Now, Lewis and Clark, a 1,800 student liberal arts college in Portland, Oregon has its new student from Iowa City.

"Not every person is willing to trade off a degree at a traditional school for a lower-cost education elsewhere," says Robert Zemsky, director of the Institute for Research in Higher Education at the University of Pennsylvania. Although increasingly, applicants are seriously looking for programs that give them the most for their money and are willing to walk away if the price is too high.

Even though college trends are in the favor of the applicant, do not assume that negotiating for a better financial aid package simply involves a request for more money. In requires a strategic approach. By using some of the following strategies you may be able to reduce the yearly cost at the college of your choice.

Room To Bargain

To fill classrooms with well qualified students, many colleges are willing to continue financial aid negotiations even after making an initial offer. On average, a school plans in their budget to collect close to one-half of its costs from students (and their parents) and the other half comes from aids: loans, grants and work/study payments that the college anticipates giving to students. This is where you, as the applicant have plenty of room to bargain.

The amount of aid, and the portion of non-repayable grants vs. repayable loans, differs widely from school to school and from applicant to applicant. Federal financial aid, on the other hand, is calculated according to a government formula. Ask for an explanation from a guidance counselor or from the colleges where you are applying.

If you can show that a college's financial aid office underestimated your merit or your need, you have an excellent change of receiving additional financial aid. An example of this is the case of the student who negotiated bigger aid packages at Brown and Harvard cited earlier. She not only sent each college copies of bigger aid packages from nine other colleges, she also reminded both colleges of her high grade point average and pointed out the unusually heavy financial burdens she and her family were under; her older sister was already in college, her mother couldn't work and her family earnings were less than $60,000 a year.

Merit Aid

There are two primary ways to boost your chances of qualifying for merit aid. One is to search out schools with "deep pockets". (By dividing a college's endowment by its enrollment, you can get a good idea of its potential per-student money to be bestowed). Second, focus on colleges where your skills are in demand. While scholastic achievement counts a great deal, other talents such as sports, musical and/or leadership ability are also important negotiating tools.

Look through college guidebooks at your local library to get an idea of which schools would be interested in your special strengths. These guidebooks note a school's special interests which can range from arts programs to engineering and zoology.

Scholarships can also provide an excellent idea of what a school values most. For instance, Cleveland's Case Western Reserve awards $8,000 annually to each student demonstrating outstanding skills in dance, theater and art.

Send Financial Aid Forms Early

Since the fall enrollment of 1995, 400+ schools are requiring a new application form, the *Financial Aid Profile*. This form is used for school sponsored grants that supplement federal need-based assistance. Check with the colleges to which you plan to apply for information on their requirements and the *Financial Aid Profile*. The earlier you get your application in, the better your chances are of receiving more money in the form of grants rather than in loans. Early applicants usually receive grants, while a higher proportion of loans go to applicants who apply closer to the colleges deadline.

Secure A Price Guarantee

Check with your college choices to get a committed price limit. A growing number of colleges are practicing this procedure to keep their students for the full four year programs. Both Michigan State and Rice Universities promise incoming freshmen that their tuition won't rise any faster than the consumer price index. Morehead State in Kentucky has frozen dormitory prices for four years and Indiana University promises that, under certain circumstances, such as declaring a major while a freshman, a student who can't graduate in four year because of over-subscribed courses will get the fifth year tuition-free.

If you decide on a college that doesn't guarantee its prices, still attempt to lock in the financial aid package for all four years. If you don't, you may have to reconsider staying at a college which has the option to lure freshmen with deep discounts that aren't repeated in subsequent years. "Cuts in aid packages after the freshman year have become a problem," observes Robert Zemsky, "Many times freshmen are given large grants, which are gifts, but are then replaced after the first year with loans, which must be paid back."

Earn Credits in Advance to Reduce Costs

You can reduce the cost of a four-year college degree by as much as 40% by:

- Taking college courses at extension sites
- Scoring well on Advance Placement exams
- Spending a year or two in a well regarded community college

Before using these strategies, be sure they are accepted and that credits can be transferred to the college you finally choose. Some private schools charge by the semester, not by the credit. In this case, you would have to accumulate enough credits to eliminate at least the cost of a semester. However, most state schools charge by the credit which can reduce the total cost as much as $600 with just one course fulfilled in advance.

Finally, you might consider accumulating some credits at a low-cost four-year college before ultimately earning a degree at a more prestigious school. A freshman at Stanford, where tuition is roughly $20,000 a year, studies summers at the University of Montana ($900 for 12 summer credits). She is allowed to gain 45 credits toward her degree to be gained outside Stanford, reducing $18,000 from her college bills and still graduate in four years with a Stanford degree.

Doing your research prior to making a college decision can ultimately reward you with many opportunities of financial resources and cost effective college degrees.

SCHOLARSHIPS

A scholarship is a sum of money or a commitment for free tuition awarded to a student on the basis of achievement, ability or financial need. A scholarship carries with it an honor in addition to providing assistance to those who have financial needs for educational purposes. Usually, scholarships are awarded as a way of training capable individuals to enhance their educational or job skills. In the long run, these individuals become valuable assets to their community and nation.

Scholarships are generally awarded for undergraduate studies. Increasingly, business, industry, labor unions as well as funds established by individuals provide thousands of scholarships annually either for general education or for specific fields of study.

Private colleges and universities generally have a scholarship program to attract outstanding students, often to specific fields such as computer science, science, medicine, engineering and the humanities. Scholarships are often funded by individuals with personal wealth and carry the name of the donor. These scholarships sometimes require certain "qualities of character or achievement" for an individual to be eligible for the scholarship.

This section contains an extensive list of sources for scholarships. If you contact sources and they cannot help you with an actual scholarship, ask them if they know of an institution or foundation that might provide the help you need. Scholarships are often obtained in this way.

S1-
AAAA SPOUSE SCHOLARSHIPS
    Army Aviation Association of America
    Scholarship Foundation
    49 Richmondville Avenue
    Westport, CT 06880-2000
    (203) 226-8184
    E-mail: aaaa@quad-a.org

COURSE STUDY: GENERAL
The purpose of this scholarship fund is to provide financial aid for the spouses of Army Aviation Association of America members who are in post-secondary education. Education may be at the undergraduate or graduate level. Each scholarship is usually at least $1,000.

S2-
ADMIRAL GRACE MURRAY HOPPER MEMORIAL SCHOLARSHIPS
    Society of Women Engineers
    120 Wall Street, 11th Floor
    New York, NY 10005-3902
    (212) 509-9577
    E-mail: 71764.743@compuserve.com

COURSE STUDY: ENGINEERING - COMPUTER SCIENCES
Any freshman female student studying engineering or computer sciences is eligible to apply for one of three annual scholarships worth $1,000 each. This is a new fund established in 1992 and dollar amounts available may increase annually.

S3-
AEI SCHOLARSHIP FUND
    c/o Society Bank - Trust Officer
    100 South Main Street
    Ann Arbor, MI 48104

COURSE STUDY: MEDICINE

Female undergraduate students accepted at or attending a medical school in the United States may apply for this financial assistance program. Applicants must be financially needy to apply. The average annual scholarship is $5,000.

S4-
AGNES E. VAGHI-CORNARO SCHOLARSHIP
>National Italian American Foundation
>Attn: Education Director
>1860 19th Street, N. W.
>Washington, DC 20009
>(202) 387-0600

COURSE STUDY: GENERAL
Any Italian American women who is enrolled or entering an accredited college or university in the United States may apply for financial assistance through this program. There are no restrictions on the major area of study. The annual award is $1,000.

S5-
AL THOMPSON JUNIOR BOWLER SCHOLARSHIP
>Young American Bowling Alliance
>5301 South 76th Street
>Greendale, WI 53129
>(414) 423-3343

COURSE STUDY: GENERAL
This unusual scholarship fund provides annual financial aid for high school seniors who actively participate in the sport of bowling with a 170 average. The recipient must be applying to any college or university in the United States. Two annual scholarships are sponsored by the Professional Bowlers Association, 1 for $1,000 and 1 for $1,500. Each scholarship may be renewed for up to 3 additional years if a 2.5 GPA is maintained.

S6-
TEYA ALBERTANI FOUNDATION FOR INVOLVEMENT, INC.
378 Whooping Loop, 1208
Altamonte Springs, FL 32701
(407) 331-3630

COURSE STUDY: GENERAL
Each year two scholarships are awarded to any graduating female high school student who has exhibited outstanding leadership qualities in her community and has excelled in school and community activities. The need for financial aid is not a criteria for selection. The scholarships range from $500 to $2,500.

S7-
ALLMAN MEDICAL SCHOLARSHIP FOUNDATION
P.O. Box 119
Atlantic City, NJ 08404
(609) 345-7571

COURSE STUDY: MEDICINE
Any female who has competed in a Miss America competition at the local, state or national level and is studying medicine may apply for the scholarship. The annual scholarship ranges from $1,00 to $1,500.

S8-
ALPHA KAPPA ALPHA FINANCIAL ASSISTANCE SCHOLARSHIPS
Alpha Kappa Alpha
5656 South Stony Island Avenue
Chicago, IL 60637
(312) 947-0026

COURSE STUDY: GENERAL
To apply for this annual scholarship award of up to $1,500 the applicant can be an undergraduate or graduate student who has completed at least one year of college level work. This work may be

completed in an accredited degree granting institution or a work in progress program in a non-institutional setting.

S9-
ALPHA KAPPA ALPHA MERIT SCHOLARSHIPS
Alpha Kappa Alpha
5656 South Stony Island Avenue
Chicago, IL 60637
(312) 947-0026

COURSE STUDY: GENERAL
Applicants must have completed one year of education at either the undergraduate or graduate level at an accredited degree granting institution and are planning to continue their education. There are 5 awards granted each year, each is $1,000 per year.

S10-
AMELIA EARHART MEMORIAL SCHOLARSHIP
Ninety-Nines, Inc.
International Women Pilots
Will Rogers World Airport
P.O. Box 59965
Oklahoma City, OK 73159
(405) 685-7969

COURSE STUDY: AVIATION
Members of the Ninety-Nines are eligible to apply for financial support in the study of advanced flight training courses in aviation. A minimum of 10 scholarships is awarded each year, each award is $1,000.

S11-
AMELIA KEMP MEMORIAL SCHOLARSHIP
Women of the Evangelical Utheran Church in America
8765 West Higgins Road
Chicago, IL 60631-4189
(312) 380-2730

COURSE STUDY: RELIGIOUS SERVICE
Financial assistance is available to lay women of color who are members of Evangelical Lutheran Church of America congregations. Applicants who are intending to enroll in college at the undergraduate, graduate, professional or vocational school level may apply. They may apply if their studies are for a career other than ordination, the diaconate, or church certified professions. The scholarship award is $2,000 annually and may be renewed for 1 additional year.

S12-
AMERICAN BUSINESS WOMEN'S ASSOCIATION COLLEGE SCHOLARSHIP PROGRAM
American Business Women's Association
P.O. Box 8728
9100 Ward Parkway
Kansas City, MO 64114-0728
(816) 361-6621

COURSE STUDY: GENERAL
Over $600,000 is awarded annually to women freshmen or sophomores in college through the 2,000 chapters of the ABWA. Applicants do not need to be members of the ABWA to apply. Most scholarships average $3,000, some are renewable.

S13-
AMERICAN COLLEGE OF NURSE-MIDWIVES SCHOLARSHIPS
American College of Nurse-Midwives Foundation
818 Connecticut Avenue, NW, Suite 900
Washington, DC 20006
(202) 728-9865

COURSE STUDY: MIDWIFERY
Applicants must be pursuing a career in midwifery and be enrolled in a college or university offering midwifery on a certificate or master's level. One semester in the midwifery program must have been

completed to apply. The award amount is $1,000 and is presented annually. The number of awards varies each year.

S14-
AMERICAN LEGION AUXILIARY NATIONAL PRESIDENT'S SCHOLARSHIP FOR JUNIOR MEMBERS

American Legion Auxiliary
777 North Meridian Street
Indianapolis, IN 46204
(317) 635-6291

COURSE STUDY: GENERAL
Applicants must be junior members of the American Legion Auxiliary for at least three years and be a senior or graduate of an accredited high school. Financial need must be shown to continue college level education. There are five awards each year, each averaging $1,000.

S15-
AMERICAN NATIONAL CATTLEWOMEN FOUNDATION SCHOLARSHIP

National FFA Center
P.O. Box 15160
5632 Mt. Vernon Memorial Highway
Alexandria, VA 22309-0160
(703) 360-3600

COURSE STUDY: FOOD OR ANIMAL SCIENCE
Applicants must be current or former FFA members and have completed 1 year of a 4 year degree program majoring in food science and nutrition or animal science. A 3.0 GPA must be maintained. There are two awards given each year, each is $1,000.

S16-
AMERICAN SOCIETY OF WOMEN ACCOUNTANTS SCHOLARSHIPS

American Society of Women Accountants
1755 Lynnfield Road, Suite 257

Memphis, TN 38119
(800) 326-2163

COURSE STUDY: ACCOUNTING
Women in undergraduate or graduate programs majoring in accounting in any college, university or professional school may apply. Candidates do not have to be members of the American Society of Women Accountants to apply. Each year four awards are given ranging for $1500 to $2,500.

S17-
AMERICA'S JUNIOR MISS
America's Junior Miss
P.O. Box 2786
Mobile, AL 36652-2786
(334) 438-3621

COURSE STUDY: GENERAL
Over $5,000,000 in college scholarships and other awards are presented at local, state and national levels each year. Amount of awards varies in each state, however, national awards exceed $100,000. Any high school senior female under the age of 19 may apply, beginning at the local Junior Miss level. No bathing suit competitions are held, each candidate must display a talent or speak on a subject of choice as part of the competition.

S18-
AMERICA'S NATIONAL TEEN-AGER SCHOLARSHIP PROGRAM
National Teen-Ager Scholarship Foundation
4708 Mill Crossing West
Colleyville, TX 76034
(817) 577-2220

COURSE STUDY: GENERAL
Over $5,000,000 is presented annually in state and regional pageants in the form of tuition scholarships, cash and awards. National awards include a $10,000 scholarship to the senior winner and $5,000 to the

junior division winner. These awards provide support for the winners college education. Junior division eligibility is all girls 13 through 15 years of age and girls 16 through 18 are eligible for the senior division.

S19-
AMS INDUSTRY UNDERGRADUATE SCHOLARSHIPS
American Meteorological Society
45 Beacon Street
Boston, MA 02108-3693
(617) 227-2426
E-mail: sarmstrg@ametsoc.org

COURSE STUDY: SCIENCES
Students enrolled in the following fields are encouraged to apply: atmospheric sciences, oceanography, hydrology, chemistry, computer sciences, engineering, environmental sciences, mathematics and physics. Applicants must have completed 2 years of study, have a 3.0 GPA and be U.S. citizens. Each year 12 awards are given to deserving candidates, each award is $2,000 and may be renewed for the final year of undergraduate study.

S20-
AMS 75TH ANNIVERSARY SCHOLARSHIP
American Meteorological Society
45 Beacon Street
Boston, MA 02108-3693
(617) 227-2426
E-mail: sarmstrg@ametsoc.org

COURSE STUDY: METEOROLOGY - SCIENCES
Applicants must be entering into their senior year of undergraduate study, have a 3.0 GPA, be a U.S. citizen and be majoring in meteorology or related atmospheric, oceanic or hydrologic sciences. Each year one award of $2,000 is given.

S21-
ANNE MAUREEN WHITNEY BARROW MEMORIAL SCHOLARSHIP
Society of Women Engineers
120 Wall Street, 11th Floor
New York, NY 10005-3902
(212) 509-9577
E-mail: 71764.743@compuserve.com

COURSE STUDY: ENGINEERING
Any female freshman studying engineering or engineering technology is eligible to apply for the $5,000 annual award. The award is renewable each year until completion of the undergraduate degree.

S22-
ANNE PEKAR MEMORIAL SCHOLARSHIP
National Federation of the Blind
Chair, Scholarship Committee
814 Fourth Avenue, Suite 200
Grinnell, IA 50112
(515) 236-3366

COURSE STUDY: GENERAL
Female blind students wanting to pursue studies at the undergraduate and graduate level will find this scholarship program outstanding. Applicants must be full time students, legally blind, and be between the ages of 17-25. The annual award is $4,000, recipients may apply for an additional 2 years of financial aid.

S23-
ANTOINETTE LIERMAN MEDLIN SCHOLARSHIP AWARD
Geological Society of America
Attn: Research Grants Administrator
3300 Penrose Place
P.O. Box 9140
Boulder, CO 80301
(303) 447-2020

COURSE STUDY: GEOLOGY
Financial support is provided to students enrolled in undergraduate and graduate studies in geology. At the master's or doctoral level, special consideration will be given to students proposing research on coal geology. The grants range from $400 to $2,500 annually.

S24-
AVON PRODUCTS FOUNDATION SCHOLARSHIP FOR WOMEN IN BUSINESS STUDIES
>Business and Professional Women's Foundation
>Attn: Scholarships
>2012 Massachusetts Avenue, NW
>Washington, DC 20036
>(202) 293-1200

COURSE STUDY: BUSINESS
Any undergraduate or graduate female student entering or advancing in a business related field (management, business administration, marketing, sales or accounting) may apply. Applicants must be 25 years of age, U.S. citizens, and enrolled in an accredited program or course of study in a U.S. institution. Each year Avon Products Foundation sponsors over 60 awards, each approximately $1,000.

S25-
AWSCPA SCHOLARSHIPS
>American Women's Society of Certified Public Accountants
>401 North Michigan Avenue
>Chicago, IL 60601
>(312) 644-6610

COURSE STUDY: ACCOUNTING, CPA
Candidates range from female high school seniors to female college seniors. Financial assistance is provided to students majoring in accounting in college and/or preparing for a career as a certified public accountant. Over 40 state and regional affiliates throughout the U.S. offer the scholarships, each with their own criteria. Annually, at least 40 awards are given, ranging from $100 to $500. In some cases, the

society's education foundation will provide matching/incentive funds to affiliates to encourage offering scholarships.

S26-
DELLA M. BAILEY INDIAN SCHOLARSHIP TRUST
    c/o First National Bank in Fairfield
    P.O. Box 30
    Fairfield, IA 52556
    (515) 472-4121

COURSE STUDY: GENERAL
Scholarship are available for female students of Native-American parentage. Applicants must be enrolled or intend to enroll in an accredited school, college or university in the United States. The number of annual awards varies according to need and range from $1,000 to $20,000+.

S27-
BANTLY CHARITABLE TRUST
    1578 Crestline Drive, c/o Trustee
    Atlanta, Georgia 30345

COURSE STUDY: RELIGIOUS STUDIES
This scholarship is open to women undergraduates in religious studies. The applicant must be working toward a degree in religious education or the ministry. Scholarship amounts vary from $500 to $3,500 annually.

S28-
BARBARA THOMAS ENTERPRISES, INC. SCHOLARSHIP
    Foundation of Research and Education
    919 North Michigan Avenue, Suite 1400
    Chicago, IL 60611-1683
    (312) 787-2672

COURSE STUDY: HEALTH INFORMATION MANAGEMENT

If you are a single parent and are an undergraduate or graduate student majoring in health information management or technology you may be eligible for scholarships offered by this foundation. You must have already been accepted for admission to a health information management or technology program or have been accepted for admission to AHIMA's independent study program. The annual award is $5,000.

S29-
STEFAN BERGMAN TRUST
  c/o Wells Fargo Bank
  P.O. Box 63954
  San Francisco, CA 94163

COURSE STUDY: MATHEMATICS
The purpose of this scholarship fund is to provide financial assistance to female students studying mathematics. One award is given yearly, the amount varies according to need.

S30-
JAMES HUBERT BLAKE TRUST
  c/o Beldock, Levine & Hoffman
  99 Park Avenue, Suite 1600
  New York NY 10016-1502

COURSE STUDY: MUSIC
Scholarships are awarded for undergraduate study to music students, particularly students interested in traditional American ragtime music. The scholarships range for $1,900 to $10,500.

S31-
BRISLEY SCHOLARSHIP LOAN FUND
  c/o Boatmen's First National Bank
  P.O. Box 419038
  Kansas City, MO 64183
  (816) 691-7481

COURSE STUDY: MEDICAL, NURSING
These scholarships are offered to two separate groups of students. First, scholarships are provided to needy medical and nursing students attending accredited schools and second, to deserving and needy students attending Methodist colleges. Annually over 50 grants are given to individuals totaling over $80,000, the highest individual grant averages $12,000, the lowest $100.

S32-
BUDWEISER-USO SCHOLARSHIP PROGRAM
>USO World Headquarters
>Attn: Scholarship Program
>Washington Navy Yard, Bldg. 198
>901 M Street, SE
>Washington, DC 20374-5096
>(202) 610-5700

COURSE STUDY: GENERAL
This program is offered to spouses and children of active-duty service members who are high school seniors or have graduated high school in the last 4 years. The annual award is $1,000 with approximately 15 awards being given each year.

S33-
CAREER ADVANCEMENT SCHOLARSHIPS
>Business and Professional Women's Foundation
>2012 Massachusetts Avenue, NW
>Washington, DC 20036-1070
>(202) 293-1200

COURSE STUDY: COMPUTER SCIENCE, EDUCATION, PARA LEGAL, ENGINEERING, M.D., J.D., D.D.S.
The purpose of this scholarship fund is to provide financial assistance to mature women who are employed or seeking employment in the job force. Also the scholarship fund has a mission of expanding the pool of women qualified for broadening their career opportunities. Applicants must be studying in the following fields: computer science, education, paralegal, engineering, science or the professions of J.D., D.D.S., M.D.

Annually over $50,000 is awarded with individual awards ranging from $500 to $1,000.

S34-
ARTHUR H. CARTER SCHOLARSHIP FUND
    c/o Cummings & Lockwood
    P.O. Box 120
    Stamford, CT 06904
    (813) 921-7747

COURSE STUDY: ACCOUNTING
The purpose of this fund is to provide financial assistance to students pursuing a career in accounting at the undergraduate or graduate level. Applicants need to have completed 2 years of accounting courses to apply. Total awards each year exceed $130,000 with each grant averaging $2,500.

S35-
CASA GRANDE UNION HIGH SCHOOL FOUNDATION, INC.
    711 East Cottonwood Lane, Suite C
    Casa Grande, AZ 85222

COURSE STUDY: GENERAL
This is an excellent resource for rural area students who otherwise would have insufficient resources to attend college or a trade school. Annual scholarship amounts range from $500 to $2,000 per individual.

S36-
CENEX FOUNDATION
    5500 Cenex Drive
    Inver Grove Heights, MN 55075
    (612) 451-5105

COURSE STUDY: GENERAL
Applicants must be enrolled in college courses at the community college level or attending vocational tech school. Also students

attending an agricultural college may apply. Awards begin at $500 per student and are awarded annually.

S37-
CHARLOTTE W. NEWCOMBE SCHOLARSHIPS FOR MATURE SECOND-CAREER WOMEN
Charlotte W. Newcombe Foundation
35 Park Place
Princeton, NJ 08542-6918
(609) 924-7022

COURSE STUDY: GENERAL
This foundation provides funding directly to the college for scholarships to fund undergraduate degrees. The college must provide a 4-year program to be eligible. The amount of each grant varies from $10,000 to $35,000, with 25 or more colleges receiving these grants each year.

S38-
CHASE MANHATTAN SCHOLARSHIP PROGRAM
Financial Women International
200 North Glebe Road, Suite 814
Arlington, VA 22203
(703) 807-2007

COURSE STUDY: FINANCIAL MANAGEMENT
The purpose of the scholarship fund is to encourage women in financial services industries to achieve their career goals and to broaden the availability of professional role models for women. Applicants must be members of the Financial Women International Organization and must be employed within the financial industry in a managerial or supervisory capacity. Applicants must be working toward an undergraduate degree or M.B.A. degree. The annual amount awarded is $1,000.

S39-
CHEVRON SCHOLARSHIPS

Society of Women Engineers
120 Wall Street, 11th Floor
New York, NY 10005-3902
(212) 509-9577
E-mail: 71764.743@compuserve.com

COURSE STUDY: ENGINEERING
Undergraduate women students entering their sophomore or junior year and majoring in chemical, mechanical or petroleum engineering at the accredited school, college or university may apply. Applicants must be U.S. citizens and have a GPA of 3.5. This is a new program and annual amounts may vary. Presently, two $2,000 awards are given each year, one for an entering sophomore and one for an entering junior.

S40-
CHINA TIMES CULTURAL FOUNDATION
43-27 36th Street
Long Island City, NY 11101
(718) 392-0995 (718)937-6110

COURSE STUDY: GENERAL
For students of Chinese ancestry who are enrolled in a college or university within the United States, this scholarship fund offers financial support at the undergraduate and graduate level. Annual scholarships vary from $500 to $4,000 with yearly awards totaling $230,000.

S41-
CHRYSLER CORPORATION SCHOLARSHIP
Society of Women Engineers
120 Wall Street, 11th Floor
New York, NY 10005-3902
(212) 509-9577
E-mail: 71764.743@compuserve.com

COURSE STUDY: ENGINEERING

Applicants must be sophomore, juniors or seniors majoring in engineering or computer science. Financial assistance is specific to minority undergraduate women or other members of an under represented group. This program was established in 1995 and annual awards may vary. Presently one award is given each year in the amount of $1,750.

S42-
THE CIT GROUP FOUNDATION, INC.
1211 Ave. of the Americas
New York, NY 10036

COURSE STUDY: GENERAL
Scholarships are available to female students enrolled in an accredited school, college or university in the United States. The annual awards and the amounts of each award varies according to need.

S43-
PAUL AND MARY COLLINS TRUST NO. 2
c/o Lyon Country State Bank
Rock Rapids, IA 51246
(712) 472-2581

COURSE STUDY: GENERAL
This fund is open to women pursuing a college education and are not a relative of Paul or Mary Collins. The dollar amount of scholarship awards varies according to the student needs.

S44-
WELSFORD STARR AND MILDRED M. CLARK MEDICAL MEMORIAL FUND
cp. Bank of Boston, Connecticut
P.O. Box 2210
Waterbury, CT 06720

COURSE STUDY: MEDICINE

The purpose of this fund is to provide female students financial assistance who are studying medicine. Applicants must be in their third year of medical school. Several grants are given, average individual amount awarded is $4,000 annually.

S45-
COLONEL HAYDEN W. WAGNER MEMORIAL FUND
Society of Daughters of the United States Army
c/o Mary Lousie Bishop
4242 East-West Highway, Apt. 910
Chevy Chase, MD 20815
(301) 652-6085

COURSE STUDY: GENERAL
The purpose of this fund is to provide financial assistance for undergraduate education to any daughter, stepdaughter, adopted daughter or granddaughter of a U.S. Army Commissioned or Warrant Officer who is on active duty, retired after 20 years of duty or retired for medical reasons or deceased. This outstanding program awards several scholarships a year each up to $1,000 and each is renewable.

S46-
COLUMBIANA COUNTY PUBLIC HEALTH LEAGUE TRUST FUND
c/o Bank One Ohio Trust Co.
235 West Schrock Rd.
Columbus, OH 43081
(614) 283-8430

COURSE STUDY: MEDICINE - SEVERAL OTHERS, SEE BELOW
This scholarship fund provides financial assistance to students studying pharmacy, medicine, medical technology training, physical therapy, nursing, dental hygiene, or occupational therapy. Applicants must be full time students and be in their second year of undergraduate study (or higher) or in the first year of their graduate studies. Applicants must be enrolled in an accredited school, college or university to apply. Annual grant amounts vary according to need.

S47-
CONTINENTAL GRAIN FOUNDATION
10 South Riverside Plaza
Chicago, IL 60606
(312) 466-6542

COURSE STUDY: GENERAL
If you are a college student and wish to travel on an exchange program to a foreign country, this foundation offers financial assistance to travel to several countries. The total giving averages $122,000, grants to individuals vary according to need.

S48-
WILLIAM AND DORIS CORRELL TRUST
234 Portage Trail
Cuyahoga Falls, OH 44222
(330) 929-0507

COURSE STUDY: GENERAL
This trust program offers financial assistance, with minimal requirements, to female undergraduate students. Applicants must be enrolled in an accredited school, college or university in the United States. Annual grant amounts vary according to need.

S49-
THE CULTURAL SOCIETY, INC.
200 West 19th Street
Panama City, FL 32405

COURSE STUDY: GENERAL
Financial assistance is available to Muslim students studying at the undergraduate level. Total annual givings are $260,000 with individual scholarship amounts varying according to student needs.

S50-
DATATEL SCHOLARS FOUNDATION
4375 Fair Lakes Court

Fairfax, VA 22033
(703) 968-9000

COURSE STUDY: GENERAL
Financial assistance is available to female students attending a school, college or university using Datatel's software. Applicants must be full time undergraduate or graduate students. Several scholarships are awarded annually averaging $1,000 each.

S51-
DAUGHTERS OF PENELOPE PAST GRAND PRESIDENT'S AWARD
Daughters of Penelope
1909 Q Street, NW, Suite 500
Washington, DC 20009-1007
(202) 234-9741

COURSE STUDY: GENERAL
Scholarships are available to Greek women who want to pursue post-secondary education. Applicants must be members of the Daughters of Penelope and whose parents or grandparents have also been a 2 year member of Daughters of Penelope or the Order of Alhepa. The annual award is $1,500 and is renewable yearly.

S52-
DAUGHTERS OF THE CINCINNATI SCHOLARSHIP PROGRAM
122 East 58th Street N
New York, NY 10022
(212) 319-6915

COURSE STUDY: GENERAL
Financial assistance is available to high school seniors entering a U.S. college or university and are daughters of regular commissioned officers (on active duty or retired) in the Army, Navy, Air Force, Coast Guard or Marines. The annual givings are $35,000, with individual scholarships from $500 to $1,500.

S53-
ADELLE DAVIS FOUNDATION
231 North Grant Ave
Monrovia, CA 91016
(818) 445-8406

COURSE STUDY: FOOD SCIENCE, NUTRITION
Financial assistance is available to female undergraduate and graduate students researching or studying in the field of food science and nutrition. Annual grant amounts vary according to need.

S54-
FRED W. DAVIS MEMORIAL FOUNDATION
c/o First Union National Bank of Florida
P.O. Box 1869
Pompano Beach, FL 33061
(305) 467-5283

COURSE STUDY: THEOLOGY
Applicants must be in their second year of study as Episcopal seminary students. The amount of each scholarship varies according to student needs.

S55-
DEED SCHOLARSHIPS
American Public Power Association
Attn: Coordinator, DEED Administration
2301 M Street, NW
Washington, DC 20037-1484
(202) 467-2910

COURSE STUDY: ENERGY RESEARCH
The purpose of this fund is to provide financial assistance to undergraduate and graduate students interested in conducting research related to public power systems. Applicants must be sponsored by a publicly owned utility participating in the Demonstration of Energy-Efficient Developments Programs in the United States, Puerto Rico,

Guam, American Samoca and the Virgin Islands. Each year 10 awards are given, $3,000 for each project.

S56-
DELAYED EDUCATION SCHOLARSHIP FOR WOMEN

American Nuclear Society
Attn: Scholarship Program
555 North Kensington Avenue
LaGrange Park, IL 60525
(708) 352-6611

COURSE STUDY: NUCLEAR FIELDS

The purpose of this scholarship fund is to provide financial support to mature women whose formal studies have been delayed or interrupted. Applicants must be majoring in the field of nuclear science, nuclear engineering or a nuclear related field. Applicants must also be a U.S. citizen or resident and be sponsored by an American Nuclear Society local section, division, student branch, committee member, or organizational member. Each year one scholarship is awarded totaling $3,500.

S57-
DELTA KAPPA GAMMA RECRUITMENT GRANTS

Delta Kappa Gamma Society International
P.O. Box 1589
Austin, TX 78767-1589
(512) 478-5748

COURSE STUDY: EDUCATION

Over 3,000 awards are given each year through this fund. Applicants need not be members of Delta Kappa Gamma to be eligible to receive awards. Applicants must be enrolled in college and be interested in a career in education. Annual amounts vary from $100 to $1,000 per scholarship.

S58-
DISPLACED HOMEMAKER'S SCHOLARSHIP

Educational Foundation for Women in Accounting
530 Church Street, Suite 700
Nashville, TN 37219
(615) 254-3687

COURSE STUDY: ACCOUNTING
This fund provides financial support for college education in accounting for women who are the sole support of their family through death, divorce, or other circumstances. Funds are available for a degree program at the undergraduate, master's or doctoral level. Each year $4,000 is awarded to one recipient.

S59-
DOG WRITERS EDUCATIONAL TRUST
2508 Teal Road
Washington Depot, CT 06794

COURSE STUDY: JOURNALISM OR VETERINARY MEDICINE
Scholarships are awarded to students with a background in dog activity and are planning on attending a U.S. college or university. Applicants must plan to major in journalism or veterinary medicine. Ten grants are given each year, each is $1,000.

S60-
HERBERT A. MIKE DONOVAN SCHOLARSHIP FUND
NationsBank
P.O. Box 26903
Richmond, VA 23261

COURSE STUDY: RELIGION
Scholarships are available to students studying in the field of religion. Two grants are given each year, each $4,000. Contact the scholarship fund for other requirements.

S61-
DORIS MULLEN MEMORIAL SCHOLARSHIP
Whirly-Girls Scholarship Fund

Executive Towers 10-D
207 West Clarendon Avenue
Phoenix, AZ 85013
(602) 263-0190

COURSE STUDY: AVIATION
This fund provides financial assistance to women helicopter pilots to advance their certification, rating or specialized training and to improve their marketability as professional pilots in the helicopter industry. Annually one award of $4,500 is given.

S62-
DOROTHY LEMKE HOWARTH SCHOLARSHIP
Society of Women Engineers
120 Wall Street, 11th Floor
New York, NY 10005-3902
(212) 509-9577
E-mail: 71764-743@compuserve.com

COURSE STUDY: ENGINEERING
This fund is available to undergraduate women majoring in engineering and are entering their sophomore year at an ABET-accredited school, college or university. They also must be U.S. citizens and have a GPA of 3.5 The award in $2,000 and 3 are given each year.

S63-
DR. DOROTHY WEITZNER KORNBLUT SCHOLARSHIP FUND
Connecticut Association of Optometrists
c/o Dr. Charles J. Connors
222 Main Street
Ansonia, CT 06401-1859
(202) 735-2241

COURSE STUDY: OPTOMETRY

Financial assistance is provided to female undergraduates enrolled in accredited colleges of optometry. Funding varies from $300 to $900 per year depending upon student needs.

S64-
THE DOW JONES NEWSPAPER FUND, INC.
P.O. Box 300
Princeton, NJ 08543-0300
(609) 452-2820

COURSE STUDY: GENERAL
The fund sponsors programs, workshops and training for minorities in college. Scholarships, grants and awards totaling $96,000 are given each year. Contact the Fund for detailed information on the variety of program and financial assistance they offer to students.

S65-
DR. PEDRO GRAD UNDERGRADUATE SCHOLARSHIP
American Meteorological Society
45 Beacon Street
Boston, MA 02108-3693

COURSE STUDY: SCIENCE
Candidates must be in their senior year of college and majoring in meteorology or related atmospheric, oceanic or hydrologic sciences. Applicants must be U.S. citizens and have a GPA of 3.0. One award is given each year in the amount of $2,500.

S66-
JOHN P. EAGER EDUCATIONAL TRUST
c/o First NH Investment Systems
P.O. Box 2770
Concord, NH 03302-2770
(301) 587-8202

COURSE STUDY: MICROGRAPHICS

Financial assistance is available to female students who are studying in the field of micro graphics. Applicants must be U. S. citizens and be enrolled in an accredited school, college or university. One grant is awarded each year in the amount of $5,000.

S67-
ECHOING GREEN FOUNDATION
800 Third Ave., Suite 3702
New York, NY 10022-3104

COURSE STUDY: GENERAL
Female students enrolled full time at an accredited school, college or university in the United States are eligible to apply for financial assistance through this foundation. Individual amounts given vary according to need.

S68-
EDUCATIONAL COMMUNICATIONS SCHOLARSHIP FOUNDATION
721 North McKinley Road
Lake Forest, IL 60045
(847) 295-6650

COURSE STUDY: GENERAL
Financial assistance is provided to students entering a U.S. college or university and have taken the SAT or ACT examinations. Each grant is $1,000 and the amount of grants given each year varies.

S69-
EDUCATIONAL FOUNDATION OF THE NATIONAL RESTAURANT ASSOCIATION
c/o National Restaurant Association
1200 17th Street, NW
Washington, DC 20036-3097

COURSE STUDY: FOOD SERVICES

Scholarships are awarded to undergraduate students studying in the food service area. Awards vary from $500 to $3,000 annually.

S70-
EDWIN G. AND LAURETTA M. MICHAEL SCHOLARSHIP
Christian Church (Disciples of Christ)
Division of Homeland Ministries
222 South Downey Avenue
P.O. Box 1986
Indianapolis, IN 46206-1986
(317) 635-3100

COURSE STUDY: GENERAL
Ministers' wives are eligible to apply for financial support to complete their education if their basic education was interrupted to allow their husbands to complete their theological education. Husbands must be employed full time in ministry and hold standing in the ministry of the Christian Church. There is limited funding and annual awards vary each year with the average award being under $1,000.

S71-
CHARLES AND ANNA ELENBERG FOUNDATION, INC.
c/o Jack Scharf
P.O. Box 630193
Spuyten Duyvil Station
Bronx, NY 10463

COURSE STUDY: GENERAL
Scholarships are awarded to needy students of Hebrew faith entering college. No grants are given to married students. The scholarships are awarded annually and vary from $100 to $1,000.

S72-
ESPN SCHOLASTIC SPORTS AMERICAN SCHOLARSHIP PROGRAM
ESPN, Inc.

Attn: Communications Department
ESPN Plaza
935 Middle Street
Bristol, CT 06010
(203) 585-2000

COURSE STUDY: GENERAL AND SPORTS
Female high school seniors entering into a college or university who have participated in interscholastic sports, have a 3.0 GPA and are U.S. citizens may apply for an award of $2,500 given annually. There are four awards given, one to a female in four regions of the country (northeast, southeast, midwest and west).

S73-
EUGENIA BRADFORD ROBERTS MEMORIAL FUND
Society of Daughters of the United States Army
c/o Janet B. Otto
7717 Rockledge Court
West Springfield, VA 22152-3854

COURSE STUDY: GENERAL
Applicants must be a daughter, stepdaughter, adopted daughter or granddaughter of a U.S. Army Commissioned or Warrant Officer who is on active duty, retired after 20 years of active duty or for medical reasons, or deceased while on active duty. Awards are granted up to $1,000 per year, several awards are given each year.

S74-
EVEREG FENESSE MESROBIAN ROUPINIAN EDUCATIONAL SOCIETY, INC.
4140 Tanglewood Court
Bloomfield Hills, MI 48301

COURSE STUDY: GENERAL
Financial assistance is available to students of Armenian descent attending Armenian day schools or are full-time undergraduate and graduate students in an accredited school, college or university in the

United States. Several awards are given each year, each grant is $236.00.

S75-
ETHEL AND EMERY FAST SCHOLARSHIP FOUNDATION, INC.
2811 Woodley Rd., NW
Washington, DC 20008
(3010 762-1102

COURSE STUDY: GENERAL
Financial assistance is provided to financially needy Native Americans who have completed at least one year of post-secondary schooling. Applicants must be full time students enrolled in an accredited school, college or university. Several awards are given each year, individual awards average $500.

S76-
FEDERAL EMPLOYEE EDUCATION & ASSISTANCE FUND SCHOLARSHIP
Federal Employee Education & Assistance Fund
Attn: Executive Director
8441 West Bowles Avenue, Suite 200
Littleton, CO 80123-3245
(303) 933-7580

COURSE STUDY: GENERAL
The purpose of this fund is to provide financial assistance for undergraduate education to civilian federal and postal employees and their dependent family members. Applicants must be civilian federal and postal employees (with 3 years of federal service) or their spouses or dependent children. Applicants must have a 3.0 GPA and be attending an accredited 2 or 4 years undergraduate, graduate or postgraduate program. 300 plus awards are given each year, each ranging from $300 to $1,500 per year.

S77-
FEMME VITALE SCHOLARSHIP AWARD
Odwalla Inc.
120 Stone Pine Road
Half Moon Bay, CA 94019
(415) 726-1888

COURSE STUDY: HEALTH AND NUTRITION
This fund provides financial assistance to women in college pursuing undergraduate or graduate degrees in health and nutrition. Preference is given to those interested in focusing on women's health and nutrition. Number of awards given each year varies, each award is $3,000 and may be renewed for a second year.

S78-
DR. PETER G. FERNANDEZ PRACTICE STARTER FOUNDATION
3491 Gandy Boulevard North
Pinellas Park, FL 34665
(813) 577-3500

COURSE STUDY: CHIROPRACTIC MEDICINE
College female students pursuing a career in chiropractic medicine may apply for financial assistance. Applicants must currently be in a chiropractic college. Annual number of grants varies, each grant between $100 and $1,000.

S79-
FLEET RESERVE ASSOCIATION SCHOLARSHIP
Fleet Reserve Association
Attn: Scholarship Administrator
125 North West Street
Alexandria, VA 22314-2754
(800) 372-1924

COURSE STUDY: GENERAL
The purpose of this fund is to provide financial assistance for undergraduate or graduate education to children or spouses of current

or former naval personnel. Applicants must be dependent children or spouses of members of U.S. Navy, Marine Corps or Coast Guard serving on active duty, retired with pay, or deceased while on active duty or retired with pay. One award is given each year, with the amount varying and depending upon the needs of the recipient.

S80-
FOREMAN FLEISHER TRUST NO. 2
    c/o PNC Bank NA
    1632 Chestnut Street
    Philadelphia, PA 19103
    (215) 585-5491

COURSE STUDY: GENERAL
Scholarships are available to Jewish women who wish to pursue secondary education and are in need of financial assistance. Applicants must be enrolled or intending to enroll in an accredited school, college or university in the United States. The number of annual awards varies, the amount per award averages $800.

S81-
THE FREEDOM FORUM
    1101 Wilson Boulevard
    Arlington, VA 22209
    (703) 528-0800

COURSE STUDY: JOURNALISM
The purpose of this scholarship fund is to provide financial assistance for journalists. Scholarships are for undergraduate and graduate journalism students. Three programs are available. Contact the Foundation for further information on each program on how to apply. The total grants to individuals is $770,000.

S82-
FUTURE HOMEMAKERS OF AMERICA SCHOLARSHIPS
    Future Homemakers of America, Inc.
    Attn: Youth/Program Assistant

1910 Association Drive
Reston, VA 22091-1584
(703) 476-4900

COURSE STUDY: HOME ECONOMICS
Financial assistance for college education is provided to students interesting in majoring in home economics. Funds come from state affiliates, each with differing eligibility requirements. Each applicant must be a member or past member of Future Homemakers of America. Award amounts range from $100 to $500 annually.

S83-
CARMELA GAGLIARDI FOUNDATION
c/o National I-A Foundation
1860 19th Street, NW
Washington, DC 20009-5599

COURSE STUDY: MEDICINE
The purpose of this program is to provide financial assistance to primarily Italian descent students who are enrolled or have been accepted in an accredited medicine program. Each year 5 grants are given, each in the amount of $5,000.

S84-
GENERAL ELECTRIC FOUNDATION SCHOLARSHIPS
Society of Women Engineers
120 Wall Street, 11th Floor
New York, NY 10005-3902
(212) 509-9577
E-mail: 71764.743@compuserve.com

COURSE STUDY: ENGINEERING
This fund provides financial assistance to outstanding freshmen women majoring in engineering at an accredited college or university. Three awards are given each year, each is $1,000.

S85-
GENERAL MOTORS FOUNDATION SCHOLARSHIPS
Society of Women Engineers
120 Wall Street, 11th Floor
New York, NY 10005-3902
(212) 509-9577
E-mail: 71764.743@compuserve.com

COURSE STUDY: ENGINEERING
Financial assistance is provided for undergraduate women majoring in engineering. Applicants must be entering their junior year of college and majoring in one of the following engineering disciplines: mechanical, electrical, chemical, industrial, materials, automotive or manufacturing. Two awards are given each year, each is $1,000.

S86-
GIRL SCOUT ACHIEVEMENT AWARD
American Legion Auxiliary
777 North Meridian Street
Indianapolis, IN 46204
(317) 635-6291

COURSE STUDY: GENERAL
Candidates must belong to the Girl Scouts and have received the Gold Award. The scholarship may be used to attend any U. S. accredited school and must be utilized within 1 year of high school graduation. The award is $1,000 annually.

S87-
GIRLS INC. SCHOLARS PROGRAM
(formerly called THE READER'S DIGEST CAREER KEY AWARDS)
Girls, Inc.
Attn: Scholarships and Awards
30 East 33rd Street
New York, NY 10016-5394
(212) 689-3700
E-mail: HN3578@handsnet.org

COURSE STUDY: GENERAL
The fund provides financial assistance for post-secondary education of Girls Inc. members who are currently in high school and have been members of Girls Inc. for at least 2 years. Ten $1,000 scholarships and 7 to 10 $10,000 scholarships are awarded each year.

S88-
GLADYS ANDERSON EMERSON SCHOLARSHIP
Iota Sigma Pi
North Central College
Department of Chemistry
P.O. Box 3063
Naperville, IL 60566-7063
(708) 420-3491

COURSE STUDY: CHEMISTRY OR BIO-CHEMISTRY
Applicants must be a female chemistry or bio-chemistry student who has junior standing at a U.S. college or university. One award is given each year in the amount of $1,000.

S89-
GLADYS C. ANDERSON MEMORIAL SCHOLARSHIP
American Foundation for the Blind
11 Penn Plaza, Suite 300
New York, NY 10001
(212) 502-7600

COURSE STUDY: RELIGIOUS OR CLASSICAL MUSIC
The scholarship fund provides financial assistance to legally blind undergraduate women studying religious or classical music. Applicants must be U.S. citizens and have been accepted in a college or university program in religious or classical music. Each year two awards are given, each is $500.

S90-
GLADYS STONE WRIGHT MEMORIAL SCHOLARSHIP

Women Band Directors National Association
c/o Gladys S. Wright
345 Overlook Drive
West Lafayette, IN 47906-1219

COURSE STUDY: MUSIC EDUCATION
If you are a female student majoring in music education with the intent of becoming an active band director you are eligible for their annual award of $300.

S91-
THE GLEANER LIFE INSURANCE SOCIETY SCHOLARSHIP FOUNDATION
5200 West U.S. Hwy. 223
Adrian, MI 49221

COURSE STUDY: GENERAL
Financial assistance is available for female students who are enrolled full time in an accredited school, college or university in the United States. Annual awards vary according to need. Contact the foundation for current application guidelines.

S92-
GONSTEAD CHIROPRACTIC EDUCATIONAL TRUST
c/o Marshall & Illsley Trust Co.
P.O. Box 2980
Milwaukee, WI 53201
(608) 252-5958

COURSE STUDY: CHIROPRACTIC MEDICINE
The purpose of this trust is to provide scholarships to students who are studying chiropractic medicine at a member college of the Council of Chiropractic Education. Applicants must have maintained a 3.0 GPA for at least two years of study to apply. Several grants are given each year, each averaging $3,500.

S93-
GRASS VALLEY GROUP, INC. SCHOLARSHIP FOUNDATION
P.O. Box 1114, MIS 8N
Grass Valley, CA 95945
(916) 478-3136

COURSE STUDY: ECONOMICS
Students enrolled in an accredited school, college or university full time may apply for financial assistance through this Foundation. Applicants must be studying economics to apply. Annual awards vary according to need, average dollar amount is $2,500.

S94-
THE HARBURG FOUNDATION
c/o Goldfine
225 West 34th Street, Suite 1200
New York, NY 10122

COURSE STUDY: POLITICAL SCIENCE
Applicants must be a full time student in at least their junior year of college study in the areas of world peace, discrimination, American political art or related socio-economical issues. Several scholarships are granted each year, each averaging $2,000.

S95-
THE HARDING FOUNDATION
c/o Harding Foundation Building
P.O. Box 130 - Fifth and Hidalgo
Raymondville, TX 78580
(512) 689-2706

COURSE STUDY: THEOLOGY
Scholarships are primarily given to seminary students. Applicants must be enrolled in an approved seminary school studying for a master's degree in theology to apply. The total givings annually are $60,000, with the highest being $3,600.

S96-
HARRIETT BARNHART WIMMER SCHOLARSHIP
　　Landscape Architecture Foundation
　　4401 Connecticut Avenue, NW, Suite 500
　　Washington, DC 20008-2302
　　(202) 686-8337

COURSE STUDY: LANDSCAPE ARCHITECTURE
Candidates who are in their senior year majoring in landscape architecture are eligible to apply. Each year one award is given in the amount of $1,000.

S97-
HAZEL CORBIN ASSISTANCE FUND
　　Maternity Center Association
　　MCA Foundation, Inc.
　　281 Part Avenue South
　　New York, NY 10010
　　(212) 777-5000

COURSE STUDY: NURSE MIDWIFERY
The purpose of this fund is to increase the number of certified nurse-midwives practicing in the United States. Candidates must be a registered nurse, nurse-midwife in the U.S. and who were trained in other countries and American nurse-midwives who are not currently working. Generally 30 to 40 awards are given each year, amounts vary depending on individual circumstances, maximum award is $1,000.

S98-
HELEN MILLER MALLOCH SCHOLARSHIP
　　National Federation of Press Women, Inc.
　　4510 West 89th Street, Suite 110
　　Prairie Village, KS 66207-2282
　　(913) 341-0165

COURSE STUDY: JOURNALISM

Female students pursuing an undergraduate or graduate degree in journalism may apply for financial assistance. Applicants must be junior or senior level college students or graduate students majoring in journalism. Each year one award is given for $1,000.

S99-
HERMIONE GRANT CALHOUN SCHOLARSHIPS
National Federation of the Blind
Chair, Scholarship Committee
805 Fifth Avenue
Grinnell, IA 50112
(515) 236-3366

COURSE STUDY: GENERAL
Financial assistance is provided to female blind students pursuing studies in any area at the undergraduate or graduate level. Applicants must be legally blind to apply. The annual award is $3,000 and may be renewed for 2 additional years.

S100-
HEWLETT-PACKARD COMPANY SCHOLARSHIPS
Society of Women Engineers
120 Wall Street, 11th Floor
New York, NY 10005-3902
(212) 509-9577
E-mail: 71764.743@compuserve.com

COURSE STUDY: ENGINEERING
The purpose of the scholarship fund is to provide financial assistance to undergraduate women majoring in engineering. Applicants must be junior or senior women majoring in either electrical engineering or computer science at an accredited school. Seven awards are given each year, four for junior women and 3 for senior women. Each scholarship is $1,000.

S101-
THE J. EDGAR HOOVER FOUNDATION

c/o McNair Law Building
50 Gull Point Road
Hilton Head Island, SC 29928

COURSE STUDY: GOVERNMENT
The purpose of this fund is to provide educational funds to women wanting to uphold the principals set forth in the constitution of the United States of America. Applicants must be studying government and be a good citizen. Total annual giving is $107,000, with a high award of $3,000.

S102-
HOWARD T. ORVILLE SCHOLARSHIP IN METEOROLOGY
American Meteorological Society
45 Beacon Street
Boston, MA 02108-3696
(617) 227-2426
E-mail: sarmstrg@ametsoc.org

COURSE STUDY: METEOROLOGY OR OTHER SCIENCES
Applicants must be entering their last year of undergraduate schooling and majoring in meteorology or other related fields of atmospheric or oceanic and hydrologic sciences. Applicants must be U.S. citizens and have a 3.0 GPA. One award per year is offered at $2,000

S103-
IDA M. POPE MEMORIAL TRUST SCHOLARSHIP
Kamehameha Schools
1887 Makuakane Street
Honolulu, HI 96817-1887
(808) 842-8216

COURSE STUDY: GENERAL
The purpose of this scholarship program is to provide assistance for undergraduate or graduate education to women of Hawaiian or part-Hawaiian ancestry. Candidates must be enrolled or plan to enroll full time in an accredited 2 or 4 year college or university in Hawaii or on the mainland. No specific area of study is required to apply. The

number of awards given each year varies, with a range of awards from $200 to $1,500.

S104-
INFORMATION HANDLING SERVICES/SAE
WOMEN ENGINEERS COMMITTEE SCHOLARSHIP
Society of Automotive Engineers
400 Commonwealth Drive
Warrendale, PA 15096-0001
(412) 772-8534
E-mail: lorile@sae.org

COURSE STUDY: ENGINEERING
Any female who is at the postsecondary level of education and majoring in engineering may apply for this scholarship. Applicants must also be U.S. citizens and graduate from high school with at least a 3.0 GPA. The scholarship amount is $1,500 and is given annually.

S105-
IVY PARKER MEMORIAL SCHOLARSHIP
Society of Women Engineers
120 Wall Street, 11th Floor
New York, NY 10005-3902
(212) 509-9577
E-mail: 71764-743@compuserve.com

COURSE STUDY: ENGINEERING
Applicants must be undergraduate women majoring in engineering. The candidate must also be in their junior or senior year at an accredited school, college or university in the U.S. One award is given each year in the amount of $2,000.

S106-
JEANNETTE RANKIN AWARD
Jeannette Rankin Foundation, Inc.
P.O. Box 6653
Athens, GA 30604

COURSE STUDY: GENERAL
Candidates must be at least 35 years of age or older and studying at the post-secondary level of education. Applicants must be U.S. citizens and may be enrolled in a certified program of training or undergraduate education. Each year seven to ten awards are given, each award is $1,000.

**S107-
JEHOVAH JIREH, INC.**
P.O. Box 795
Clifton Park, NY 12065
(518) 383-1864

COURSE STUDY: THEOLOGY
Any women studying theology may apply for this scholarship program. The annual range of scholarship awards is from $500 to $12,000.

**S108-
JOHN AND MURIEL LANDIS SCHOLARSHIP AWARD**
American Nuclear Society
Attn: Scholarship Program
555 North Kensington Avenue
La Grange Park, IL 60525
(708) 352-6611

COURSE STUDY: NUCLEAR SCIENCE
The purpose of this scholarship program is to assist undergraduate or graduate students interested in a career in nuclear science, nuclear engineering or other nuclear-related fields. Applicants must be enrolled in a college or university located in the United States. Generally 5 awards are given each year, in the amount of $3,000 each.

**S109-
MYRNA M. JOHNSON MEMORIAL TRUST SCHOLARSHIP FUND**
1515 Charleston Avenue

Mattoon, IL 61938

COURSE STUDY: NURSING, MUSIC, ART
This program offers financial assistance to students who want to develop a career in music, art or nursing. Each year several awards are given averaging $800 per scholarships.

S110-
THE HARVEY AND BERNICE JONES CHARITALBE TRUST NO.2
c/o First National Bank
P.O. Box 249
Springdale, AR 72765

COURSE STUDY: GENERAL
Scholarships are awarded to any female full time student in an accredited school, college or university in the United States. Annual number of awards and dollar amounts vary with need.

S111-
JUDITH RESNIK MEMORIAL SCHOLARSHIP
Society of Women Engineers
120 Wall Street 11th Floor
New York, NY 10005-3902
(202) 509-9577
E-mail: 71764-743@compuserve.com

COURSE STUDY: ENGINEERING
Financial assistance is offered to women seniors majoring in an engineering field with a space related major. Each year one scholarship is offered in the amount of $2,000.

S112-
JUST FOUNDATION
5844 Heather Ridge
Gurnee, IL 60031
(847) 680-7002

COURSE STUDY: JOURNALISM OR BROADCASTING
Applicants must be entering their first year of undergraduate study in the fields of newspaper business, journalism or broadcasting. Applicants must be in the upper half of their class to apply. Dollar amount of the annual awards will not exceed $4,000.

S113-
KARLA SCHERER FOUNDATION SCHOLARSHIP
    Karla Scherer Foundation
    100 Renaissance Center, Suite 1680
    Detroit, MI 48243
    (313) 259-4520

COURSE STUDY: BUSINESS
The purpose of this scholarship program is to provide financial assistance to women who are undergraduate students, graduate students, re-entry women or women who have never attended college before. Applicants must be preparing for a career in business with a focus on finance and/or economics. Each year the foundation awards numerous scholarships, the amount of each award varies according to need.

S114-
KEHILAT KAMINETZ TRUST
    c/o Max Wasser
    132 Nassau Street
    New York, NY 10038

COURSE STUDY: RELIGIOUS STUDIES
The purpose of this trust fund is to provide financial assistance to serious students studying the Torah. Grants are awarded annually and the amounts vary according to need.

S115-
THE KIMBO FOUNDATION
    c/o Korea Central Daily, S.F.

685 Harrison Street
San Francisco, CA 94107
(415) 974-6500

COURSE STUDY: GENERAL
Scholarships are offered to individuals of Korean descent to further their education. Twenty grants per year are given ranging from $1,000 to several thousand dollars.

S116-
KNIGHTS OF COLUMBUS-BISHOP CHARLES P. GRECO GRADUATE FELLOWSHIPS

Knights of Columbus
Attn: Scholarship Department
P.O. Box 1670
New Haven, CT 06507-0901
(203) 772-2130

COURSE STUDY: TEACHER
Financial assistance is offered for graduate education of wives/widows, children and members of the Knights of Columbus. Candidates must be enrolled or accepted for full time graduate study and be planning to develop a career as a teacher of mentally retarded children. Awards are up to $5000 per semester and are renewable for up to three additional semesters.

S117-
LA FRA SCHOLARSHIP

Ladies Auxiliary of the Fleet Reserve Association
Attn: Scholarship Administrator
125 North West Street
Alexandria, VA 22314-2754
(800) 372-1924

COURSE STUDY: GENERAL
The purpose of this program is to provide financial assistance for the post-secondary education of daughters and granddaughters of naval personnel. One award is given each year in the amount of $2,500.

S118-
LILLIAN MOLLER GILBRETH SCHOLARSHIP
Society of Women Engineers
120 Wall Street, 11th Floor
New York, NY 10005-3902
(212) 509-9577
E-mail: 71764.743@compuserve.com

COURSE STUDY: ENGINEERING
Financial assistance is available to undergraduate women majoring in engineering. Junior and senior undergraduates enrolled at an accredited college, university or school and maintain a 3.5 GPA may apply. There is one scholarship given each year for $5,000.

S119-
LINDA RIDDLE/SGMA SCHOLARSHIP
Women's Sports Foundation
Eisenhower Park
1899 Hempstead Turnpike, Suite 400
East Meadow, NY 11554-1000
(516) 542-4700
E-mail: wosport@aol.com

COURSE STUDY: GENERAL-SPORTS
The purpose of this scholarship fund is to provide young female athletes of limited financial means with the opportunity to advance their sports career while pursuing their college education. Candidates must be a senior in high school preparing to enter college the following fall full-time at an accredited 2-4 year college or university. The number of awards varies each year and the amount of each award is $1,500.

S120-
MANA NATIONAL SCHOLARSHIP PROGRAM
MANA, A National Latina Organization
1725 K Street, NW Suite 501
Washington, D.C. 20006
(202) 833-0060

COURSE STUDY: GENERAL
Financial support is available to Latina women who wish to continue their education at the undergraduate or graduate level. Applicants must be enrolled as a full time student at an accredited college or university in the U.S. Each year 20 + awards are given, each for $1,000.

S121-
MARK J. SCHROEDER SCHOLARSHIP IN METEOROLOGY
American Meteorological Society
45 Beacon Street
Boston, MA 02106-3693
(617) 227-2426
E-mail: sarmstrg@ametsoc.org

COURSE STUDY: METEOROLOGY - OTHER SCIENCES
Students in their senior year of undergraduate study and majoring in meteorology or any related atmospheric sciences may apply. Candidates must be U.S. citizens, enrolled in an accredited college or university and have a 3.0 GPA. One award is given each year in the amount of $3,000.

S122-
MARY PAOLOZZI MEMBERSHIP SCHOLARSHIP
Navy Wives' Club of America
P.O. Box 6971
Washington, DC 20032

COURSE STUDY: GENERAL
Financial assistance is provided to members of the Navy Wives' Club of America for post-secondary education. Several awards are given each year ranging from $500 to $1,000 each.

S123-
MARY'S PENCE GRANT PROGRAM
Mary's Pence
P.O. Box 29078

Chicago, IL 60629-9078
(708) 499-3771

COURSE STUDY: SOCIAL STUDIES
Any Catholic woman living in the United States and wanting to advance her education in the areas of social structures may apply. Two programs are available to Catholic women, one related to direct service with women and one for education and study. Grants for direct service are up to $3,000 and for education and study up to $1,500.

S124-
MASWE MEMORIAL SCHOLARSHIP
Society of Women Engineers
120 Wall Street, 11th Floor
New York, NY 10005-3902
(212) 509-9577
E-mail: 71764-743@compuserve.com

COURSE STUDY: ENGINEERING
Financial assistance is available to junior or senior college women majoring in the field of engineering. Candidates must be attending an accredited school, college or university in the United States. Each year two awards are given, each for $2,000.

S125-
W.H. McCLENNAN SCHOLARSHIP FUND
c/o The International Assn. of Fire Fighters
1750 New York Ave., NW
Washington, DC 20006-5395
(202) 737-8484

COURSE STUDY: GENERAL
Scholarships are available to children or dependents of fire fighters who died in the line of duty. Applicants must be enrolled or intend to enroll in an accredited school, college or university in the United States and must maintain a 2.0 GPA. Ten grants are awarded, each $2,500.

S126-
VERNE-CATT McDOWELL CORPORATION
P.O. Box 128
Albany, OR 97321

COURSE STUDY: THEOLOGY
Financial assistance is available for graduate theological studies. Applicants must be members the Christian Church and be studying in the United States. Individual amounts and number of grants vary with each year according to needs.

S127-
WILLIAM J. McMANNIS & A. HASKELL McMANNIS EDUCATIONAL FUND
c/o Marine Bank Trust Department
P.O. Box 8480
Erie, PA 16553
(814) 871-9597

COURSE STUDY: GENERAL
Women studying for a baccalaureate or graduate degree and who are U.S. citizens may apply for financial assistance. Several awards are given each year varying from $300 to $2,000.

S128-
ARTHUR AND ANN MARCIANO SCHOLARSHIP AND CHARITABLE TRUST
18 Baldwin Farms North
Greenwich, CT 06830
(203) 869-9187

COURSE STUDY: GENERAL
Financial assistance is available to female students enrolled full time in an accredited school, college or university. Applicants must be U.S. citizens and be studying at the undergraduate level. Eight awards are given annually in the amount of $500 each.

S129-
MEAT CUTTERS EDUCATIONAL TRUST
    7018 Lindsley
    Dallas, TX 75223-1116

COURSE STUDY: GENERAL

This special interest group offers financial assistance to daughters of members of UFCW Unions. Candidates must be high school seniors and have completed SAT or ACT tests. Annual awards total $13,000, with individual amounts varying according to need.

S130-
MICROSOFT CORPORATION SCHOLARSHIPS
    Society of Women Engineers
    120 Wall Street, 11th Floor
    New York, NY 10005-3902
    (212) 509-9577
    E-mail: 71764.748@compuserve.com

COURSE STUDY: ENGINEERING

Microsoft Corporation scholarships are provided to undergraduate or graduate women studying computer sciences or computer engineering. There are ten awards given each year, each is $1,000.

S131-
JOHN MISKOFF FOUNDATION
    9605 North East 79th Avenue, No. 16
    Hialeah Gardens, FL 33016
    (305) 754-5169

COURSE STUDY: GENERAL

Any female student who has completed her sophomore year of college is eligible to apply for financial assistance through this foundation. Annual amounts vary according to need and range from $1,000 to $6,000 each.

S132-
MISS AMERICA PAGEANT SCHOLARSHIP
    Miss America Pageant
    Attn: Executive Vice President
    P.O. Box 119
    Atlantic City, NJ 08404
    (609) 345-7571

COURSE STUDY: GENERAL
The purpose of this scholarship fund is to provide educational scholarships as rewards to local, state and national level winners of the Miss America Pageant. Applicants must be between ages of 17 and 26, single, U.S. citizens and female. $29,000,000 is awarded annually, with individual scholarships ranging from $2,500 to $35,000.

S133-
MISS INDIAN USA SCHOLARSHIP PROGRAM
    American Indian Heritage Foundation
    6051 Arlington Boulevard
    Falls Church, VA 22044-2788
    (202) INDIANS

COURSE STUDY: GENERAL
Miss Indian USA scholarship program is awarded through the pageants held as local, state and national levels. Candidates must be of Native American decent, exhibit a talent, be 18 to 26 years of age, high school graduates and never married. Over $12,000 in scholarships is awarded each year.

S134-
MISS NATIONAL TEEN-AGER SCHOLARSHIP PROGRAM
    National Teen-Ager Foundation
    Attn: Cherly Snow
    P.O. Box 610187
    Dallas, TX 75261
    (817) 540-0313

COURSE STUDY: GENERAL

America's talented teens are recognized at a local, regional and national level through this scholarship fund. Applicants must be 13 to 18 years of age. More than $2.5 million in cash, tuition scholarships and awards are presented in state and regional pageants. Financial support also comes from several academic institutions who offer scholarships to the state and national winners.

S135-
MISS T.E.E.N PAGEANT

Miss T.E.E.N Pageant
c/o Diane Brandes
Box 329
Long Prairie, MN 56347
(612) 732-2115

COURSE STUDY: GENERAL

Applicants must be women, single and between the ages of 13 and 18 to qualify for entry into the Miss T.E.E.N. Pageant at any level. Over $100,00 is awarded in cash each year in scholarships and prizes.

S136-
MISS TEENAGE AMERICA PAGEANT

Miss Teenage America Program
c/o Teen Magazine
Peterson Publishing Co.
6420 Wilshire Boulevard
Los Angeles, CA 90048-5515
(213) 782-2950

COURSE STUDY: GENERAL

Outstanding female high school students residing in the United States are eligible to enter the Miss Teenage America Pageant program. Applicants must be 13 to 18 years of age and never married. $15,000 in college scholarships and $5,000 in modeling contracts is annually awarded.

S137-
MOBILE MEDICAL MISSION HOSPITAL, INC.
1919 Plaza Tower
Knoxville, TN 37929

COURSE STUDY: MEDICINE
Scholarships are available to full time students who are pursuing a career in medicine. Candidates are required to volunteer ten percent of their time to care for low-income citizens. The number and dollar amount of the awards varies according to need.

S138-
THE MODGLIN FAMILY FOUNDATION
P.O. Box 1338
Huntington Beach, CA 92647

COURSE STUDY: THEOLOGY
Financial assistance is provided to students attending a theological seminary and are planning a career in this field of study. Individual grants are given annually and vary from $1,500 to $31,000.

S139-
NATIONAL ASSOCIATION OF NEGRO BUSINESS AND PROFESSIONAL WOMEN'S CLUBS SCHOLARSHIP PROGRAMS
National Associations of Negro Business and Professional Women's Clubs
1806 New Hampshire Avenue, NW
Washington, DC 20009-3208
(202) 483-4206

COURSE STUDY: GENERAL
Financial assistance is available to young black women advancing their education to post-secondary levels. Awards are given through the local Negro Business and Professional Women's Clubs. Applicants must be a high school senior or first level college student. The amount of each of the annual awards varies with a minimum of $1,000 each award.

S140-
NATIONAL ASSOCIATION OF WOMEN IN CONSTRUCTION MEMBER SCHOLARSHIPS

National Association of Women in Construction Education Foundation
327 South Adams
Fort Worth, TX, 76104
(817) 877-5551

COURSE STUDY: CONSTRUCTION, GENERAL

Financial assistance is available to members of the National Association of Women in Construction for special courses or apprenticeships and for degrees. Candidates must be intending to study at an approved vocational school, college or university. The annual number of awards varies according to need, however over $25,000 per year is awarded in scholarships.

S141-
NATIONAL HISPANIC DESIGNERS MODEL SEARCH

JC Penney Company, Inc.,
P.O. Box 10001
Dallas, TX, 75301-8105
(214) 431-4182

COURSE STUDY: GENERAL

This program is available to women of Hispanic descent and who are between the ages of 16 and 22. Applicants must have a nonprofessional modeling status. Applicants can receive awards at the local, regional and national level. Scholarships range from $2,500 to $500, plus numerous cash and merchandise awards.

S142-
NATIONAL TOP FEMALE "MATHLETE"

American Association of University Women Educational Foundation
1111 16th Street, NW
Washington, DC 20036-4873
(202) 785-7700

E-mail: foundation@mail.aauw.org

COURSE STUDY: MATHEMATICS
Through the annual Mathcounts National Competition, a college scholarship is awarded to outstanding female mathematicians. Each year one scholarship is awarded in the amount of $3,000.

S143-
NAVY-MARINE CORPS RELIEF SOCIETY SPOUSE TUITION AID PROGRAM
>Navy-Marine Corps Relief Society
>Attn: Education Programs
>801 North Randolph Street, Suite 1228
>Arlington, VA 22203-1978
>(703) 696-4904

COURSE STUDY: GENERAL
Financial assistance is provided for undergraduate or graduate studies to the spouses of active duty Navy and Marine service members. The program is open to spouses who reside at overseas locations and where education is available. The number of awards varies each year with a maximum per term of $300 for undergraduate study and $350 per term for graduate study. The maximum for any one recipient per academic year is $1,500.

S144-
NEW YORK LIFE FOUNDATION SCHOLARSHIP PROGRAM FOR WOMEN IN THE HEALTH PROFESSIONS
>Business and Professional Women's Foundation
>2012 Massachusetts Avenue, NW
>Washington, DC 20036
>(202) 293-1200

COURSE STUDY: HEALTH CARE PROFESSIONS
Financial assistance is available to women interested in pursuing studies in the health care fields. Applicants must be 25 years of age or older and be a U.S. citizen. Applicants must also be enrolled in an

accredited program or course of study. A total of $50,000 is granted annually with individual scholarships ranging from $500 to $1,000.

S145-
NFPW JUNIOR/SENIOR SCHOLARSHIP
National Federation of Press Women
4510 West 89th Street, Suite 110
Prairie Village, KS 66207-2282
(913) 341-0165

COURSE STUDY: COMMUNICATIONS
Candidate must be in their junior or senior year of college study in the field of communications and planning to pursue a career in the communications industry. Also, candidates must be graduating with a degree in journalism. Annual award amount is $500, funds are used to pay tuition.

S146-
NIAF-CORNARO SCHOLARSHIP
National Italian American Foundation
Attn: Education Director
666 11th Street, NW, Suite 800
Washington, DC 20001-4596
(202) 638-0220

COURSE STUDY: GENERAL
Any Italian-American woman who is planning to enter or has entered college as a graduate or undergraduate student may apply for financial assistance through this program. Each year one award is given in the amount of $1,000.

S147-
NIH UNDERGRADUATE SCHOLARSHIP PROGRAM FOR INDIVIDUALS FROM DISADVANTAGED BACKGROUNDS
National Institutes of Health
Attn: Loan Repayment and Scholarship Programs
Federal Building, Room 604

7550 Wisconsin Avenue NSC 9015
Bethesda, MD 20892-9015
(800) 528-7689
E-mail: kk10b@nih.gov

COURSE STUDY: LIFE SCIENCES, BIOMEDICAL RESEARCH
Any female undergraduate student who is majoring in the life sciences, planning to pursue a career in biomedical research and is from a disadvantaged background may apply for financial aid through this program. Applicants must be U.S. citizens, and a full time student at a qualified accredited school, college or university. Applicants must contact the above program for information on definition of disadvantaged. Annually 15 awards are given and can be as high as $20,000 per year. Awards may be renewed for up to 3 additional years.

S148-
NORTHROP CORPORATION FOUNDERS SCHOLARSHIP
Society of Women Engineers
120 Wall Street, 11th Floor
New York, NY 10005-3902
(212) 509-9577
E-mail: 71764.743@compuserve.com

COURSE STUDY: ENGINEERING
Female students entering their sophomore year at an accredited school, college or university are eligible to apply. Applicant must also be majoring in engineering and be a U.S. citizen and have a 3.5 GPA. One award is given each year in the amount of $1,000.

S149-
NSPE-AUXILIARY SCHOLARSHIP
National Society of Professional Engineers
Attn: Educational Foundation
1420 King Street
Alexandria, VA 22314-2794
(703) 684-2858

COURSE STUDY: ENGINEERING
Female students majoring in engineering and maintaining a 3.0 GPA may apply for financial aid through this program. Applicants must also be U.S. citizens and be enrolled in an accredited school, college or university. One award is given each year in the amount of $1,000.

S150-
OLIVE LYNN SALEMBIER SCHOLARSHIP
Society of Women Engineers
120 Wall Street, 11th Floor
New York, NY 10005-3902
(212) 509-9577
E-mail: 71764.743@compuserve.com

COURSE STUDY: ENGINEERING
Female applicants who are undergraduate or graduate students and have been away from the engineering market for a minimum of 2 years may apply for financial aid. Applicants must intend to return to school to complete their education in engineering and be planning to obtain the credentials necessary to reenter the job market as an engineer. The annual award is given in the amount of $2,000.

S151-
PAUL H. KUTSCHENREUTER SCHOLARSHIP
American Meteorological Society
45 Beacon Street
Boston, MA 02108-3693
(617) 227-2426
E-mail: sarmstrg@ametsoc.org

COURSE STUDY: METEOROLOGY - SCIENCE
Applicants must be in their final year of undergraduate study in the field of meteorology or related study of atmospheric, oceanic or hydrologic sciences and intend to make the major area of study their profession. Applicants must also be U.S. citizens and have a 3.0 GPA. One award is given each year in the amount of $5,000.

S152-
P.E.O. PROGRAM FOR CONTINUING EDUCATION
P.E.O. Sisterhood
Attn: Executive Office
3700 Grand Avenue
Des Moines, IA 50312-2899
(515) 255-3153

COURSE STUDY: GENERAL
Any female from the United States or any other country can apply for financial aid to resume their college education. Applicants must be sponsored by a local chapter of the P.E.O. Sisterhood. The annual amounts vary and number of awards vary according to need.

S153-
P.H.P., INC.
P.O. Box 319
Hopkinsville, KY 42240

COURSE STUDY: GENERAL
Students enrolled in or planning to enroll in an accredited school may apply for financial assistance through this program. Financial assistance is not based on area of study. Applicants must prove need for financial assistance to continue secondary education. Annual grants are given ranging from $500 to $5,000 each award.

S154-
PHI CHI THETA SCHOLARSHIP PROGRAM
Phi Chi Theta Foundation
Attn: Scholarship Committee
8656 Totempole Drive
Cincinnati, OH 45249

COURSE STUDY: BUSINESS ADMINISTRATION - ECONOMICS
Female students who have enrolled as a full time student in business administration or economics are eligible to apply for financial aid through this program. Applicants must be enrolled in an approved

college or university. The annual award averages $1,000, three awards are given each year.

S155-
POLONSKY BROTHERS FOUNDATION
151 Harding Rd.
Red Bank, NJ, 07701
(908) 741-8438

COURSE STUDY: GENERAL
The purpose of this scholarship fund is to provide financial assistance to disadvantaged urban youths to help cover tuition, books, travel and fees for schooling. Applicants must be enrolled in or planning to enroll in an accredited school, college or university in the United States. Thirty five grants have been given in the past ranging from $100 to $6,000.

S156-
RAQUEL MARQUEZ FRANKEL SCHOLARSHIP FOR HISPANIC WOMEN
Mexican American Women's National Association (MANA)
1725 K Street, NW Suite 501
Washington, DC 20006
(202) 833-0060

COURSE STUDY: GENERAL
The purpose of this program is to provide financial assistance to Latina women studying at the undergraduate or graduate level. Applicants must be enrolled at a post-secondary or vocational institution. One or more awards are given each year. The awards range from $200 to $1,000.

S157-
RAWLINGS MEMORIAL SCHOLARSHIP FUND, INC.
925 Euclid Ave., No. 1525
Cleveland, OH 44115-1407

COURSE STUDY: GENERAL
The purpose of this scholarship fund is to provide financial assistance to graduate students who have participated in college baseball for four years and lettered in baseball at least one year. Applicants can apply for the annual grants through their collegiate baseball coaches. Number of annual awards and dollar amounts vary according to need.

S158-
RITA DIMARITINO SCHOLARSHIP IN COMMUNICATIONS

MANA A National Latina Organization
1725 K Street, NW, Suite 501
Washington, DC 20006
(202) 833-0060

COURSE STUDY: COMMUNICATIONS
Any Latina women who is enrolled in an accredited school, college or university and is majoring in communications may apply. Applicants must be intending to use their education in the field of communication to advance Latino interests and the Latino community. One award is given each year in the amount of $1,000.

S159-
RITA LEVINE MEMORIAL SCHOLARSHIP

American Mensa Education and Research Foundation
201 Main Street, Suite 1101
Fort Worth, TX 76102-3115
(817) 332-2600

COURSE STUDY: GENERAL
Any woman who has been away from her field of study at an accredited school, college or university for at least 7 years is eligible to apply. The purpose of the fund is to provide financial assistance to these women to continue their education. Annually there is one award, the amount varies according to need.

S160-
THE RETIRED OFFICERS ASSOCIATION SCHOLARSHIP FUND
    201 North Washington Street
    Alexandria, VA 22314-2539
    (703) 549-2311

COURSE STUDY: GENERAL
Scholarship awards are available to any dependent children of active, retired or decreased military officers or enlisted personnel or members of the Association. Applicants must be enrolled or are planning to enroll full time in an accredited school, college or university in the United States. Applicants must be single, under the age of 24 and have not yet received their bachelor's degree. Number and dollar amount of annual awards varies according to need, with the average award being $2,000.

S161-
RAYMOND A. RICH CHARITABLE FOUNDATION
    Rose Tree Ranch
    HCI Box 15
    Elgin, AZ 85611

COURSE STUDY: GENERAL
Scholarships are available to students who are enrolled or are planning to enroll full time in an accredited school, college or university in the United States. The average annual awards are $3,500.

S162-
JACKIE ROBINSON FOUNDATION, INC.
    Three West 35th Street
    New York, NY 10001-2204

COURSE STUDY: GENERAL
This program provides financial assistance to minority youth who wish to enroll in a 4 year degree program at an accredited school, college or university. The program offers various annual awards and the amounts of each award varies with need.

S163-
THE ROOTHBERT FUND, INC.
475 Riverside Drive, Room 252
New York NY 10115
(212) 870-3116

COURSE STUDY: TEACHING
The purpose of this program is to provide financial assistance to female undergraduate and graduate students enrolled in a degree program for teachers. The annual awards vary with individual amounts between $1,000 and $2,000.

S164-
CHARLES M. ROSS TRUST
c/o Henry Phillips
113 West Walnut Street
Fairbury, IL 61739
(815) 692-4336

COURSE STUDY: RELIGION, SOCIOLOGY, MEDICINE, TEACHING
Scholarships are provided for graduate students studying in the fields of religion, sociology, medicine or teaching. The annual awards vary and the dollar amount varies with need. Awards can range from $500 to $2,000 each.

S165-
S. EVELYN LEWIS MEMORIAL SCHOLARSHIP IN MEDICAL HEALTH SCIENCES
Zeta Phi Beta Sorority, Inc.
1734 New Hampshire Avenue, NW
Washington, DC 20009
(202) 387-3103

COURSE STUDY: MEDICINE, HEALTH SCIENCES
The purpose of this program is to assist women who are pursuing a career in medicine or health sciences at the undergraduate or graduate level. Candidates must be enrolled in an institution offering a degree

in medicine or health sciences and be enrolled in either program. One or more awards is given each year ranging from $500 to $1,000.

S166-
LEOPOLD SCHEPP FOUNDATION
551 Fifth Avenue, Suite 3000
New York, NY 10176
(212) 986-3078

COURSE STUDY: GENERAL
This fund provides financial assistance in the form of a scholarship to any full-time student studying at the undergraduate level at an accredited college or university. Applicants must be U.S. citizens. The annual givings vary from $1,000 to $20,000 per award.

S167-
WILLIAM E. SCHMIDT FOUNDATION, INC.
4445 Commerce Street
Evansville, IN 47710

COURSE STUDY: GENERAL
Financial assistance is available to female students enrolled or planning to enroll as a part time or full time student in an accredited school, college or university in the United States. Applicants must be between the ages of 16 and 20 and have written proof of GPA. Three grants are awarded each year, ranging between $10,000 and $5,000 each.

S168-
THE SCHOLARSHIPS FOUNDATION, INC.
Canal St. Station
P.O. Box 6020
New York, NY 10128

COURSE STUDY: GENERAL
The purpose of this unique program is to provide scholarships to undergraduate and graduate students with priority given to those who do not fit into defined scholarship categories. Applicants must be at

least 20 years of age and have two years remaining in their course of study. Annual awards vary, amounts range from $2,000 to $500 each.

S169-
SPORTSGIRL OF THE YEAR
'Teen Magazine
6420 Wilshire Boulevard
Los Angeles, CA 90048-5515
(213) 782-2950

COURSE STUDY: GENERAL- SPORTS
Financial assistance is provided to reward teenage females who are outstanding athletes and pursuing post-secondary education. Candidates must be teenage female athletes who excel in sports and are between the ages of 12 and 19. Two awards are given per year, one for $10,000 and a second for $3,000.

S170-
THE STATLER FOUNDATION
Statler Towers, Suite 508
Buffalo, NY 14202
(716) 852-1104

COURSE STUDY: HOTEL - FOOD SERVICE MANAGEMENT
The Statler Foundation offers numerous scholarships to students majoring in hotel or food service management. Contact the foundation for specific information on the requirements for the annual awards.

S171-
'TEEN ATHLETE OF THE YEAR
'Teen Magazine
Peterson Publishing Company
6420 Wilshire Boulevard
P.O. Box 48994
Los Angeles, CA 90048-5515
(213) 782-2950

COURSE STUDY: GENERAL-SPORTS
The purpose of this program is to offer financial assistance to outstanding female high school athletes attending school in the United States. Applicants must be between the ages of 13 and 18 to apply and do not hold any professional standing in a sport. This annual award is a $10,000 college scholarship plus several additional prizes.

S172-
TEXACO FOUNDATION SCHOLARSHIPS
Society of Women Engineers
120 Wall Street, 11th Floor
New York, NY 10005-3902
(212) 509-9577
E-mail: 71764.743@compuserve.com

COURSE STUDY: ENGINEERING
This scholarship program is open to women students who are members of the Society of Women Engineers, are U.S. citizens, and in the junior year of college study and are majoring in chemical or mechanical engineering. Each year two awards are given in the amount of $2,000 each. Each award is renewable if the recipient is in the top 20 percent of her class.

S173-
THEOFANI AND JOHN GEO-KARIS MEMORIAL AWARD
Daughters of Penolope
Attn: National Scholarship Chair
1909 Q Street, NW, Suite 500
Washington, DC 20009-1007
(202) 234-9741

COURSE STUDY: GENERAL
The purpose of this program is to provide financial assistance to Greek women who wish to pursue post-secondary educational studies. Applicants must have been a member of the Daughters of Penolope or the Maids of Alhepa for at least 2 years and be applying to a college, university or accredited technical school. The annual award is $1,000 and is renewable for 2 additional years at a rate of $500 per year.

S174-
TRAINING AWARDS PROGRAM
Soroptimist International of the Americas, Inc.
1616 Walnut Street
Philadelphia, PA 19103-5313
(215) 732-0512

COURSE STUDY: GENERAL
The purpose of this program is to help women, particularly women reentering the job market, upgrade their economic status through education. Candidates must be 30 years of age or older. They must be heads of their household or have families dependent on them and have not yet completed a college degree. Fifty-four regional awards and one finalist are chosen each year. Each regional award is $3,000 and one finalist is given $10,000 for education.

S175-
ULLERY CHARITABLE TRUST
c/o Liberty Bank & Trust Co. of Tulsa, N.A.
P.O. Box 1
Tulsa, OK 74193
(918) 586-5594

COURSE STUDY: THEOLOGY
The purpose of this scholarship fund is to provide financial assistance to students entering into the study of theology and plan to develop a career in this area of service. Individual awards and the number of awards given each year varies with need.

S176-
UNDERGRADUATE AWARD FOR EXCELLENCE IN CHEMISTRY
Iota Sigma Pi
North Central College
Department of Chemistry
P.O. Box 3063
Naperville, IL 60566-7063
(708) 420-3491

COURSE STUDY: CHEMISTRY
This program honors female undergraduate student who excel in chemistry. The applicant must be a senior woman chemistry student at an accredited college or university. The award of $300 is given each year.

S177-
UPS SCHOLARSHIP FOR FEMALE STUDENTS
Institute of Industrial Engineers
25 Technology Park/Atlanta
Norcross, GA 30092-3295
(770) 449-0460

COURSE STUDY: INDUSTRIAL ENGINEERING
The purpose of this program is to provide financial assistance to any female undergraduate student who will be or is enrolled in a degree program in industrial engineering at an accredited college, school or university. Applicants must maintain a 3.4 GPA and completed 5 full quarters or 3 full semesters of study. The annual award is $2,500.

S178-
USO DESERT STORM EDUCATION FUND
USO World Headquarters
Attn: Scholarship Program
Washington Navy Yard, Building 198
901 M Street, SE
Washington, DC 20374-5096
(202) 610-5700

COURSE STUDY: GENERAL
The purpose of this program is to provide financial assistance for academic or vocational education of spouses and children of military personnel who died in the Persian Gulf War. Department of Defense guidelines will be used to determine eligibility. USO will distribute all the funds to eligible persons in equal amounts. All eligible survivors will receive funding.

S179-
USPA & IRA EDUCATIONAL FOUNDATION
P.O. Box 2387
Fort Worth, TX 76113

COURSE STUDY: GENERAL
The purpose of this program is to provide scholarships to undergraduates who are a family member of an active duty, retired, or deceased military person. Several annual awards are given and individual amounts vary according to need.

S180-
USTA/NATIONAL JUNIOR TENNIS LEAGUE, INC.
70 West Red Oaks Lane
White Plains, NY 10604-3602
(914) 696-7231

COURSE STUDY: GENERAL-SPORTS
The purpose of this scholarship fund is to provide financial assistance to National Junior Tennis League players who need support. Applicants may apply for three different scholarships; Secondary School Educational Scholarships, Individual Player Scholarships, and College Educational Scholarships. Grant amounts vary according to the scholarship fund and individual need.

S181-
VIRGINIA D. HENRY SCHOLARSHIP
National Society of Professional Engineers
1420 King Street
Alexandria, VA 22314-2794
(703) 684-2800

COURSE STUDY: ENGINEERING
This program offers financial assistance to high school female students who are pursuing a 4 year degree program in engineering. Applicants must have a 3.0 GPA and be a U.S. citizen. One award is given each year in the amount of $1,000.

S182-
WESTINGHOUSE BERTHA LAMME SCHOLARSHIPS
Society of Women Engineers
120 Wall Street, 11th Floor
New York, NY 10005-3902
(212) 509-9577
E-mail: 71764.743@compuserve.com

COURSE STUDY: ENGINEERING
Any female freshman student majoring in engineering at an accredited school, college or university may apply for this scholarship program. Applicants must be U.S. citizens. The annual award is $1,000 and three are given each year.

S183-
WHIRLY-GIRLS HELICOPTER FLIGHT TRAINING SCHOLARSHIP
Whirly-Girls Scholarship Fund
Executive Towers 10-D
207 West Clarendon Avenue
Phoenix, AZ 85013
(602) 263-0190

COURSE STUDY: HELICOPTER LICENSING
Financial assistance is available to women pilots who are pursuing their additional rotorcraft helicopter rating. Applicants must have a FAA, airplane balloon, or glider pilot license to apply. The annual award is $4,500.

S184-
KATHRYN M. WHITTEN TRUST
c/o Farmers & Merchants Trust Company
P.O. Box 891
Long Beach CA 90801

COURSE STUDY: GENERAL
Financial assistance is available to full-time students studying in the United States at an accredited school, college or university in any field

of study. Candidates must maintain a "B" average. Several annual awards are given, varying from $3,500 to $500.

S185-
OLIVER WIGHT EDUCATIONAL FOUNDATION, INC.
c/o Kutak, Rock & Campbell
4400 Georgia Pacific Center
133 Peachtree St, NE
Atlanta, GA 30303
(603)763-9707

COURSE STUDY: MANUFACTURING
This scholarship fund provides financial assistance to students at the undergraduate level wishing to advance their career in the field of manufacturing. Number and dollar amount of awards varies according to need.

S186-
DAVID H. WINTON FOUNDATION, INC.
c/o Kirlin, Campbell & Keating
14 Wall Street, 23rd Floor
New York NY 10005
(212) 732-5520

COURSE STUDY: GENERAL
The purpose of this program is to provide scholarships based on financial need to students attending colleges and universities throughout the U.S. Any area of study will be accepted, students must prove financial need. Over $7,500 is available annually.

S187-
WOMEN IN ACCOUNTING UNDERGRADUATE SCHOLARSHIPS
Educational Foundation for Women in Accounting
530 Church Street, Suite 700
Nashville, TN 37219
(615) 254-3687

COURSE STUDY: ACCOUNTING
Female students majoring in a 4 year degree program in accounting may apply for financial support through this program. The yearly amount and number of awards varies each year with need.

S188-
WOMEN IN GEOGRAPHIC EDUCATION SCHOLARSHIPS
>National Council for Geographic Education
>16A Leonard Hall
>Indiana University of Pennsylvania
>Indiana, PA 15705
>(412) 357-6290

COURSE STUDY: GEOGRAPHIC STUDIES
Female students, both undergraduate and graduate women, are eligible for financial assistance offered through this fund if their major field of study is geographic education. One award is given each year in the amount of $300.

S189-
WOMEN'S TRANSPORTATION SEMINAR UNDERGRADUATE SCHOLARSHIPS
>Women's Transportation Seminar
>One Walnut Street
>Boston, MA 02108-3616
>(617) 367-3273
>wts@tec.ccmail.compuserve.com

COURSE STUDY: TRANSPORTATION
This program offers financial assistance to female undergraduate students majoring in a career in a transportation related field. Applicants must be enrolled or planning to enroll in an accredited school, college or university in the United States. The annual award varies in dollar amount depending upon the need.

S190-
WOMEN'S WESTERN GOLF FOUNDATION SCHOLARSHIP
Women's Western Golf Foundation
c/o Mrs. Richard Willis
393 Ramsay Road
Deerfield, IL 60015

COURSE STUDY: GENERAL-SPORTS
Any female undergraduate who is interested in the sport of golf may apply for financial assistance through this program. Applicants need not excel in the game of golf to apply and receive the scholarship. Applicants must plan to enroll in an accredited school, college or university in the United States. The annual award is $3,000.

S191-
MARY BYRD WYMAN MEMORIAL ASSOCIATION OF BALTIMORE CITY
3130 Golf Course Road West
Owing Mills, MD 21117
(410) 363-1395

COURSE STUDY: GENERAL
The purpose of this program is to provide financial assistance to female students studying any major at the undergraduate level. Annual awards and amounts vary according to need.

S192-
YOUTH MINISTRY, INC.
P.O. Box 16764
Greensboro, NC 27416-0764
(901) 299-5201

COURSE STUDY: THEOLOGY
Financial assistance is available to students who are studying biblical and theological fields with the goal of developing a career in these fields of interest. Applicants must have not received their ordination to apply for funds. Annuals awards vary according to need, the range of awards is from $32,000 to $100 each.

GRANTS

Grants are programs that provide funds to support women's efforts, travel, projects, creative activities or research on any level. They can apply to a range from undergraduate to post-doctorate, professional or other interests.

In some cases, proposals may be submitted by institutions or organizations which contribute to the betterment of women with their programs. If you represent such an organization, pay special attention to what is listed in this category.

G1-
AAUW DISSERTATION FELLOWSHIPS
American Association of University Women
Attn: Educational Foundation
2201 North Dodge Street
Iowa City, IA 52243-4030
(319) 337-1716

INTEREST AREA: DISSERTATION
The purpose of this grant is to provide financial assistance to women in the final year of writing their dissertation. Applicants must be citizens of the United States and have completed all required course work and examinations. Students requesting financial assistance who are in engineering need to apply for a separate grant offered by the AAUW. Fifty awards are given each year, the individual award amount is $14,500.

G2-
AAUW POSTDOCTORAL FELLOWSHIPS
American Association of University Women
Attn: Educational Foundation
2201 North Dodge Street
Iowa City, IA 52243-4030
(319) 337-1716

INTEREST AREA: POSTDOCTORAL RESEARCH
The purpose of this grant is to reward women who have achieved distinction in their fields of scholarly work. Applicants must be working on postdoctoral research and are U.S. citizens. One award is set aside specifically for an under represented minority woman. Ten awards are given each year. Awards range from $20,000 to $25,000.

G3-
AAUW SUMMER FELLOWSHIPS
American Association of University Women
Attention: Educational Foundation
2201 North Dodge Street
Iowa City, IA 52242-4030

(319) 337-1716

INTEREST AREA: POSTDOCTORAL STUDIES
The purpose of this grant fund is to provide summer fellowships to women scholars for their postdoctoral research. There are no restrictions on place of study, field of study or age of applicants. Each year 6 fellowship awards are granted, each is $5,000.

G4-
ACADEMIC CAREER AWARDS
>National Institutes of Health
>Attention: Office of Extramural Research
>Extramural Outreach and Information Resources Office
>6701 Rockledge Drive, Room 6207
>MSC 7910
>Bethesda, MD 20892-7910
>(301) 435-0714
>E-mail: asknih@odrockm1.od.nih.gov

INTEREST AREA: SCIENCE RESEARCH
NIH provides financial support to individuals who are developing or improving curriculum in a particular scientific field with the intention of improving the educational or research capacity of the institution granting the financial aid. Contact the National Institutes of Health for specific information on the programs offered. The NIH provides salary and fringe benefits for the candidate.

G5-
ACADEMIC RESEARCH ENHANCEMENT AWARD
>National Institutes of Health
>Attention: Office of Extramural Research
>Extramural Outreach and Information Resources Office
>6701 Rockledge Drive, Room 6207
>MSC 7910
>Bethesda, MD 20892-7910
>(301) 435-0714
>E-mail: asknih@odrockm1.od.nih.gov

INTEREST AREA: RESEARCH
This program offers grant monies to researchers at educational institutions which have not received more than $2 million per year from NIH for other research studies. Minority and women's institutions are encouraged to apply. Up to $75,000 in available per year.

G6-
ADHF/AGA STUDENT RESEARCH FELLOWSHIPS
American Digestive Health Foundation
7910 Woodmont Avenue, Suite 700
Bethesda, MD 20814-3015
(301) 654-2635

INTEREST AREA: DIGESTIVE-NUTRITION RESEARCH
Funds for this program are available to high school, undergraduate, graduate or medical students in the U.S. Each grant is $2,500 and there are up to 35 grants awarded each year.

G7-
AGING WOMEN AND BREAST CANCER GRANTS
National Institutes of Health
Attention: National Institute on Aging
Geriatrics Program
Building 31, Suite 5C05
31 Center Drive
Bethesda, MD 20892
(301) 496-5278
E-mail: ry3e@nih.gov

INTEREST AREA: BREAST CANCER
Financial assistance is available to support research that focuses on the conditions of older women with breast cancer. Monies go to the institution and not directly to the researcher/investigator. The amount of the award depends on the nature of the proposal and the number of awards varies each year.

G8-
RITA ALLEN FOUNDATION, INC.
550 Park Avenue
New York, NY 10021

INTEREST AREA: RESEARCH
The purpose of this financial assistance is to provide medical research grants to university research scientists. Research must be in the fields of cancer, multiple sclerosis, cerebral palsy, andeuphorics and analgesics related to the terminally ill. Grants for research total $405,500, individual amounts vary.

G9-
ALLIANCES FOR MINORITY PARTICIPATION GRANTS
National Science Foundation
Attention: Directorate for Education and Human Resources
Division of Human Resource Development
4201 Wilson Boulevard, Room 815
Arlington, VA 22230
(703) 306-1632
E-mail: hrdamp@nsf.gov

INTEREST AREA: SCIENCE - ENGINEERING
The purpose of this financial assistance program is to support college programs designed to increase the quality and quantity of undergraduate students in science and engineering fields. Grants up to $1 million per year are available and there are approximately 5 grants awarded each year.

G10-
ALZHEIMER'S ASSOCIATION INVESTIGATOR-INITIATED RESEARCH GRANTS
Alzheimer's Association
Attention: Medical and Scientific Affairs
919 North Michigan Avenue, Suite 1000
Chicago, IL 60611-1676
(312) 335-8700

INTEREST AREA: RESEARCH
The purpose of this financial assistance is to provide funding for research on Alzheimer's Disease to investigators with at least 3 years post-doctoral experience and who are working in nonprofit institutions. Each year $50,000 is available for grants, there can be as many as 15 awards each year.

G11-
AMERICAN HEART ASSOCIATION ESTABLISHED INVESTIGATOR GRANT
    American Heart Association
    Attention: Division of Research Administration
    7272 Greenville Avenue
    Dallas, TX 75231-4596
    (214) 706-1453
    E-mail: ncrp@amhrt.org

INTEREST AREA: CARDIOVASCULAR RESEARCHERS
Financial assistance is available to help develop the careers of clinician-scientists who wish to continue their profession as cardiovascular investigators. Applicants must be U.S. citizens and hold an M.D., Ph.D. D.O. or equivalent degree. Contact the AHA for requirements for application. Four awards are given annually, each is $75,000 and up to $40,000 for project support costs.

G12-
AMERICAN HEART ASSOCIATION GRANT-IN-AID
    American Heart Association
    Attention: Division of Research Administration
    7272 Greenville Avenue
    Dallas, TX 75231-4596
    (214) 706-1453
    E-mail: ncrp@amhrt.org

INTEREST AREA: HEART DISEASE RESEARCH
The purpose of this fund is to provide financial assistance to investigators who have developed well defined research proposals in

the areas of cardiovascular function and disease, stroke, basic science, clinical or public health problems. Each year 100 awards are given, each up to $55,000.

G13-
AMERICANS FOR MIDDLE EAST UNDERSTANDING, INC.
475 Riverside Drive
New York, NY 10115
(212) 870-2053

INTEREST AREA: RESEARCH: MIDDLE EAST
The purpose of this fund is to provide financial assistance in the form of grants to support studies, research and other projects concerning the Middle East. Annual grants to individuals vary according to need.

G14-
ANNIE JUMP CANNON AWARD IN ASTRONOMY
American Association of University Women
Attn: Educational Foundation, Department AJC
1111 16th Street, NW
Washington, DC 20036-4873
(800) 821-4364

INTEREST AREA: ASTRONOMY
The purpose of this financial aid is to assist women in their research in astronomy. Applicants must be under age 35 and plan a career in astronomy. Each year one award is given in the amount of $5,000.

G15-
ARTISTS' BOOK RESIDENCY GRANTS
Women's Studio Workshop
P.O. Box 489
Rosendale, NY 12472
(914) 658-9133

INTEREST AREA: BOOK ARTISTS

Financial assistance and a residency to women book artists is provided by this grant. Grant is $1,800, plus $450 for material and housing while in residence. The number of grants varies each year.

G16-
ASPEN INSTITUTE NONPROFIT SECTOR RESEARCH FUND
Aspen Institute
1333 New Hampshire Avenue, NW, Suite 1070
Washington, DC 20036
(202) 736-5800
E-mail: nsrfund1@aol.com

INTEREST AREA: RESEARCH
Research by scholars and practitioners on the underlying values, capacity and effectiveness of nonprofit organizations and philanthropies will be considered for financial support through this fund. Grants are awarded in two categories, contact the Aspen Institute for detailed information. One grant is for $20,000 and one is for $50,000.

G17-
ASPIRE HIGHER GRANTS FOR GIRLS
Women's Sports Foundation
Eisenhower Park
1899 Hempstead Turnpike, Suite 400
East Meadow, NY 11554-1000
(516) 542-4700
E-mail: wosport@aol.com

INTEREST AREA: WOMEN - SPORTS
Financial support is provided for projects or programs submitted by individuals, clubs, institutions or other organizations seeking to promote sports and fitness opportunities for women. Number of awards varies each year, grants up to $5,000 are awarded.

G18-
BAAUSCH & LOMB CONTACT LENS DIVISION RESEARCH GRANT
>Women's Sports Foundation
>Eisenhower Park
>1899 Hempstead Turnpike, Suite 400
>East Meadow, NY 11554-1000
>(516) 542-4700

INTEREST AREA: VISION AND SPORTS
This program provides financial assistant for research related to vision and sports performance of female athletes. Any researcher, whether university affiliated, organizational affiliated or independent may apply. One award is given each year in the amount of $5,000.

G19-
THE BAGBY FOUNDATION FOR THE MUSICAL ARTS, INC.
>501 Fifth Avenue
>New York, NY 10017

INTEREST AREA: MUSIC
The Foundation provides financial assistance in the form of grants for musical study. Grants are awarded based on talent and need. Number and dollar amount of awards varies each year according to need.

G20-
BANTLY CHARITABLE TRUST
>1578 Crestline Drive
>Atlanta, GA 30345

INTEREST AREA: RELIGIOUS - MEDICAL RESEARCH
The purpose of this trust is to provide monies for religious study and medical research. Program descriptions for medical and religious study need to be requested from the Trust. Each year approximately $12,000 is available for funding. Individual grants range from $3,500 to $500.

G21-
BELLAGIO CENTER RESIDENCY
> Rockefeller Foundation
> 1133 Avenue of the Americas
> New York, NY 10036
> (212) 869-8500

INTEREST AREA: GENERAL
The Foundation is very flexible in the area of study and provides financial and other support to women wanting a place to engage in creative activities. Scholars in any discipline, writers and composers are eligible. Women and minorities are encouraged to apply. Free room and board are awarded for 5 week durations. Two or three awards are given for each residency period.

G22-
THE BILL BALDWIN FUND, INC.
> 176 Third Street,
> Troy, NY 12180-4459

INTEREST AREA: PERIODICAL INDUSTRY
The purpose of this fund is to provide grants for people in the periodical industry. Details for grant application can be obtained by contacting the foundation. Grants to individuals have annually totaled at least $8,500.

G23-
BEHAVIORAL SCIENCES RESEARCH TRAINING FELLOWSHIPS
> Epilepsy Foundation of America
> Attention: Dept. of Research and Professional Education
> 4351 Garden City Drive
> Landover, MD 20785
> 800-EFA-1000
> E-mail: postmaster@efa.org

INTEREST AREA: RESEARCH

Financial assistance is available for research in epilepsy treatment. Applicants must have their doctoral degree in a field of the behavioral sciences. Up to $30,000 per year is available for individual research projects.

G24-
BERLEX FOUNDATION, INC.
530 Fifth Avenue, 25th Floor
New York, NY 10036
(212) 719-5613

INTEREST AREA: MEDICAL RESEARCH
Financial assistance is available in the form of grants to medical doctors for research in the field of reproductive medicine. Doctors must be affiliated with a university or laboratory institution. Number and dollar amount of grants varies each year according to need.

G25-
BIOMEDICAL RESEARCH FELLOWSHIP PROGRAM
Mary Ingraham Bunting Institute
Attn: Fellowship Office
Radcliffe College
34 Concord Avenue
Cambridge, MA 02138
(617) 495-8212
E-mail: bunting_fellowships@radcliffe.harvard.edu

INTEREST AREA: RESEARCH
Financial assistance is available to women with doctorates in biomedical sciences and are interested in research study at the Mary Ingraham Bunting Institute. The fellows receive $34,000 per year plus up to $3,000 in research expenses. Each year two awards are given.

G26-
BRUCE L. "BIFF" REED AWARD
Geological Society of America
Attn: Research Grants Administrator

3000 Penrose Place
P.O. Box 9140
Boulder, CO 80301-9140
(303) 447-2020
E-mail: jforstro@geosociety.org

INTEREST AREA: GEOLOGICAL RESEARCH
This program is available to graduate students in geology who are at the master's or doctoral level. Applicants do not need to be members of the society to apply. The number of awards given each year varies, each grant is approximately $1,600.

G27-
BUDGET RENT-A-CAR LEADERSHIP DEVELOPMENT GRANTS
Women's Sports Foundation
Eisenhower Park
1899 Hempstead Turnpike, Suite 400
East Meadow, NY 11554-1000
(800) 227-3988
E-mail: wosport@aol.com

INTEREST AREA: WOMEN - SPORTS TRAINERS
The purpose of this fund is to provide training for women as sports leaders, coaches, officials and administrators of girls' and women's sports. Organizations, schools, sports clubs and individuals may apply. The number of awards varies, grants range from a high of $4,000 to a low of $500.

G28-
CAMPUS MINISTRY ADVANCEMENT, INC.
1602 Northbrook Drive
Indianapolis, IN 46260

INTEREST AREA: MINISTERY
Grant money is available to students for the purpose of strengthening and advancing campus ministry in the United States. The grants are

made to institutions on behalf of the individual recipient. This program has approximately $15,000 to provide as financial assistance.

G29-
CARNEGIE CORPORATION OF NEW YORK
437 Madison Avenue
New York, NY 10022
(212) 371-3200

INTEREST AREA: RESEARCH
The purpose of this financial assistance fund is to provide monies for research in specific interest areas. There are four major areas of research interest: The Education and Healthy Development of Children and Youth; Strengthening Human Resources in Developing Countries (concentrated efforts are on the development of women leadership); Cooperative Security and Special Projects. Total givings are approximately $42,500,000, individual amounts vary according to need.

G30-
CAREER ADVANCEMENT AWARDS FOR WOMEN SCIENTISTS AND ENGINEERS
National Science Foundation
Attn: Directorate for Education and Human Resources
Senior Staff Associate for Cross Directorate Programs
4201 Wilson Boulevard, Room 805
Arlington, VA 22230
(703) 306-1603

INTEREST AREA: RESEARCH - SCIENCE OR ENGINEERING
Financial assistance is available in the form of grants to experienced women researchers in the field of science or engineering and wish to expand their research career. The maximum award per year per individual is $50,000 with a possible additional $10,000 for equipment.

G31-
JAMES McKEEN CATTELL FUND

Department of Psychology, Duke University
Durham, NC 27706
(919)-684-3902

INTEREST AREA: SABBATICAL SUPPORT
Financial assistance is available in the form of grants given for postdoctoral training to supplement sabbatical allowances for psychologists. Applicants must be teaching at universities in North America. The grants enable a faculty member to take a full year sabbatical rather than only half a year. Depending on budget, 5-6 grants are awarded annually up to a maximum of $20,000 per grant.

G32-
CENTER FOR ECONOMIC POLICY RESEARCH INTERNATIONAL FOUNDATION
c/o Portes, Sharp, Herbst, and Kravets
333 West Wacker Drive, Suite 500
Chicago, IL 60606

INTEREST AREA: RESEARCH PUBLICATION
Grants are available for the production of scholarly papers suitable for publication by the Center. Applicants must be established professional economists to apply. The dollar amount of the grants varies with need.

G33-
CHESED AVRHOM HACOHN FOUNDATION
c/o Gateway Bancorp, Inc.
60 Bay Street
Staten Island, NY 10301
(718) 948-7643

INTEREST AREA: RELIGIOUS INSTRUCTION
Grants are provided for the continued education of rabbinical scholars. Two awards are given each year to assist serious students wanting to become rabbis, teachers and leaders or instructors. The number and dollar amount of each grant varies according to need.

G34-
CHINA TIMES CULTURAL FOUNDATION
43-27 36th Street
Long Island City, NY 11101
(718) 392-0995

INTEREST AREA: TRAVEL RELATED TO CHINESE HISTORY
Grant money is available for Chinese scholars to attend conferences relating to the history and development of China. Applicants must be of Chinese ancestry. The number and dollar amount of each grant varies according to need.

G35-
CISE POSTDOCTORAL RESEARCH ASSOCIATES IN COMPUTATIONAL SCIENCE AND ENGINEERING
National Science Foundation
Attn: Directorate for Computer and Information Science and Engineering
Division of Advanced Scientific Computing
New Technologies Program
4201 Wilson Boulevard
Arlington, VA 22230
(703) 306-1970
E-mail: ntpd@nsf.gov

INTEREST AREA: FACULTY APPOINTMENT
Grant monies are available to provide financial resources to academic institutions wanting to increase the number of women faculty members who are trained to do research in the fields of Computer and Information Science and Engineering. Awards include a salary range of $25,000 to $38,000, research expense allowance of $4,000, and travel, publication and other related expense allowance of $4,200. Each year 15 awards are given by the National Science Foundation for this project.

G36-
THE COMMONWEALTH FUND
One East 75th Street

New York NY 10021-2692
(212) 535-0400

INTEREST AREA: NURSING - MEDICINE
The purpose of this grant fund is to provide grants in nursing and medicine for minority students. Over 60 grants have been issued, the number and dollar amount varies with need, individual grants have ranged from $15,000 to $6,000.

G37-
CLARE BOOTHE LUCE JUNIOR FACULTY APPOINTMENT
Clare Boothe Luce Fund
c/o Henry Luce Foundation, Inc.
111 West 50th Street
New York, NY 10020
(212) 489-7700

INTEREST AREA: FACULTY FUNDING
A five year contract for additional women faculty is available to academic institutions who wish to increase the number of women on their faculty. Candidates must submit the nature of the teaching and research projects. Over 9 institutions have recently received this award. Each award is between $225,000 and $430,000 for a 5 year teaching period.

G38-
COLLABORATIVES FOR EXCELLENCE IN TEACHING PREPARATION PROGRAM
National Science Foundation
Attn: Directorate for Education and Human Resources
Division of Undergraduate Education
4201 Wilson Boulevard, Room 835
Arlington, VA 22230
(703) 306--1669
E-mail: undergrad@nsf.gov

INTEREST AREA: ADVANCE K-12 TEACHERS

The purpose of this program is to provide financial resources to support the design and implementation of teacher preparation programs which result in the advancement of K-12 teachers who have demonstrated the most advanced thinking and learning for science and mathematics. Contact the Foundation for details of application. The range of sponsorship is between $200,000 and $1 million per year.

G39-
COMMUNITY ACTION GRANTS
American Association of University Women
Attn: Educational Foundation
2201 North Dodge Street
Iowa City, IA 52243-4030
(319) 337-1716

INTEREST AREA: EDUCATION
The purpose of this grant fund is to provide financial assistance for branches or divisions of the American Association of University Women or to persons (women) for projects and/or research (non-degree) that promotes education and equity for women and girls. Proposals must have a direct community or public impact. Approximately 45 grants are giving each year ranging from $500 to $5,000 each.

G40-
COMMUNITY HOSPITAL FOUNDATION, INC.
P.O. Box 24185
Houston, TX 77229

INTEREST AREA: MEDICINE
The purpose of this fund is to provide grants to graduate students seeking a degree in medical related education. Total giving, $265,000, grants to individuals varies according to need.

G41-
CONTINENTAL GRAIN FOUNDATION
10 South Riverside Plaza

Chicago, IL 60606
(312) 466-6542

INTEREST AREA: EXCHANGE PROGRAMS
The program provides grants to students for exchange programs between the U.S. and other countries. Total giving, $122,180, grants to individuals vary according to need.

G42-
COUNCIL ON LIBRARY RESOURCES, INC.
1785 Massachusetts Avenue, NW No. 313
Washington, DC 20036-2117
(202) 483-7474

INTEREST AREA: LIBRARIANS
Financial assistance is available in the form of grants to provide support to librarians for research grants and the Academic Library Management Intern Program. Total giving, $623,000 grants to individuals vary according to need.

G43-
COURSE AND CURRICULUM DEVELOPMENT PROGRAM
National Science Foundation
Attn: Directorate for Education and Human Resources
Division of Undergraduate Education
4201 Wilson Boulevard, Room 835
Arlington, VA 22230
(703) 306-1681
E-mail: undergrad@nsf.gov

INTEREST AREA: SCIENCE, MATH, ENGINEERING, TECHNOLOGY
Funding is available to academic institutions and organizations intending to revitalize their undergraduate programs in science, mathematics, engineering and technology. Details for application can be obtained by writing to NSF. Grants can range from $30,000 to $800,000 depending the scope of the projects.

G44-
TRUSTEES UNDER THE WILL OF LOTTA M. CRABTREE
294 Washington Street, Room 636
Boston, MA 02108
(617) 451-0698

INTEREST AREA: THEATRE
The purpose of this program is to provide monies for young women training in the theatrical profession. Grants to individuals vary in number and dollar amount according to need.

G45-
OPAL DANCEY MEMORIAL FOUNDATION
c/o Manufacturers National Bank of Detroit,
Trust Tax Department
100 Renaissance Center
Detroit, MI 48243

INTEREST AREA: THEOLOGY
The purpose of this fund is to provide grants for students attending seminaries and schools of theology. Grants to individuals vary according to need ranging from $700 to $12,000.

G46-
DECISION MAKING PROCESSES IN WOMEN'S HEALTH
National Institutes of Health
Attn: National Institute of Nursing Research
Natcher Building, Room 3AN-12
45 Center Drive MSC 6300
Bethesda, MD 20892-6300
(301) 594-5966
E-mail: pmoritz@ep.ninr.nih.gov

INTEREST AREA: RESEARCH WOMENS HEALTH
Financial assistance for research is provided to investigators at universities, colleges, hospitals, units of state and local government, and eligible agencies from the federal government. Research must be

on the treatment and intervention processes related to non-cancerous health problems of women where the decisions often result in a hysterectomy. The number of and dollar amount of awards given each year varies according to the nature of the proposals and availability of funds.

G47-
THE GLADYS KRIEBLE DELMAS FOUNDATION
c/o Reid and Priest
40 West 57th Street, 27th Floor
New York, NY 10019
(212) 603-2302

INTEREST AREA: RESEARCH - VENICE ITALY
The purpose of this grant fund is to provide financial assistance for predoctoral or postdoctoral research only. Research is for the study of Venice, Italy and for travel to Venice, Italy. Applicants must be U.S. citizens. Grant amounts vary according to need and availability of funds.

G48-
THE DIABETES RESEARCH & EDUCATION FOUNDATION, INC.
P.O. Box 6168
Bridgewater, NJ 08807-9998
(908) 658-9322

INTEREST AREA: DIABETES RESEARCH & EDUCATION
Financial assistance is provided in the form of grants for diabetes research and education initiatives that would usually not be considered for funding by traditional research Foundations. The Foundation underwrites granted projects in basic and clinical research and education. The Foundation has in recent years awarded 65 grants to individuals, ranging from $20,000 to $2,300.

G49-
DIABETES TREATMENT CENTERS OF AMERICA FOUNDATION
One Burton Hills Boulevard, Suite 300
Nashville, TN 37215

INTEREST AREA: RESEARCH - DIABETES
The purpose of this fund is to provide monies for research grants for the study of diabetes. Specifications for grant monies can be obtained through the Diabetes Treatment Centers of American Foundation office. The range of individual giving is from $45,000 to $2,400.

G50-
DIRECTING WORKSHOP FOR WOMEN
American Film Institute
Attn: Production Training
2021 North Western Avenue
P.O. Box 27999
Los Angeles, CA 90027-1625
(213) 856-7721

INTEREST AREA: FILM AND TELEVISION
Financial assistance is provided to assist professional women in the film and television arts to acquire skills to increase their talents as film and television directors. Candidates need to have experience in television, film video or the dramatic arts and must be U. S. citizens. The workshop is an 18 month time commitment to direct a 30-minute video. Twelve candidates are chosen and each receives $5,000 per project.

G51-
DIVERSITY ACTION GRANTS
American Society of Mechanical Engineers
Attn: Board of Minorities and Women
1828 L Street, NW, Suite 906
Washington, DC 20036-5104
(202) 785-3756
E-mail: engles@asme.org

INTEREST AREA: STUDENT INVOLVEMENT ON CAMPUS
Funding is provided to student sections of the American Society of Mechanical Engineers to increase the participation of women students in any of the ASME student activities. The number of awards varies each year, the dollar amount ranges from $500 to $1,500.

G52-
DOE LABORATORY COOPERATIVE POSTGRADUATE RESEARCH TRAINING PROGRAM
>Oak Ridge Institute for Science and Education
>Attn: Science/Engineering Education Division
>P.O. Box 117
>Oak Ridge, TN 37831-0117
>(800) 569-7749
>E-mail: lbcooppr@orau.gov

INTEREST AREA: POSTGRADUATE RESEARCH - ENERGY & ENGINEERING FIELDS
Funding is provided for postgraduate research and training at the research facilities of the U.S. Department of Energy (DOE). Applicants must have completed a graduate degree in life sciences, earth sciences, physical sciences, computer sciences, mathematics, engineering, environmental sciences or other scientific disciplines. The award amount depends upon the research area and degree, the number of awards each year varies.

G53-
DOE LABORATORY GRADUATE PARTICIPATION PROGRAM
>Oak Ridge Institute for Science and Education
>Attn: Science/Engineering Education Division
>P.O. Box 117
>Oak Ridge, TN 37831-0117
>(800) 569-7749
>E-mail: labgpp@orau.gov

INTEREST AREA: GRADUATE RESEARCH

Funding is provided for graduate thesis or dissertation research at selected U.S. Department of Energy research laboratories. Applicants must be degreed in life sciences, physical sciences, social sciences, mathematics or engineering and have completed all degree requirements except their thesis or dissertation research. Annual financial assistance is $14,000 with tuition and fees of $3,500 paid per year. Approximately 15 awards are given each year.

G54-
DOROTHY LEET GRANTS
International Federation of University Women
c/o American Association of University Women
1111 16th Street, NW
Washington, DC 20036-4873
(202) 785-7700

INTEREST AREA: GRADUATE RESEARCH/STUDY

Funding is provided to assist women graduates who are interested in pursuing additional study or research in another country. Applicants must be members of the Association or the Federation. The number and dollar amount of grants varies each year. Recently, 18 grants were award in one year.

G55-
DRUG ABUSE PREVENTION INTERVENTION FOR WOMEN AND MINORITIES
National Institutes of Health
Attn: National Institute of Drug Abuse
Division of Epidemiology and Prevention Research
Parklawn Building, Room 9A-53
5600 Fishers Lane
Rockville, MD 20857
(301) 443-1514
E-mail: rn29e@nih.gov

INTEREST AREA: INTERVENTION - DRUG ABUSE & WOMEN/MINORITIES

The purpose of this program is to provide financial assistance for advanced research in the study of drug abuse prevention and intervention for minorities and women. Applicants are accepted from public, nonprofit or for-profit institutions, and local, state or federal government agencies. The amount awarded varies depending upon the funds available and the scope of the projects.

G56-
DRUG ABUSE TREATMENT FOR WOMEN OF CHILDBEARING AGE AND THEIR CHILDREN
National Institutes of Health
Attn: National Institute on Drug Abuse
Division of Clinical and Services Research
Parklawn Building, Room 10A-30
5600 Fishers Lane
Rockville, MD 20857
(301) 443-4060
E-mail: ft10v@nih.gov

INTEREST AREA: DRUG ABUSE AND WOMEN
Funds are provided for research to improve the effectiveness of drug abuse treatment programs for women of childbearing age and their children. Applicants must be researchers from public, non-profit or for-profit institutions and local, state or federal government agencies. The number and dollar amount of each grant varies according to need and the scope of the programs being supported.

G57-
JOHN P. EAGER EDUCATIONAL TRUST
P.O. Box 1017
Concord, NH 03302-1017

INTEREST AREA: MICROGRAPHICS
The purpose of this grant fund is to provide financial assistance to students with an interest in micrographics. Applicants must be U.S. citizens to apply. Grant amounts and the number of grants vary according to need.

G58-
ECONOMIC JUSTICE FOR WOMEN GRANTS
Rockefeller Family Fund
1290 Avenue of the Americas
New York, NY 10104
(2120 373-4252
E-mail: rff@mcimail.com

INTEREST AREA: JUSTICE FOR WOMEN
The fund supports projects that are designed to promote economic justice for women in the United States. In the past, this fund has supported projects which provide equal employment opportunities, opportunities of employment into nontraditional jobs; litigation to upgrade job status and salaries for women of color and research and education efforts to achieve equal pay for women. Only tax-exempt organizations promoting educational and charitable activities of national significance may apply. Grants range from $15,000 to $30,000 and last for one year. Usually the Fund awards 15 grants a year.

G59-
EDUCATIONAL FOUNDATION OF THE NATIONAL RESTAURANT ASSOCIATION
c/o National Restaurant Association
1200 17th Street, NW
Washington, DC 20036-3097
(312) 715-1010

INTEREST AREA: FOOD SERVICE
The purpose of this fund is to provide monies for studies in the food service area. Work-study grants are awarded to teachers and administrators in the food service area. Grants to individuals range from a high of $3,000, to a low of $750.

G60-
ELEANOR ROOSEVELT FUND RESEARCH AND DEVELOPMENT AWARD

American Association of University Women
Attn: Educational Foundation
1111 16th Street, NW
Washington, DC 20036-4873
(202) 785-7700
E-mail: foundation@mail.aauw.org

INTEREST AREA: EQUAL EDUCATION FOR WOMEN
The purpose of this fund is to provide financial support to individuals, organizations, institutions or projects that provide equal school environments for women and girls. The annual awards range from $2,000 to $5,000 and usually there is only one award per year.

G61-
ELEANOR ROOSEVELT TEACHER FELLOWSHIPS
American Association of University Women
Attn: Educational Foundation
2201 North Dodge Street
Iowa City, IA 52243-4030
(319) 337-1716

INTEREST AREA: TEACHERS
Women public school teachers who have taught for at least 3 consecutive years in grades K through 12 may apply. Applicants have to be teaching mathematics, science or technology courses for at-risk girls. Applicants must also be U.S. citizens. The dollar amount per award varies from $1,000 to $10,000 depending upon the proposed program. Each year 15 awards are granted.

G62-
ELOISE GERRY FELLOWSHIPS
Sigma Delta Epsilon - Graduate Women in Science, Inc.
P.O. Box 19947
San Diego, CA 92159
(610) 583-4856
E-mail: dcbrown@crash.cts.com

INTEREST AREA: RESEARCH - BIOLOGICAL/CHEMICAL SCIENCES
Graduate and postgraduate women students who are interested in scientific research are eligible to apply. Generally the annual awards range from $1,000 to $4,000 and up to 8 awards are given each year.

G63-
ENGINEERING DISSERTATION FELLOWSHIPS
>American Association of University Women
Attn: Educational Foundation
2201 North Dodge Street
Iowa City, IA 52243-4030
(319) 337-1716

INTEREST AREA: DISSERTATION - ENGINEERING
The program offers financial assistance to women who are working on their doctoral dissertations and are majoring in engineering. Candidates must be U.S. citizens. The award is $14,500 and the funds are not to be used to cover tuition for additional course work.

G64-
THE EPPLEY FOUNDATION FOR RESEARCH, INC.
>c/o Turk, Marsh, Kelly & Hoare
575 Lexington Avenue
New York, NY 10022
(212) 371-1660

INTEREST AREA: RESEARCH: PHYSICAL/BIOLOGICAL SCIENCES
Grants are provided primarily for postdoctoral research in the physical and biological sciences. Applicants must be associated with a recognized educational and charitable organization. The annual grants to individuals varies with need ranging from $25,000 to $2,100.

G65-
ERNST & YOUNG FOUNDATION
>c/o Ernst & Young

787 Seventh Avenue
New York, NY 10019
(212) 773-3000

INTEREST AREA: RESEARCH: FINANCE- ACCOUNTING
Funds are available in the form of grants to doctoral candidates in the fields of tax research, accounting and auditing. Annually over 15 grants are given to individuals ranging from $28,500 to $13,000.

G66-
ETIOLOGY, CONSEQUENCES AND BEHAVIORAL PHARMACOLOGY OF FEMALE DRUG ABUSE
National Institutes of Health
Attn: National Institute on Drug Abuse
Division of Epidemiology and Prevention Research
Parklawn Building, Room 9A-53
5600 Fishers Lane
Rockville, MD 20857
(301) 443-6637
E-mail: cj39g@nih.gov

INTEREST AREA: RESEARCH - DRUG ABUSE & WOMEN
Financial assistance is offered to investigators at public, non-profit or for-profit institutions and local, state or federal government agencies studying the etiology, natural history and consequences of drug abuse unique to women. The amount awarded each year varies depending upon the funds available and the scope of the proposed programs.

G67-
EVEN START FAMILY LITERACY PROGRAM IN A WOMAN'S PRISON
Department of Education
Attn: Office of Elementary and Secondary Education
Compensatory Education Programs
Portals Building, Room 4400
600 Independence Avenue, SW
Washington, DC 20202-6132
(202) 260-0991

INTEREST AREA: EDUCATION OF PRISON WOMEN AND THEIR CHILDREN
Funds are available for a program for low-income families with mothers in prison. The purpose of the program is to integrate early childhood education, adult literacy or adult basic education into a unified family literacy program. Applications are accepted from a prison (not a federal prison) that houses women and their preschool aged children, an institution of higher education, a local educational agency, a hospital or other public or private organization. Up to $200,000 is available for this program which is awarded once a year.

G68-
EVIAN RESEARCH GRANT
    Women's Sports Foundation
    Eisenhower Park
    1899 Hempstead Turnpike, Suite 400
    East Meadow, NY 11554-1000
    (516) 542-4716
    E-mail: wosport@aol.com

INTEREST AREA: SPORTS PERFORMANCE
Financial assistance is provided for research on re-hydration and the sports performance of female athletes. Independent and/or university affiliated researchers may apply. There is one award given each year in the amount of $5,000.

G69-
FACULTY RESEARCH ENHANCEMENT SUPPORT PROGRAM
    National Institutes of Health
    Attn: Extramural Associates Program
    Rockledge, II, Room 6187A
    6701 Rockledge Drive MSC 7910
    Bethesda, MD 20892-7910
    (301) 435-2692
    E-mail: mk51q@nih.gov

INTEREST AREA: RESEARCH: BIOMEDICAL
Financial assistance is available in the form of grant monies for salaries to women who wish to participate in and contribute to biomedical research. The program sponsors the researcher for a 10 week tenure at the NIH. The dollar amount is comparable to salary being received by the associate at the time of selection. The number of awards varies each year.

G70-
FEMINIST THEOLOGY AWARD
> Unitarian Universalist Association
> Attn: Women's Federation
> 25 Beacon Street
> Boston, MA 02108
> (617) 742-2100

INTEREST AREA: THEOLOGY AND FEMINISM
The purpose of this financial assistance is to provide monies for the advancement of scholarly and/or creative works in feminist theology. Proposed projects must be finished within 2 years. Applicants must be Unitarian Universalist women. Three awards are given each year ranging from $2,500 to $1,000.

G71-
THE REGINALD A. FESSENDEN EDUCATIONAL FUND, INC.
> P.O. Box 3490
> San Diego, CA 92163
> (619) 488-4991

INTEREST AREA: EDUCATION
The purpose of this fund is to provide grants for education. Recipients are chosen based on their service to humanity. The number of grants awarded each year varies according to the need. Grants range from $6,500 to $1,500.

G72-
FOUNDATION FOR NUTRITIONAL ADVANCEMENT

600 New Hampshire Avenue, NW No. 720
Washington, DC 20037
(202) 337-4442

INTEREST AREA: NUTRITION
The purpose of this program is to provide grants primarily for research on micro-nutrition and health and nutrition in the treatment and prevention of diseases. Grants to individuals have annually totaled over $90,000.

G73-
THE FRANCIS FAMILIES FOUNDATION
800 West 47th Street, Suite 604
Kansas City, MO 64112
(816) 531-0077

INTEREST AREA: PULMONARY DISEASE
The purpose of this program is to provide grants for research in pulmonary disease or anesthesiology. Over $2,000,000 is available through this fund, annual dollar amounts and number of awards vary with need and scope of program submitted.

G74-
THOMAS GERBER & KAY GERBER FOUNDATION
c/o Bess Brill
5600 Wisconsin Avenue, No. 1307
Chevy Chase, MD 20815

INTEREST AREA: MEDICAL RESEARCH
The purpose of this fund is to provide funding for medical research. Up to $12,000 is available on an annual basis.

G75-
J. PAUL GETTY TRUST
401 Wilshire Boulevard, Suite 1000
Santa Monica, CA 90401-1455
(310) 395-0388

INTEREST AREA: HISTORY: ARTS AND HUMANITIES
The purpose of this fund is to provide grants for study of the history of arts and humanities. Applicants must be in their postdoctoral study or senior research projects. Grants range from $70,000 to $2,000.

G76-
GLOBAL FUND FOR WOMEN GRANTS
Global Fund for Women
425 Sherman Avenue, Suite 300
Palo Alto, CA 94306-1823
(415) 853-8305
E-mail: gfw@igc.apc.org

INTEREST AREA: WOMEN & SOCIAL IMPROVEMENTS
Funds are available for programs sponsored by organizations committed to the improvement of women in society. Applicants must be organizations in countries other than the United States and must be run by women. The focus is on women's rights, communications and economic development. Grants range from $3,000 to $10,000 each and usually more than 80 grants are given each year.

G77-
GRANTS TO COMBAT VIOLENT CRIMES AGAINST WOMEN
Department of Justice
Attn: Office of Justice Programs
Violence Against Women Program Office
633 Indiana Avenue, NW, Fourth Floor
Washington, DC 20531
(202) 307-6026

INTEREST AREA: LAW ENFORCEMENT
The purpose of this program is to provide financial assistance to develop programs for victim services in cases involving violent crimes against women. Monies are provided to develop and strengthen law enforcement and prosecution strategies. Funds may be used to provide personnel, training, technical assistance, date collection, equipment,

etc. Over $130 million has been available for grants to states under this program. Each state is eligible to receive funding through this program.

G78-
GRETCHEN L. BLECHSCHMIDT AWARD
Geological Society of America
Attn: Research Grants Administrator
3300 Penrose Place
P.O. Box 9140
Boulder, CO 80301-9140
(303) 447-2020 ext. 137
E-mail: jforstro@geosociety.org

INTEREST AREA: RESEARCH: GEOLOGY
Funds are provided for women conducting research related to their Ph.D. in geology. Women candidates must be interested in a career in academic research. Annual grants are up to $2,500 each, one award is given each year.

G79-
THE HARRY FRANK GUGGENHEIM FOUNDATION
527 Madison Avenue, 15th floor
New York, NY 10022-4301
(212) 644-4907

INTEREST AREA: RESEARCH: SCIENCES
The purpose of this fund is to provide monies for doctoral and postdoctoral research in behavioral, social and biological sciences. Separate grants are given for research and dissertations. Up to 40 grants have been given to individuals ranging from $37,500 to $2,000.

G80-
HEWLETT-PACKARD NATIONAL CONTRIBUTIONS PROGRAM
Hewlett-Packard Company
Attn: National Contributions Manager

P.O. Box 10301
MS 20 AH
Palo Alto, CA 94303-0890

INTEREST AREA: WOMEN - DISABILITIES
The purpose of this program is to provide financial support for the development of underrepresented minorities, women or people with disabilities. No funding is granted to individual researchers or organizations requesting funds for conferences, political or religious activities. The number of awards varies each year. Cash grants range from $5,000 to $20,000, equipment grants range from $10,000 to $75,000.

G81-
HISTORICAL RESEARCH FOUNDATION, INC.
c/o National Review Publications, Inc.
135 East 35th Street
New York, NY 10016

INTEREST AREA: RESEARCH
Financial assistance is provided in the form of grants given for historic or philosophic research and studies. The number of grants awarded each year varies according to need and ranges between $25,000 and $3,000.

G82-
THE J. EDGAR HOOVER FOUNDATION
c/o McNair Law Building
Ten Pope Avenue, P.O. Box 5914
Hilton Head Island, SC 29938

INTEREST AREA: GOVERNMENT
Funds are provided to present award monies for the study of government and good citizenship. Applicants should write to the Foundation for specific details. Grants to individuals range from a high of $3,000, to a low of $500.

G83-
HOWARD HUGHES MEDICAL INSTITUTE PRECOLLEGE AND PUBLIC SCIENCE EDUCATION PROGRAM

Howard Hughes Medical Institute
Attn: Office of Grants and Special Programs
4000 Jones Bridge Road
Chevy Chase, MD 20815-6789
(301) 215-8873
E-mail: grantvpr@hhmi.org

INTEREST AREA: WOMEN - SCIENCE EDUCATION
The purpose of this program is to provide funds for support to institutions providing science education for women and minority students. Since this program began in 1991, over $21 million has been disbursed in grants. The dollar amount of number of grants varies according to scope of proposed programs.

G84-
HOWARD HUGHES MEDICAL INSTITUTE UNDERGRADUATE BIOLOGICAL SCIENCES EDUCATION INITIATIVE

Howard Hughes Medical Institute
Attn: Office of Grants and Special Programs
4000 Jones Bridge Road
Chevy Chase, MD 20815-6789
(301) 215-8872
E-mail: barkanic@hq.hhmi.org

INTEREST AREA: UNDERGRADUATE BIOLOGICAL SCIENCE EDUCATION
Financial assistance is provided to advance undergraduate biological science education for women and minority students. Applications are accepted from academic institutions directly supportive of the objectives of the Howard Hughes Medical Institute. The dollar amount and number of awards varies each year. Grants range from $600,000 to $1,600,000 and have totaled approximately over $43 million.

G85-
HUMANE STUDIES FOUNDATION
P.O. Box 2256
Wichita, KS 67201

INTEREST AREA: RESEARCH - SCIENCES
Financial assistance is given in the form of grants to support research with emphasis on the social sciences. Applicants should write to the Foundation for compete information. Grants range from $4,700 to $2,000.

G86-
IFUW STUDY AND ACTION PROGRAMME (SAAP) FELLOWSHIPS
International Federation of University Women
8 rue de l'Ancien-Port
CH-1201 Geneva
Switzerland
Phone: 41 22 731 23 80

INTEREST AREA: RESEARCH - WOMEN STUDIES
Financial assistance is provided to women who are wishing to conduct research on women's studies. Applicants must be graduates and a member of the International Federation of University Women or a member of the American Association of University Women. The award ranges from 8,000 to 10,000 Swiss francs, one award is given on even numbered years.

G87-
AGNES AND SOPHIE DALLAS IRWIN MEMORIAL FUND
200 Stevens Drive
Lester, PA 19112

INTEREST AREA: TEACHERS - GIRLS' SCHOOLS
Financial assistance is provided in the form of grants to teachers in private girls' schools who have earned the right to retire and to provide opportunities for travel, study, research or retirement benefits. Annual amounts vary according to need and range from $7,000 to $1,000.

G88-
JEANNE HUMPHREY BLOCK DISSERTATION AWARD
Henry A. Murray Research Center
Attn: Grants Administrator
Radcliffe College
10 Garden Street
Cambridge, MA 02138
(617) 495-8140

INTEREST AREA: WOMEN - PSYCHOLGOCIAL DEVELOPMENT
This program provides financial assistance to women graduate students researching women's psychological development. Applicants must be in a doctoral program and have completed their course work when award is made. One award is given each year up to $2,500.

G89-
BARBARA PIASECKA JOHNSON FOUNDATION
c/o Danser, Balaam, and Frank
Five Independent Way
Princeton, NJ 08540
(609) 921-1200

INTEREST AREA: SCIENCE AND ARTS
Financial assistance is provided in the form of grants to defray expenses of scientific or artistic endeavors, including costs of equipment, supplies, tuition, basic living expenses and related costs. Several grants are given annually; the highest is $31,000, lowest is $2,000.

G90-
JOHN F. KENNEDY LIBRARY FOUNDATION
John F. Kennedy Library
Columbia Point
Boston, MA 02125
(617) 929-4524

INTEREST AREA: RESEARCH
The purpose of the fund is to provide grants to scholars doing significant research using the holdings of the Library. Several grants and fellowships are given under different departments. Contact to Foundation for specific grant monies available under each department.

G91-
THE KIMBO FOUNDATION
    c/o Korea Central Daily, S.F.
    430 Shotwell Street
    San Francisco, CA 94110

INTEREST AREA: KOREAN CULTURE
Financial assistance is available in the form of grants and is awarded to students of Korean descent to further their education. Several grants are awarded each year, each grant is $1,000.

G92-
KOSCIUSZKO FOUNDATION, INC.
    15 East 65th Street
    New York, NY 1021-4552
    (212) 734-2130

INTEREST AREA: STUDY/RESEARCH PROGRAMS: POLISH DESCENT
The purpose of this program is to offer domestic scholarships for Americans of Polish descent and study/research programs for Americans in Poland. Applicants must be of Polish descent. Recently, 195 grants were awarded to individuals ranging from $11,000 to $500.

G93-
LEADERSHIP ENRICHMENT FUND GRANTS
    Ms. Foundation for Women
    120 Wall Street, 33rd Floor
    New York, NY 10005
    (212) 742-2300

INTEREST AREA: WOMEN'S ORGANIZATIONS
Funds are provided to assist local and national organizations for women which help women expand their social fields and remove barriers facing women of color, low-income women, older women, lesbians and women with disabilities. Awards are up to $2,000 and number of awards varies each year.

G94-
LENA LAKE FORREST FELLOWSHIP/BPW RESEARCH GRANTS
    Business and Professional Women's Foundation
    Attn: Research Grants
    2012 Massachusetts Avenue, NW
    Washington, DC 20036-1070
    (202) 293-1200

INTEREST AREA: RESEARCH
Funds are provided to women working in historical research related to issues of importance to today's working women. Candidates must be doctoral candidates or post-doctoral scholars whose proposal for research has been approved by the academic committee. Grants range from $500 to $2,500, with the average award being $2,000. One to five awards are given each year.

G95-
LIEBIG FOUNDATION
    112 Bauer Drive
    Oakland, NJ 07436
    (201) 337-6126

INTEREST AREA: RESEARCH - VASCULAR SURGERY
The purpose of this fund is to provide financial assistance in the form of grants awarded to individuals conducting research in vascular surgery. Contact the Foundation for scope of program. Approximately $11,000 is available for grants.

G96-
THE CHARLES A. LINDBERGH FUND
708 South Third Street, Suite 110
Minneapolis, MN 55415
(612) 338-1703

INTEREST AREA: RESEARCH
Monies in the form of grants are available to support research and educational projects that address the balance between technology and the environment. Application is open to citizens of all countries. Nine grants are awarded annually to individuals.

G97-
LUISE MEYER-SCHUTZMEISTER AWARD
Association for Women in Science
1522 K Street, NW, Suite 820
Washington, DC 20005
(202) 408-0742
E-mail: awis@awis.org

INTEREST AREA: PHYSICS
Financial assistance is available to women graduate students studying physics and intend to pursue a career in physics. Applicants should be in the dissertation stage of their graduate work. Awards range from $500 to $1,000 and funds may be used for tuition, books, housing, research, etc. One award is given each year.

G98-
JOHN D. AND CATHERINE T. MAC ARTHUR FOUNDATION
140 South Dearborn Street, Suite 700
Chicago, IL 60603
(312) 726-8000

INTEREST AREA: RESEARCH
The purpose of this fund is to provide assistance for research and writing grants to explore peace and cooperation issues. Grants are not limited to scholarly studies, the writing projects can be directed to policy makers and the general public as well as scholars. Individual

grants are given annually, dollar amounts and number of grants varies with need.

G99-
VAROON MAHAJAN MEMORIAL TRUST, INC.
199 Bon Air Avenue
New Rochelle, NY 10824

INTEREST AREA: MEDICINE
Financial assistance is provided in the form of grants to individuals for medical training who demonstrate an interest in providing medical care in India and the U.S. Several grants are given each year, amounts vary according to need.

G100-
EDWARD MALLINCKRODT, JR. FOUNDATION
One North Jefferson
St. Louis, MO 63105
(314) 289-3000

INTEREST AREA: BIOMEDICAL RESEARCH
The purpose of this program is to provide financial assistance in the form of research grants to individuals in biomedical areas. Applicants must be connected with a U.S. university. Annual grants vary in dollar amount and number, individual grants range from $70,000 to $10,000.

G101-
MARTA SUTTON WEEKS GRANT
American Association of Petroleum Geologists Foundation
Attn: Chair, AAPG Grants-in-Aid Committee
1444 South Boulder
P.O. Box 979
Tulsa, OK 74101-0979
(918) 584-2555

INTEREST AREA: RESEARCH EARTH SCIENCES

Funds are available in the form of grants to support women who are conducting graduate research related to the field of earth sciences. Candidates may be students working toward their master's degree or their doctoral degree. The award in given each year in the amount of $2,000.

G102-
MARY INGRAHAM BUNTING INSTITUTE AFFILIATION PROGRAM

>Mary Ingraham Bunting Institute
>Attn: Fellowships Office
>Radcliffe College
>34 Concord Avenue
>Cambridge, MA 02138
>(617) 495-8212
>E-mail: bunting_fellowships@radcliffe.harvard.edu

INTEREST AREA: GENERAL & THE ARTS
Financial assistance is provided for women who are pursuing education and career advancement in academic and professional fields and in the creative arts fields. Applicants from the field of creative arts must be nominated and invited to apply. Women scholars in any other field may apply directly if they have earned their doctorate at least 2 years prior to the award. Ten to twenty awards are given each year.

G103-
MARY'S PENCE GRANT PROGRAM

>Mary's Pence
>P.O. Box 29078
>Chicago, IL 60629-9078
>(708) 499-3771

INTEREST AREA: CATHOLIC WOMEN
Funding is provided for Catholic women residing in the United States who are working to improve the lives of women through Catholic teachings and services. Individual grants range up to $3,000 for direct service projects and up to $1,500 for study projects. The number of grants varies with need.

G104-
MAX GOLDENSON AND KAREN HANSEN WOMEN AND CHILDREN IN WAR GRANT
Women in Film Foundation
6464 Sunset Boulevard, Suite 530
Los Angeles, CA 90028
(213) 463-6040

INTEREST AREA: FILMS - WOMEN/CHILDREN - WAR
This program offers financial assistance to women in the film industry to complete or create a film or video on women, children and war. The theme should be heroism and peace. Grants up to $3,000 are available on an annual basis.

G104-
CHAIM MAYER FOUNDATION, INC.
c/o Stockel and Press
39 Broadway
New York, NY 10006
(212) 269-4444

INTEREST AREA: RELIGIOUS STUDIES
The foundation provides grants to rabbis and other persons for research and study of the bible, the Talmud, and similar theological works. Grants to individuals totaling $10,000 are available on an annual basis.

G106-
THE MC KNIGHT FOUNDATION
600 TCF Tower
121 South Eighth Street
Minneapolis, MN 55402
(612) 233-4220

INTEREST AREA: RESEARCH

Financial assistance is provided in the form of grants to provide research in plant biology. Applicants must be proven researchers in plant biology. Annually several grants are available to individuals, the number and dollar amounts vary according to need and availability of funds.

G107-
MEDICAL RESEARCH FOUNDATION OF BOSTON, INC.
127 Bay State Road
Boston, MA 02215-1711
(617) 536-5037

INTEREST AREA: MEDICAL RESEARCH
The purpose of this program is to provide grants for medical research. Annual grants are available, number of and dollar amount of grants varies according to funds available.

G108-
MINORITY FELLOWSHIPS IN TRANSPLANTATION
National Institutes of Health
Attn: National Institute of Allergy and Infectious Diseases
Division of Allergy, Immunology and Transplantation
Solar Building, Room 4A-14
6003 Executive Boulevard MSC 7640
Bethesda, MD 20892-7640
(301) 496-5598
E-mail: sr8j@nih.gov

INTEREST AREA:RESEARCH
Financial assistance is provided for programs offering women and persons with disabilities advancement within the fields of science and transplant rejection. Projects may cover research training on etiology, pathogenesis, diagnosis and treatment and prevention. Applicants must be U.S. citizens and hold a Ph.D., M.D., D.O., D.D.S., O.D., D.P.M., Sc.D., Eng.D. or equivalent degree. Award amounts vary according to funds available, two awards are given each year.

G109-
MINORITY SCIENCE IMPROVEMENT PROGRAM
Department of Education
Attn: Office of Postsecondary Education
Division of Higher Education Incentive Programs
Portals Building, Suite C-80
600 Independence Avenue, SW
Washington, DC 20202-5329
(202) 260-3261
E-mail: argelia_velez_rodriquez@ed.gov

INTEREST AREA: RESEARCH
Financial assistance is provided in the form of grants to increase opportunities for women in the fields of sciences and engineering. Contact the NIH for information and details on the various options available through this fund. The range of financial support is from $16,000 to $20,000 for individuals and approximately $290,000 for institutional grants and/or cooperative grants. Approximately 29 grants are given each year.

G110-
THE JOHN AND CLIFFORD MIRIKITANI FOUNDATION
2336 Oahu Avenue
Honolulu, HI 96822

INTEREST AREA: MEDICAL RESEARCH
Financial assistance is provided for women who are involved in medical research. Each year two grants are given, the dollar amount varies according to need.

G111-
THE VANGEE L. MOORE MEMORIAL FOUNDATION
Route 4, Box 88
Richmond, TX 77469
(713) 342-7150

INTEREST AREA: MEDICAL RESEARCH

Grant monies are provided for research to professionals with a Ph.D. or to a physician with five or fewer years in medical research. Applicants must be members of a teaching or research faculty. Annual amounts and number of grants varies according to need.

G112-
MS. FOUNDATION COLLARBORATIVE GRANTS
Ms. Foundation for Women
120 Wall Street, 33rd Floor
New York, NY 10005
(212) 742-2300

INTEREST AREA: WOMEN & ADVANCEMENT
Grant monies are provided to fund women's organizations in the United States in collaboration with other funders. Applications are accepted for nonprofit, tax-exempt women's organizations working to advance women in all areas of work, social, government and home environments. The number and dollar amount of these grants varies according to need.

G113-
MS. FOUNDATION GENERAL GRANTS
Ms. Foundation for Women
120 Wall Street, 33rd Floor
New York, NY 10005
(212) 742-2300

INTEREST AREA: WOMEN & ADVANCEMENT
Financial assistance is provided to organizations working to open areas of advancement for women which have been closed to them due to color, low income, age, and/or disabilities. Applying organizations must be tax-exempt and working on issues of concern to women. Awards range from $5,000 to $25,000 and the number of awards varies each year.

G114-
NASA GRADUATE STUDENT RESEARCHERS PROGRAM

National Graduate Student Researchers
Attn: Office of Human Resources and Education
Code FE
Headquarters Room 4D-45
Washington, DC 20546-0001
(202) 358-1517
E-mail: anurrid@hq.nasa.gov

INTEREST AREA: RESEARCH : SPACE, AERONAUTICS
Financial assistance is provided to students enrolled or planning to enroll in an accredited graduate program in a university or college in the United States. Research is to be done in the areas of aeronautics, space science, space applications and space technology. There is a $16,000 student stipend and a $6,000 allowance to cover costs such as tuition, books, etc. Grants are annual and are renewable. There are a minimum of 150 grants given each year.

G115-
NATIONAL CENTER FOR ATMOSPHERIC RESEARCH POSTDOCTORAL PROGRAM

National Center for Atmospheric Research
Attn: Advanced Study Program
P.O. Box 3000
Boulder, CO 80307-3000
(303) 497-1650
E-mail: barbm@asp2.ucar.edu

INTEREST AREA: RESEARCH
This fund provides monies for atmospheric scientists (who have recently received their Ph.D.'s) to continue their research interests and gain experience in their professional fields. Applicants who may apply are physicists, chemists, applied mathematicians, engineers and specialists from other natural scientific disciplines. Applications from women are especially encouraged. Annually 8 to 10 grants are awarded, each grant approximately $33,400 and each grant may be renewed.

G116-
NATIONAL CENTER FOR TOXICOLOGICAL RESEARCH POSTGRADUATE RESEARCH
> Oak Ridge Institute for Science and Education
> Attn: Science/Engineering Education Division
> P.O. Box 117
> Oak Ridge, TN 37831-0117
> (423) 576-3190
> E0mail: prpnctr@orau.gov

INTEREST AREA: RESEARCH: TOXIC CHEMICAL EFFECTS
Funding is available to postgraduate students who are doing and wish to participate in research on the biological effects of potentially toxic chemical. Study is done at the National Center for Toxicological Research in Arkansas. Applicants must have a graduate degree in one of the following areas; toxicology, pharmacology, biological sciences, mathematics, chemistry, medicine, computer science or other related scientific disciplines. The individual dollar amount is based on research area and degree. The number of awards varies each year.

G117-
NAVAL AIR WARFARE CENTER TRAINING SYSTEMS DIVISION POSTGRADUATE RESEARCH PARTICIPATION PROGRAM
> Oak Ridge Institute for Science and Education
> Attn: Science/Engineering Education Division
> P.O. Box 117
> Oak Ridge, TN 37831-0117
> (423) 569-7749
> E-mail: prpnawct@orau.gov

INTEREST AREA: TRAINING SYSTEMS
Funding is provided for postgraduates who wish to participate in research on advanced simulation and training systems at the Training Center in Orlando, Florida. Candidates must have completed their master's or doctoral degrees in behavioral sciences, computer science or engineering within the part three years. The number and dollar amount of awards varies each year.

G118-
NIAID/MODELL MINORITY FELLOWSHIPS IN PRIMARY IMMUNE DEFICIENCY
National Institutes of Health
Attn: National Institute of Allergy and Infectious Diseases
Division of Allergy, Immunology and Transplantation
Solar Building, Room 4A-19
6003 Executive Boulevard MSC 7640
Bethesda, MD 20892-7640
(301) 496-7104
E0mail: hd7e@nih.gov

INTEREST AREA: RESERACH IMMUNE DEFICIENCY DISEASES
Funding is provided for women who hold a Ph.D., M.D. or equivalent doctoral degree, who have disabilities and who are interested in conducting research on the etiology, pathogenesis, diagnosis and/or treatment of immune deficiency diseases. Two awards are given each year, each approximately $32,000.

G119-
NIDR SUMMER RESEARCH TRAINING FOR MINORITY AND WOMEN STUDENTS IN DENTAL SCHOOL
National Institutes of Health
Attn: National Institute of Dental Research
Division of Extramural Research
Natcher Building, Room 4AN-18J
45 Center Drive MSC 6402
Bethesda, MD 20892-6402
(301) 594-2618
E-mail: jl46d@nih.gov

INTEREST AREA: RESEARCH: DENTAL SCIENCES
Funds are provided for women dental students who wish to be involved in research training in the dental sciences. Applicants must be U.S. citizens and have successfully completed at least 1 semester in a dental school in the United States. The award covers a two month summer

time period and is approximately $800 per month. The number of awards varies each year.

G120-
NIH INDIVIDUAL RESERACH PROJECT GRANTS
National Institutes of Health
Attn: Office of Extramural Research
Extramural Outreach and Information Resources Office
6701 Rockledge Drive, Room 6207
MSC 7910
Bethesda, MD 20892-7910
(301) 435-0714
E-mail: asknih@odrockm1.od.nih.gov

INTEREST AREA: BIOMEDICAL - BEHAVIROAL RESEARCH
This program provides financial assistance for research in the biomedical and behavioral fields. Application is accepted from investigators at nonprofit and for-profit, public and private organizations. The funding amount varies according to the scope of proposed research and the number of awards also varies each year according to accepted projects.

G121-
NLM FELLOWSHIP IN APPLIED INFORMATICS
National Institutes of Health
Attn: National Library of Medicine
Division of Extramural Programs
Building 38A, Suite 5S-518
Bethesda, MD 20894
(301) 496-4221
E-mail: pc49n@nih.gov

INTEREST AREA: TRAINING: MEDICAL INFORMATION SYSTEMS
Financial assistance is provided for health science librarians, researchers, administrators and others in health care who are pursuing a career or certification in medical information system application and/or development. Annual award is up to $58,000 per year. The

applicant's institution may request an additional $3,000 for the institution to support expenses relating to supplies, equipment, tuition, fees and other training-related costs. The number of awards varies each year.

G122-
NURSE PRACTITIONER AND NURSE MIDWIFERY GRANTS
Heath Resources and Services Administration
Attn: Bureau of Health Professions
Division of Nursing
Parklawn Building, Room 9-36
5600 Fishers Lane
Rockville, MD 20857
(301) 443-6333

INTEREST AREA: EDUCATION IN NURSING
Grants are provided to schools of nursing who offer degrees or certifications for nurse practitioners and/or nurse midwives. Applications are accepted from public and private nonprofit schools of nursing. Approximately 70 grants are awarded each year, the average grant has been $240,000.

G123-
OCEAN SPRAY TRAVEL AND TRAINING FUND
Women's Sports Foundation
Eisenhower Park
1899 Hempstead Turnpike, Suite 400
East Meadow, NY 11554-1000
(516) 542-4700
E-mail: wosport@aol.com

INTEREST AREA: ATHELETIC TRAINING
Financial assistance is provided to female amateur athletes who need funding to train and travel to scheduled competitions in their events. Applicants must have a regional ranking to be eligible to apply for support. Individual requests may be up to $1,500 and a team may request up to $5,000 each year. The annual amount available is $100,000, the number of awards varies each year.

G124-
PARAPSYCHOLOGY FOUNDATION, INC.
228 East 71st Street
New York, NY 10021
(212) 628-1550

INTEREST AREA: RESEARCH IN PARAPSYCHOLOGY
The purpose of this fund is to assist scientists and others engaged in study, research and experiments pertaining to parapsychology and parapsychological phenomena. The number and dollar amount of grants varies according to scope of project. The average amount given is $2,500.

G125-
PEACE FELLOWSHIP
Mary Ingraham Bunting Institute
Attn: Fellowships Office
Radcliffe College
34 Concord Avenue
Cambridge, MA 02138
(617) 495-8212
E-mail: bunting_fellowships@radcliffe.harvard.edu

INTEREST AREA: RESEARCH: CONFLICT RESOLUTIONS
Financial assistance is offered to women interested in or conducting research on the resolution of conflicts in peaceful ways between groups and/or nations. Applicants must be an activist or a scholar. The annual award is $30,000, plus office space, access to libraries and other resources at Radcliffe College and Harvard University.

G126-
PERGAMON - NWSA GRADUATE SCHOLARSHIP IN WOMEN'S STUDIES
National Women's Studies Association
7100 Baltimore Avenue, Suite 301
College Park, MD 20740

(301) 403-0525
E-mail: nwsa@umail.umd.edu

INTEREST AREA: RESEARCH: WOMEN'S STUDIES
Funding is provided for graduate research in women's studies. The research must be for a master's thesis or Ph.D. dissertation in the field of women's studies. Scholarships are between $500 and $1,000 and 2 are given each year.

G127-
POSTDOCTORAL/FACULTY LEAVE FELLOWSHIPS
American Association of University Women
Attn: Educational Foundation
2201 North Dodge Street
Iowa City, IA 52243-4030
(319) 337-1716

INTEREST AREA: RESEARCH
Financial assistance is provided for American women scholars who are working on postdoctoral research in any field. The annual stipend ranges from $20,000 to $25,000, ten awards are given out each year.

G128-
QUAKER RESEARCH GRANT
Women's Sports Foundation
Eisenhower Park
1899 Hempstead Turnpike, Suite 400
East Meadow, NY 11554-1000
(516) 542-4700
E-mail: wosport@aol.com

INTEREST AREA: RESEARCH: NUTRITION AND FEMALE ATHELETES
Financial assistance is provided for research into the field of female sports and fitness and what part exercise and nutrition play in achievement. Any researcher, independent or affiliated with a university or organization may apply. One award is given each year in the amount of $5,000.

G129- REPRODUCTIVE RIGHTS COALITION FUND GRANTS
Ms. Foundation for Women
120 Wall Street, 33rd Floor
New York, NY 10005
(212) 742-2300

INTEREST AREA: SUPPORT OF REPRODUCTIVE RIGHTS
Financial assistance is provided to organizations who support reproductive rights. Funds may be used to support development and growth of coalitions supporting reproductive rights and health issues. Grants range for $10,000 to $15,000, the number of grants varies each year.

G130- RESEARCH FUND OF THE AMERICAN OTOLOGICAL SOCIETY
c/o University of California
Otology Lab, 1159 Surge 3rd Street
Davis, CA 95616-8649
(916) 752-8931

INTEREST AREA: RESEARCH: OTOSCLEROSIS
The purpose of this fund is to provide monies for the research and study of otosclerosis. Grants are awarded to U.S. and Canadian citizens only for research in the field of otosclerosis. Each year five grants are awarded, individual amounts vary according to scope of research proposal.

G131- RUTH SATTER MEMORIAL AWARD
Association for Women in Science
1522 K Street, NW, Suite 820
Washington, DC 20005
(202) 408-8321
E-mail: awis@awis.org

INTEREST AREA: DOCTORAL DEGREE SUPPORT
Financial assistance is provided for any female re-entering into education and working on her doctoral degree in the sciences. Applicants must be enrolled in any life science, physical science, social science or engineering program with the intention of obtaining a Ph.D. degree. Applicants must also be U.S. citizens and have had their education interrupted for 3 or more years to raise a family. One award is given each year and is approximately $750.

G132-
SALLY BUTLER MEMORIAL FUND FOR LATINA RESEARCH

    Business and Professional Women's Foundation
    Attn: Research Grants
    2012 Massachusetts Avenue, NW
    Washington, DC 20036-1070
    (202) 293-1200

INTEREST AREA: RESEARCH
Financial assistance is provided for Latina women who wish to conduct research supporting equity for Latinas. Applicants must be Latin Americans conducting research at the postdoctoral level. Up to 5 awards are given each year ranging from $500 to $2,500 each.

G133-
SCHOLARSHIP IN JEWISH WOMEN'S STUDIES

    National Women's Studies Association
    7100 Baltimore Avenue, Suite 301
    College Park, MD 20740
    (301) 403-0525
    E-mail: nwsa@umail.umd.edu

INTEREST AREA: GRADUATE RESEARCH
The purpose of this fund is to provide financial assistance to support research on Jewish women. Candidates must be enrolled full time as a graduate student and engaged in research for a master's thesis or Ph.D. dissertation. The project must be directly related to the study of Jewish

women and feminism. One award is granted each year in the amount of $500.

G134-
SIGMA DELTA EPSILON FELLOWSHIPS
Sigma Delta Epsilon - Graduate Women in Science, Inc.
P.O. Box 19947
San Diego, CA 92159
(619) 583-4856
E-mail: dcbrown@crash.cts.com

INTEREST AREA: RESEARCH: NATURAL SCIENCES
Funding is provided for female graduate students doing research in the natural sciences. Applicants must be U.S. citizens and be doing their research at the postdoctoral level. The stipends range from $1,000 to $4,000 a year, usually 4 awards are given each year.

G135-
SPECIAL SUPPLEMENTAL NUTRITION PROGRAM FOR WOMEN, INFANTS, AND CHILDREN
Department of Agriculture
Attn: Food and Consumer Service
Supplemental Food Programs Division
3101 Park Center Drive
Alexandria, VA 22302
(703) 305-2286

INTEREST AREA: WOMEN, CHILDREN & NUTRITION
The purpose of this fund is to provide financial assistance to state health departments or comparable agencies to assist low-income, pregnant, postpartum or breast-feeding women, infants and children and to improve their nutritional status during developmental stages of growth. Each year Congress decides the amount of grant money available for this program. In recent years Congress has provided over $3.7 billion which is available for all 50 states, the District of Columbia, Puerto Rico, the Virgin Islands and Guam.

G136-
THE SPENCER FOUNDATION
900 North Michigan Avenue, Suite 2800
Chicago, IL 60611
(312) 337-7000

INTEREST AREA: RESEARCH
The purpose of this fund is to provide financial assistance to individuals or teams of investigators to do research aimed at expanding the knowledge, understanding and practice of education. Applicants must have doctoral degrees in education or liberal arts disciplines, working under the auspices of an institution. The annual grants vary in amount and range from $345,000 to $4,800.

G137-
SPONSORED RESEARCH INFRASTRUCTURE PROGRAM
National Institutes of Health
Attn: Extramural Associates Program
Rockledge II, Room 6187A
6701 Rockledge Drive MSC 7910
Bethesda, MD 20892-7910
(301) 435-2692
E-mail: mk51q@nih.gov

INTEREST AREA: BIOMEDICAL RESEARCH
Financial assistance is provided to women researchers who are a scientific faculty member or academic administrator at an educational institution which promotes the advancement of women in careers and education. The applicant will participate in a research program at the National Institutes of Health for 5 months and receive funding comparable to her salary during the time of selection. The number of awards varies each year.

G138-
STROKE IN BLACKS, OTHER MINORITIES, AND WOMEN RESEARCH GRANTS
National Institutes of Health
Attn: National Institute of Neurological Disorders and Stroke

Division of Stroke and Trauma

Federal Building, Room 8A13
7550 Wisconsin Avenue
Bethesda, MD 20892
(301) 496-4226

INTEREST AREA: RESEARCH: CEREBROVASCULAR DISEASE
Financial support is provided through this grant fund for research into cerebrovascular disease in Blacks, other minorities and women. Investigators at nonprofit and for-profit organizations are eligible to apply. The amount of the award varies each year as does the total amount of awards given each year.

G139-
SUPPLEMENTS TO PROMOTE REENTRY INTO BIOMEDICAL AND BEHAVIORAL RESEARCH CAREERS
National Institutes of Health
Attn: Office of Extramural Research
Extramural Outreach and Information Resources Office
6701 Rockledge Drive, Room 6207
MSC 7910
Bethesda, MD 20892-7910
(301) 435-0714
E-mail: asknih@odrockm1.od.nih.gov

INTEREST AREA: REENTRY INTO RESEARCH FIELD
Financial assistance is provided for women to reenter into a career in research after taking time off from their chosen career to raise families, care for parents or attend to other family responsibilities. Candidates must have a doctoral degree (M.D., D.D.S., Ph.D., O.D., D.V.M., or equivalent). The maximum award is $50,000 per year and the award is renewable annually. The number of awards varies each year.

G140-
THANKS BE TO GRANDMOTHER WINIFRED FOUNDATION GRANTS
Thanks Be to Grandmother Winifred Foundation
P.O. Box 1449

Wainscott, NY 11975-1449
(516) 725-0323

INTEREST AREA: OLDER WOMEN
This unique fund provides financial assistance to women at least 54 years of age who are developing and implementing projects, programs or policies that enhance the lives of women, including themselves. Grants may be used for education, improvement of a literary, artistic, musical, scientific or teaching skill or talent. Approximately 30 grants are awards each year, ranging from $500 to $5,000.

**G141-
THRASHER RESEARCH FUND**
50 East North Temple Street, Seventh Floor
Salt Lake City, UT 84150
(801) 240-4753

INTEREST AREA: CHILD HEALTH RESEARCH
The purpose of this fund is to promote national and international child health research. Applicants must be affiliated with a nonprofit academic and research institution. Grants totaled over $2,000,000, individual amounts vary each year.

**G142-
UNITED NATIONS DEVELOPMENT FUND FOR WOMEN (UNIFEM)**
United Nations
30e East 45th Street, Room 608
New York, NY 10017
(212) 906-6400

INTEREST AREA: ECONOMIC AND POLITICAL EMPOWERMENT OF WOMEN
Financial assistance is provided to develop projects that promote the advancement of women in economic and political environments. This program is extensive and applicants are encouraged to contact the UN to become aware of the various projects being supported. The average grant is $95,000, since 1978 the fund has made over $30 million available for projects. The number of grants varies each year.

G143-
W. E. UPJOHN UNEMPLOYMENT TRUSTEE CORPORATION
300 South Westridge Avenue
Kalamazoo, MI 49007
(616) 343-5541

INTEREST AREA: RESEARCH
The purpose of this fund is to provide financial assistance into the research of the causes, effects, prevention and alleviation of unemployment. Program description may be requested from the Foundation. Total annual funds are approximately $285,000, grants to individuals varies according to scope of project.

G144-
VIOLENCE AND TRAUMATIC STRESS RESEARCH GRANTS
National Institutes of Health
Attn: National Institute of Mental Health
Violence and Traumatic Stress Research Branch
Parklawn Building, Room 10C-24
5600 Fishers Lane
Rockville, MD 20857
(301) 443-3728
E-mail: ss75f@nih.gov

INTEREST AREA: RESEARCH
Funds are provided to research the prevention and treatment of antisocial behavior, particularly rape and other sexual assaults. Both individuals and organization may apply. Contact the NIH for specific areas of research to be financially supported. There is over $3,500,000 per year available through this fund, the average grant is $175,000 and there are 20 awards granted each year.

G145-
VISHAY MACCABIAH GAMES FUND
Women's Sports Foundation
Eisenhower Park
1899 Hempstead Turnpike, Suite 400
East Meadow, NY 11554-1000

(516) 542-4700
E-mail: wosport@aol.com

INTEREST AREA: FEMALE ATHELETES
Financial support is provided to female athletes or teams who are competing in the MacCabiah Games and grants are awarded in the years in which the Games are held. Call (215) 561-6900 for details on Games scheduling. Up to $3,500 is awarded in grants, the number varies according to need.

G146-
VISITING PROFESSORSHIPS FOR WOMEN
National Science Foundation
Attn: Directorate for Education and Human Resources
Division of Human Resource Development
Programs for Women and Girls
4201 Wilson Boulevard, Room 815
Arlington, VA 22230
(703) 306-1637
E-mail: vpw@nsf.gov

INTEREST AREA: RESEARCH AND TEACHING
Financial assistance is provided through this fund for doctoral women scientists and engineers who wish to advance their research and teaching careers at host institutions. Applicants must have a doctorate in a field of research supported by NSF, be a U.S. citizen and not have a salaried position at the host institution. Over 15 grants are given each year, the individual amounts vary according to need and scope of service.

G147-
WAWH GRADUATE STUDENT FELLOWSHIP AWARD
Western Association of Women Historians
c/o Emily Rader, Treasurer
436 Lime Avenue, #6
Long Beach, CA 90802

INTEREST AREA: GRADUATE STUDY NEEDS

Financial assistance is provided for women who are members of the WAWH and are writing their dissertation at the time of application. One award is given each year in the amount of $1,000.

G148-
CLARA WHEELER TRUST
c/o Colorado National Bank of Denver
P.O. Box 5168-TA
Denver, CO 80217

INTEREST AREA: RESEARCH: CANCER
The purpose of this fund is to provide financial assistance for research for the prevention, treatment or cure of cancer. Contact the Trust Officer for program description. Annually 25 grants are awarded to individuals totaling $161,000 and ranging from $9,500 to $3,500.

G149-
WILLIAM GIBSON RESERACH SCHOLARSHIP FOR MEDICAL WOMEN
Royal Society of Medicine
Attn: General Services Secretary
1 Wimpole Street
London W1M 8AE
England
0171 290 2900
E-mail: 100673,2422@compuserve.com

INTEREST AREA: RESEARCH
The purpose of this fund is to provide financial assistance to medically qualified women to investigate medical research in the United Kingdom or abroad. The amount awarded is approximately 750 pounds and one award is given every 2-3 years.

G150-
WINIFRED CULLIS GRANTS
International Federation of University Women
8 rue de l'Ancien-Port

CH-1201 Geneva, Switzerland
41 22 731 23 80

INTEREST AREA: RESEARCH
The purpose of this fund is to provide financial assistance to women graduates who are interested in continuing research in their field of study in another country. Applicants must be a member of 1 of the 67 national federations or associations affiliated with the International Federation of University Women. The stipend is 3,000 to 6,000 Swiss francs and number of awards given each year varies. In recent years up to 18 awards per year have been given.

G151-
WOMEN IN UNITED METHODIST HISTORY RESEARCH GRANT

United Methodist Church
General Commission on Archives and History
Attn: Assistance General Secretary
36 Madison Avenue
P.O. Box 127
Madison, NJ 07940
(210) 408-3189

INTEREST AREA: RESEARCH: WOMEN
The fund provides financial assistance for the research and study of the history of women in the United Methodist church. Grants are given annually and range from $500 to $1,000.

G152-
WOMEN LAWYERS' PUBLIC ACTION SUMMER LAW CLERKSHIP

Women Lawyers' Public Action Grant Foundation
P.O. Box 480197
Los Angles, CA 90048-1197
(213) 897-2682

INTEREST AREA: WOMEN LAW STUDENTS

This fund provides financial assistance to female law students wishing to conduct research on projects that benefit individuals or groups who have not received governmental or social service agency attention to their needs. The annual grants are up to $5,000 and number of grants given each year varies.

G153-
WOMEN'S EDUCATIONAL EQUITY ACT PROGRAM GRANTS
>Department of Education
>Attn: Office of Elementary and Secondary Education
>Equity and Educational Excellence Division
>Portals Building, Room 4500
>600 Independence Avenue, SW
>Washington, DC 20202-6140
>(202) 260-2670

INTEREST AREA: WOMEN'S EQUITY PROJECTS
Financial assistance is provided for funding for projects that promote equity for women. Two fields of support are considered: implementation of gender equity programs and grants for research and development of equity programs. Grants awarded range from $310,000 to $80,000, with approximately $4 million available each year. The number of awards varies each year.

G154-
WOMEN'S HEALTH OVER THE LIFECOURSE: SOCIAL AND BEHAVIORAL ASPECTS GRANTS
>National Institutes of Health
>Attn: National Institute of Aging
>Behavioral and Social Research Program
>Gateway Building, Suite 2C231
>7201 Wisconsin Avenue MSC 9205
>Bethesda, MD 20892-9205
>(301) 496-3136
>E-mail: mo12x@nih.gov

INTEREST AREA: RESEARCH

Financial assistance is provided to investigators from public or private, nonprofit or for profit organizations for the support of research on the social and behavioral development of women's health during their adult lifetime. All aspects of a woman's life and the effect of health issues on her quality of life are to be studied. The amount of each award and the number of annual awards varies each year.

G155-
WOMEN'S HIV RISK AND PROTECTIVE BEHAVIORS RESEARCH GRANTS
>National Institutes of Health
>Attn: National Institute on Drug Abuse
>Division of Epidemiology and Prevention Research
>Parklawn Building, Room 9A-42
>5600 Fishers Lane
>Rockville, MD 20857
>(301) 443-6720
>E-mail: sc91m@nih.gov

INTEREST AREA: RESEARCH

The purpose of this fund is to provide financial assistance for the study of women and the prevention or reduction of risk behaviors and risk taking environments. Contact the National Institute on Drug Abuse for all the various areas of research in this field of study. The number of and dollar amount of awards varies each year with scope of projects.

G156-
WOMEN'S MENTAL HEALTH RESEARCH GRANTS
>National Institutes of Health
>Attn: National Institute of Mental Health
>Office for Special Populations
>Parklawn Building, Room 17C-14
>5600 Fishers Lane MSC 8030
>Rockville, MD 20857-8030
>E-mail: dp23@nih.gov

INTEREST AREA: RESEARCH: MENTAL DISORDERS

Financial assistance is available for research on mental disorders in women during their lifetime. Applicants may be investigators from nonprofit, for profit, public or private organizations and eligible agencies of the federal government. The number of and dollar amount of annual awards varies according to scope of projects.

G157-
WOMEN'S PEACEPOWER FOUNDATION GRANTS
Women's Peacepower Foundation
Attn: Director
P.O. Box 1281
San Antonio, FL 33576
(352) 567-9116

INTEREST AREA: WOMEN AND ANTIVIOLENCE
The fund provides financial assistance for start-up projects developing interventions for violence against women and their children. Applications may come from organizations with annual budgets not over $75,000. The number and dollar amount of the annual grants varies according to scope of projects.

G158-
WOMEN'S RESEARCH AWARDS
National Association of Women in Education
c/o Dr. Anna Roman-Koller
Chair, NAWE Research Awards
University of Pittsburgh School of Medicine
Department of Pathology
3550 Terrace Street, Room S-701
Pittsburgh, PA 15261
(412) 648-9466
E-mail: koller@a1.isd.upmc.edu

INTEREST AREA: RESEARCH
Financial assistance is provided for research by, for and about women. The research may be relevant to the education, personal and/or professional lives of women. Two awards are given each year in the amount of $750 each.

G159-
WOMEN'S SPORTS FOUNDATION SPORTING CHANCE AWARD
    Women's Sports Foundation
    Eisenhower Park
    1899 Hempstead Turnpike, Suite 400
    East Meadow, NY 11554-1000
    (516) 542-4700
    E-mail: wosport@aol.com

INTEREST AREA: SPORTS PROGRAMS AND WOMEN ATHELETES
Financial assistance is provided in the form of a grant for the development of a nontraditional and well structured sports program from women athletes. One award is given each year in the amount of $1,500.

G160-
WOMEN'S STUDIES DISSERTATION FELLOWSHIP
    Women's Studies Program
    University of California at Santa Barbara
    Santa Barbara, CA 93106-7110
    (805) 893-4330

INTEREST AREA: WOMEN'S STUDIES
Financial assistance is provided to graduate students for the completion of their dissertation on women's studies. Applicants may apply who are enrolled in any university in the United States and are U.S. citizens. The stipend is $18,000 and two awards are given annually.

G161-
WOODROW WILSON DISSERTATION GRANTS IN WOMEN'S STUDIES
    Woodrow Wilson National Fellowship Foundation
    5 Vaughn Drive, Suite 300
    CN 5281

Princeton, NJ 08543-5281
(609) 452-7007
E-mail: maryh@woodrow.org

INTEREST AREA: RESEARCH

Financial assistance is provided for research on the evolution of women's roles in society, history, health care, literature and on the psychology of women. Applicants must be enrolled in a university or college in the U.S. and have completed all pre-dissertation requirements. Over 15 grants are awarded annually, each is $1,500 and is to be used for expenses related to the dissertation costs.

G162-
WOODROW WILSON - JOHNSON & JOHNSON DISSERTATION GRANTS IN WOMEN'S HEALTH
Woodrow Wilson National Fellowship Foundation
Department WS
CN 5281
Princeton, NJ 08543-5281
(609) 452-7007
E-mail: charlott@woodrow.org

INTEREST AREA: RESEARCH

The purpose of this fund is to provide financial assistance for research on any major issues related to women's health. Applicants must be completing their doctoral programs at any college or university in the United States. The annual individual grant amount is $2,000, the number of grants varies each year with need and scope of projects.

G163-
WOODWARD FOUNDATION, INC.
5418 South State Route 202
Tipp City, OH 45371
(513) 667-7012

INTEREST AREA: HOMEOPATHIC MEDICINE

The purpose of this fund is to provide assistance for preceptorships for M.D.'s and D.O.'s in homeopathic medicine. Annually one grant totaling $12,000 is awarded.

FELLOWSHIPS

Fellowships are financial support programs designed to fund studies on the graduate and higher levels of educational pursuits. Usually there is no expected return of service or repayment of monies required to receive a fellowship.

F1-
AAAA SPOUSE SCHOLARSHIPS
Army Aviation Association of America Scholarship Foundation
49 Richmondville Avenue
Westport, CT 06880-2000
(203) 226-8184
E-mail: aaaa@quad-a.org

INTEREST AREA: GENERAL EDUCATION
The purpose of this fellowship is to provide financial assistance to spouses of Army Aviation Association of America members. Recipients must be a member of AAAA and be pursuing college studies at the graduate level. The number of awards given each year varies, minimum of 2 per year, each $1,000.

F2-
AAWD/COLGATE-PALMOLIVE AWARD FOR WOMEN DENTAL STUDENTS
American Association of Women Dentists
401 North Michigan Avenue
Chicago, IL 60611-4267
(312) 644-6610

INTEREST AREA: DENTISTRY
The purpose of this fund is to provide financial support to women dental students for dental study. Grants are awarded to 10 dental schools, the school in turn awards grants of $500 maximum per chosen student. Ten (10) awards are given each year.

F3-
ALLAN V. COX AWARD
Geological Society of American
Attn: Research Grants Administrator
3300 Penrose Place
P.O. Box 9140
Boulder, CO 80301
(303) 447-2020

INTEREST AREA: GEOLOGICAL RESEARCH
This fund provides financial support to graduate students for geological research. Graduate students must be at the master's or doctoral level to apply. One or more awards is given each year ranging from $2,500 to $400.

F4-
ALPHA EPSILON IOTA SCHOLARSHIP FUND
    Society Bank, Michigan
    c/o Betty Kelsea
    P.O. Box 8612
    Ann Arbor, MI 48107-8612
    (313) 994-5555

INTEREST AREA: MEDICINE
Financial assistance is available to provide financial support to women pursuing degrees at accredited schools or colleges of medicine in the United States. Applicants must already be enrolled or admitted for acceptance at any accredited schools or college of medicine in the U.S. Two awards are given each year up to $4,000, renewal of award is possible.

F5-
AMELIA KEMP MEMORIAL SCHOLARSHIP
    Women of the Evangelical Lutheran Church in America
    8765 West Higgins Road
    Chicago, IL 50531-4189
    (312) 380-2730
    E-mail: womnelca@elca.org

INTEREST AREA: GENERAL EDUCATION
Financial assistance is provided to lay women of color who are members of Evangelical Lutheran Church of America local congregations. Applicants may apply who are pursuing post-secondary education on the undergraduate, graduate, professional or vocational school level. The number of awards varies each year, each award is approximately $2,000.

F6-
AMERICAN BUSINESS WOMEN'S ASSOCIATION FOUNDERS SCHOLARSHIP
>American Business Women's Association
>P.O. Box 8728
>9100 Ward Parkway
>Kansas City, MO 64114-0728
>(816) 361-6621

INTEREST AREA: PROFESSIONAL AND TECHNICAL FIELDS
This fund provides financial support to women developing careers in professions and technical fields not usually entered by women. Recipients must be doing graduate work in above fields. The scholarship is usually offered every 5 years with the award totaling $3,000.

F7-
AMERICAN BUSINESS WOMEN'S ASSOCIATION PRESIDENT'S SCHOLARSHIP
>American Business Women's Association
>P.O. Box 8728
>9100 Ward Parkway
>Kansas City, MO 64114-0728
>(816) 361-6621

INTEREST AREA: BUSINESS
This fund provides financial support to women developing careers in the business field. Recipients are selected by the national board of directors. Recipients must be involved in graduate level work. The award is granted each year for 4 years between the Founders Scholarship which is given every 5 years. The number of awards varies each year, stipend is $3,000.

F8-
AMERICAN COLLEGE OF NURSE-MIDWIVES SCHOLARSHIPS
>American College of Nurse-Midwives Foundation

818 Connecticut Avenue, NW, Suite 900
Washington, DC 20006
(202) 728-9865

INTEREST AREA: MIDWIFERY
Financial assistance is provided for students interested in a career in midwifery. Students must be enrolled in a college or university offering midwifery through a certification program or as a master's level course. Five (5) awards are given each year, $1,000 each.

F9- AMERICAN HEART ASSOCIATION CLINICIAN SCIENTIST AWARD

American Heart Association
Attn: Division of Research Administration
7272 Greenville Avenue
Dallas, TX, 75231-4596
(214) 706-1453

INTEREST AREA: RESEARCH
This fund provides monies for research and training to clinically trained physicians pursuing careers in investigative science research. Three participants must qualify to receive monies; the applicant, a U.S. sponsor (clinical department) and a research preceptor (laboratory may be in U.S. or abroad). Sponsor and preceptor may not be the same person. Annual financial support ranges from $40,000 to $44,000 plus benefits and $33,000 for project support in third and fourth years of research. Monies may be extended into additional 2 year period.

F10- AMERICAN HEART ASSOCIATION GRANT-IN-AID

American Heart Association
Attn: Division of Research Administration
7272 Greenville Avenue
Dallas, TX 75231-4596
(214) 706-1453

INTEREST AREA: RESEARCH

Financial assistance is available to support research by independent investigators and established investigators advancing research in the following health areas: cardiovascular, stroke, clinical or public health problems. Research must be located at accredited universities, colleges, medical or dental schools, schools of public health, accredited hospitals and laboratories and other qualifying non-profit research institutions. Financial support is annually up to $40,000 for a maximum of 3 years.

F11-
AMERICAN SOCIETY OF WOMEN ACCOUNTANTS SCHOLARSHIPS

American Society of Women Accountants
Attn: Executive Director
1755 Lynnfield Road, Suite 257
Memphis, TN 38119
(901) 680-0470

INTEREST AREA: ACCOUNTING CAREER
This fund provides monies for women enrolled in college studying for a degree in accounting. Application is taken through the local chapter of ASWA. Five (5) awards are given each year, ranging from $5,000 to $1,000.

F12-
AMS INDUSTRY GRADUATE FELLOWSHIPS

American Meteorological Society
45 Beacon Street
Boston, MA 02108-3693
(617) 227-2426
E-mail: sarmstrg@ametsoc.org

INTEREST AREA: OCEANIC SCIENCES
Funds are available to first year graduate students in the fields of atmospheric sciences, oceanography, hydrology, chemistry, computer sciences, engineering, environmental sciences, mathematics and physics. Approximately 8 awards are given each year, each in the amount of $15,000 per academic year.

F13-
ANNE PEKAR MEMORIAL SCHOLARSHIP
>National Federation of the Blind
>Attn: Chair, Scholarship Committee
>814 Fourth Avenue, Suite 200
>Grinnell, IA 50112
>(515) 236-3366

INTEREST AREA: BLIND STUDENTS
Financial assistance is provided for women ages 17-25 who are legally blind and are pursuing undergraduate or graduate studies full time. One award is given each year in the amount of $4,000.

F14-
ANNIE JUMP CANNON AWARD IN ASTRONOMY
>American Association of University Women
>Attn: Educational Foundation, Department AJC
>1111 16th Street, NW
>Washington, DC 20036-4873
>(202) 785-7700

INTEREST AREA: ASTRONOMY
The purpose of this fund is to provide research monies for women studying in the field of astronomy. Women must be under the age of 35, preference is given to women with a Ph.D. in astronomy. One award is given each year in the amount of $5,000.

F15-
APPLIED HEALTH PHYSICS FELLOWSHIP PROGRAM
>Oak Ridge Institute for Science and Education
>P.O. Box 117
>Oak Ridge, TN 37831-0117
>(423) 576-9279
>E-mail: ahpfp@orau.gov

INTEREST AREA: APPLIED HEALTH PHYSICS

Funding is available for graduate study and work experience in the field of applied health physics. Applicants must be working on a master's degree in this field at an accredited college, university or school in the United States. The number of awards varies each year, each award provides full payment of tuition and fees and $14,000 yearly.

F16-
ASME GRADUATE TEACHING FELLOWSHIP
American Society of Mechanical Engineers
Attn: Director of Engineering Education
345 East 47th Street
New York, NY 10017-2392
(212) 705-7177

INTEREST AREA: MECHANICAL ENGINEERING
Funding is available to graduate students to pursue a doctorate in mechanical engineering and to select teaching engineering sciences as a career. Applicants must have an undergraduate degree from an ABET accredited program. The number of awards given each year varies, each award is $5,000 per year.

F17-
ASA/NSF/NIST SENIOR RESEARCH FELLOW AND ASSOCIATE PROGRAM
American Statistical Association
1429 Duke Street
Alexandria, VA 22314-3402
(703) 684-1221

INTEREST AREA: RESEARCH
Funding is available to financially support research conducted at the National Institute of Standards and Technology and managed by associate or senior researchers. Senior researchers (Ph.D.'s) and graduate students (must have completed 2 years of graduate study) qualify for the fellowship. Senior researchers may receive up to $95,000 annually, associates may receive up to $43,000 annually.

F18-
ASME GRADUATE FELLOWSHIP
American Society of Mechanical Engineers
345 East 47th Street
New York, NY 10017
(212) 705-7177

INTEREST AREA: ENGINEERING
This fund provides financial assistance to women pursuing careers in engineering and to assist in doctorate studies in mechanical engineering. Applicants must belong to the American Society of Mechanical Engineers and meet their requirements. Fellowship amount is $5,000 per year, may be renewed up to three years.

F19-
ASTRA MERCK ADVANCED RESEARCH TRAINING AWARDS
American Digestive Health Foundation
7910 Woodmont Avenue, Suite 700
Bethesda, MD 20814-3015
(301) 654-2635

INTEREST AREA: MEDICAL RESEARCH
Funding is provided for research training in the fields of gastrointestinal or liver functions. Applicants must be M.D.s and currently hold a gastroenterology related fellowship at an accredited North American institution. Six fellowships are awarded each year, each in the amount of $36,000.

F20-
AVON PRODUCTS FOUNDATION SCHOLARSHIP FOR WOMEN IN BUSINESS STUDIES
Business and Professional Women's Foundation
Attn: Scholarships
2012 Massachusetts Avenue, NW
Washington, DC 20036

(202) 293-1200

INTEREST AREA: BUSINESS
Funds are available to provide women with financial support entering undergraduate or graduate studies in the field of business. Applicants must be women at least 25 years old, U.S. citizens and accepted into an accredited program or course of study. The award is $1,000 per year, the number of awards given each year varies with need.

F21-
AWIS PREDOCTORAL AWARDS
Association for Women in Science
1522 K Street, NW, Suite 820
Washington, DC 20005
(202) 408-0742

INTEREST AREA: SCIENCE EDUCATION
The purpose of this fund is to provide monies to women pre-doctoral studying in any field of science; physical, natural, social, behavioral, engineering, mathematics. Women at the dissertation stage of their graduate studies are favored for this award. Four awards are given each year, each approximately $500.

F22-
BARBARA THOMAS ENTERPRISES, INC. SCHOLARSHIP
Foundation of Research and Education
919 North Michigan Avenue, Suite 1400
Chicago, IL 60611
(312) 787-2672

INTEREST AREA: HEALTH INFORMATION FIELD
The purpose of this fund is to provide financial assistance to women studying at the undergraduate or graduate level in the area of health information management or technology. Applicants must be a member of AHIMA, be a single parent, have or be working toward a bachelor's degree in the health information management profession. One award is given each year in the amount of $5,000.

F23- BEHAVIORAL SCIENCES RESEARCH TRAINING FELLOWSHIPS

Epilepsy Foundation of America
Attn: Department of Research and Professional Education
4351 Garden City Drive
Landover, MD 20785
(301) 459-3700
E-mail: postmaster@efa.org

INTEREST AREA: EPILEPSY RESEARCH

The purpose of this fund is to provide financial assistance to women pursuing additional postgraduate research in the field of epilepsy. Applicants must have received their doctoral degree in behavioral sciences prior to fellowship award. The number of awards varies each year, awards may go as high as $30,000 per year and are based on experience and qualifications of applicant, scope of project and duration of research.

F24- BISHOP CHARLES P. GRECO GRADUATE FELLOWSHIPS

Knights of Columbus
P.O. Box 1670
New Haven, CT 06507-0901
(203) 772-2130

INTEREST AREA: GRADUATE EDUCATION

Financial assistance is provided for members of the Knights of Columbus, their wives, children, widows and children of deceased members for graduate education. Applicants must be full time students and plan to pursue a career in teaching mentally retarded children The number of awards given each year varies, each is in the amount of $500.

F25- BUNTING FELLOWSHIP PROGRAM

Mary Ingraham Bunting Institute

Attn: Fellowships Office
Radcliffe College
34 Concord Avenue
Cambridge, MA 02138
(617) 495-8212

INTEREST AREA: GENERAL
Financial support is available for women conducting study at the Bunting Institute in the following areas: academic or professional fields, creative writing, all the arts. Applicants who receive the awards must be full time students for one year and maintain residence in the Boston area during that time. The number of awards varies each year from 4 to 9. Each fellowship includes $30,000 annually, office\studio space, auditing allowances, access to several resources at Redcliffe and Harvard.

F26-
CAREER ADVANCEMENT SCHOLARSHIPS
Business and Professional Women's Foundation
2012 Massachusetts Avenue, NW
Washington, DC 20036
(202) 293-1200

INTEREST AREA: EDUCATION, COMPUTER SCIENCE
The purpose of this fund is to provide women in transition financial support to increase their educational levels and compete for qualified positions in chosen careers. Applicants must be 30 years of age and studying in the following fields; computer science, education, paralegal, engineering, science or as a J.D., D.D.S., or M.D. Awards total $50,000 each year, with the average award being $750, over 100 awards are given each year.

F27-
CAREER DEVELOPMENT GRANTS
American Association of University Women
Attn: Educational Foundation
2201 North Dodge Street
Iowa City, IA 52243-4030

(319) 337-1716

INTEREST AREA: EDUCATIONAL ADVANCEMENT
The purpose of this fund it to provide financial assistance to women with degrees who had their educational studies interrupted and to provide opportunity to working women with degrees to update their professional skills through advanced studies. Applicants must have received their bachelor's degree, be a U.S. citizen, and plan to pursue an degree from an accredited school, college or university. Each year 75 awards are given, the range is between $1,000 and $5,000 each.

F28-
CHASE MANHATTAN SCHOLARSHIP PROGRAM
Financial Women International
200 North Glebe Road, Suite 814
Arlington, VA 22203
(703) 807-2007

INTEREST AREA: FINANCIAL INDUSTRY
This fund provides financial support to women in the banking and financial services industry to further their career goals through advanced education. Applicants must be members of Financial Women International and be employed within the financial industry as a manager or supervisor. One award is given each year in the amount of $2,300.

F29-
CHICANA DISSERTATION FELLOWSHIP
Department of Chicano Studies
Attn: Administrative Adviser
University of California at Santa Barbara
Santa Barbara, CA 93106
(805) 893-3012

INTEREST AREA: CHICANA STUDENTS
Funding is provided to assist Chicana students with the completion of their dissertations. Applicants must be enrolled in a doctoral program

in the field of humanities of social sciences. Two awards are given each year, $18,000 each.

F30-
CHILDREN'S HOSPITAL-REDCLIFFE COLLEGE JOINT FELLOWSHIP ON FAMILY VIOLENCE

Mary Ingraham Bunting Institute
Attn: Fellowships Office
Radcliffe College
34 Concord Avenue
Cambridge, MA 02138
(617) 495-8212
E-mail: bunting_fellowships@radcliffe.harvard.edu

INTEREST AREA: FAMILY VIOLENCE STUDIES

The purpose of this fund is to provide financial assistance to women with Ph.D.s and wish to participate at Children's Hospital furthering the study of family violence. Applicants must hold a doctoral degree in sociology, psychology, anthropology, medicine, social work, or nursing. One award is given each year ranging from $18,000 to $32,000, depending upon the postdoctoral experience of the applicant.

F31-
CLARE BOOTHE LUCE GRADUATE FELLOWSHIPS IN SCIENCE AND ENGINEERING

Clare Boothe Luce Fund
c/o Henry Luce Foundation, Inc.
111 West 50th Street
New York, NY 10020
(212) 489-7700

INTEREST AREA: SCIENCES

This fund provides financial assistance for women in the following areas: physics, chemistry, biology, meteorology, engineering, computer sciences and mathematics. Applicant must have a master's degree or be a candidate for a master's degree or a doctoral degree in the above areas, be a U.S. citizen and intend to work in the chosen field of study. Amount of fellowship varies according to individual assessment by participating institutions. Duration of the award is 2 years, with renewal for a third optional.

F32-
CLARE BOOTHE LUCE JUNIOR FACULTY APPOINTMENT
Clare Boothe Luce Fund
c/o Henry Luce Foundation, Inc.
111 West 50th Street
New York, NY 10020
(212) 489-7700

INTEREST AREA: SCIENTIST-ENGINEERS FACULTY POSITIONS

The purpose of this fund is to provide support for women scientists and engineers of outstanding caliber who are currently under represented or un-represented on the faculty of the requesting facility. Preference is given in the fields of physics, chemistry, biology, meteorology, engineering, computer science and mathematics. Application is processed through the requesting institution where research and residency will take place. Awards are for 5 years of study and research and can range from $225,000 to $400,000. Exact amount depends upon seniority of candidate, nature of study and research planned.

F33-
CONGRESSIONAL FELLOWSHIPS ON WOMEN AND PUBLIC POLICY
Women's Research and Education Institute
Attn: Fellowship Program
1700 18th Street, NW, Suite 400
Washington, DC 20009
(202) 328-7070

INTEREST AREA: GOVERNMENT STUDIES

Financial assistance is available to provide one year of study at George Washington University and be interned to a congressional committee staff member during that time. The purpose is to develop specialists in policy issues regarding women. Applicants must be in a graduate or professional program in the United States. Applicant must demonstrate interest in research or political activity within women's studies. Monies are provided for living and tuition expenses, individual amounts average approximately $9,500 yearly. Six (6) or more awards are given each year.

F34-
CORPORATE EXECUTIVES FELLOWS PROGRAM
National Urban Fellows, Inc.
55 West 44th Street, Suite 600
New York, NY 10036
(212) 921-9400

INTEREST AREA: ADMINISTRATIVE-MANAGERIAL ASSISTANCE
The purpose of this fund is to offer financial assistance and a mentorship to women working in upper level management with experience in administrative or managerial positions. Applicants must be U.S. citizens, have a bachelor's degree and have significant work experience. Participants will study at either Columbia University or Stanford University (Graduate School of Business at both universities) and will receive an MBA degree from either Columbia or Stanford. Approximately 6 awards are given each year ranging from $16,000 to $18,000. Including full time academic work, the participants undertake a 9 month mentorship.

F35-
DEED SCHOLARSHIPS
American Public Power Association
Attn: Coordinator, DEED Administration
2301 M Street, NW
Washington, DC 20037-1484
(202) 467-2960

INTEREST AREA: RESEARCH POWER SYSTEMS
This program offers financial assistance to undergraduate and graduate women researching in the fields of public power systems. Applicants must be sponsored by a publicly owned utility participating in the Demonstrations of Energy Efficient Developments DEED programs

and be doing research on projects approved by sponsoring utility. Ten (10) awards are given each year, each ranging $3,000 per project.

F36-
DISPLACED HOMEMAKER'S SCHOLARSHIP
Educational Foundation for Women in Accounting
530 Church Street, Suite 700
Nashville, TN 37219
(615) 254-3687

INTEREST AREA: ACCOUNTING

This program provides financial support for women who have become the sole support for their family and wish to advance their education in the field of accounting. Education levels include a degree in accounting at the undergraduate, master's or doctoral level. One award is given each year in the amount of $4,000.

F37-
DISSERTATION FELLOWSHIP ON PEACE AND SECURITY IN A CHANGING WORLD
Social Science Research Council
810 Seventh Avenue
New York, NY 10019
(212) 377-2700

INTEREST AREA: DOCTORAL RESEARCH

Funds are provided to students completing their doctoral research in the fields of security and security issues with concerns for worldwide cultural, social and economic changes. Applicants must be working the fields of social and/or behavioral sciences. Each year 7 awards are given, each is approximately $17, 500.

F38-
DOROTHY HARRIS SCHOLARSHIP
Women's Sports Foundation
Eisenhower Park
1899 Hempstead Turnpike, Suite 400

East Meadow, NY 11554-1000
(516) 542-4700
E-mail: wosport@aol.com

INTEREST AREA: SPORTS CAREER INTERESTS
The purpose of this fund is to provide monies for female graduate students participating in full time graduate studies in the field of athletics. Applicants must be enrolled or planning to enroll in one of the following programs; physical education, sport management, sport psychology or sport sociology. Number of awards varies each, each award is $1,500.

F39-
DOROTHY LEET GRANTS
American Association of University Women
1111 16th Street, NW
Washington, DC 20036-4873
(202) 785-7700

INTEREST AREA: GENERAL-OUTSIDE THE U.S.
This program provides financial assistance in the training of graduate women students wanting to work in countries with low per capita income and who can make a significant contribution within that country with research in their chosen profession. Applicants must be a member of a national federation or association affiliated with the International Federation of University Women. The awards are given in even numbered years and average 20 per award period. The average award is 3,000 to 6,000 Swiss francs.

F40-
ELAINE OSBORNE JACOBSON SCHOLARSHIP FOR WOMEN WORKING IN HEALTH CARE LAW
Roscoe Pound Foundation
1050 31st Street, NW
Washington, DC 20007
(202) 965-3500 ext. 380

INTEREST AREA: HEALTH CARE LAW

Financial assistance is provided to women law students who are interested in advancing their career studies in the field of health care law. Applicants must be attending an accredited law school approved by the ABA. Two awards are given each year, one for $2,000 and one for $1,000.

F41-
ELEANOR ROOSEVELT TEACHER FELLOWSHIPS
American Association of University Women
2201 North Dodge Street
Iowa City, IA 52243-4030
(310) 337-1716

INTEREST AREA: TEACHERS: MATHEMATICS/SCIENCE
Funds are provided to advance the education of women public school teachers who work with girls-at-risk and are responsible for mathematics, science or technology courses for these children. Applicants must be U.S. citizens and be committed to at least 3 years of teaching after the fellowship year. Each year 15 awards are given out. The dollar amount varies depending upon the proposed sabbatical program.

F42-
ENVIRONMENTAL SCIENCE AND MANAGEMENT FELLOWS PROGRAM
National Urban Fellows, Inc.
55 West 44th Street, Suite 600
New York, NY 10036
(212) 921-9400

INTEREST AREA: ENVIRONMENTAL PROTECTION-MANAGEMENT
This is a unique program for women in the field of environmental protection and management. After successful completion of the fellowship requirement, candidates will be granted a master of science degree from Tufts University. Applicants must be U.S. citizens, have a bachelor's degree and at least 3 years work experience as a full time administrator or manager. Each year 15 awards are given out. The

fellowship in a 2 year award covering tuition, other program related expenses and a stipend.

F43-
EPILEPSY FOUNDATION OF AMERICAN RESEARCH TRAINING FELLOWSHIPS
Epilepsy Foundation of America
Department of Research and Professional Education
4351 Garden City Drive
Landover, MD 20785
(301) 459-3700
E-mail: postmaster@efa.org

INTEREST AREA: EPILEPSY RESEARCH
Funds are provided to develop expertise in epilepsy research. Applicants must be physicians or Ph.D. neuroscientists interested in postdoctoral research. Each year 3 awards are given out, each is approximately $40,000. This foundation also offers fellowships for clinical training. Seven awards are given each year in the amount of $40,000

F44-
FEMME VITALE SCHOLARSHIP AWARDS
Odwalla, Inc.
120 Stone Pine Road
Half Moon Bay, CA 94019
(415) 726-1888

INTEREST AREA: HEALTH AND NUTRITION
Financial assistance is provided to women working on a degree in health and nutrition. Applicants may be pursuing an undergraduate or graduate degree. Each year one or more awards is given, each in the amount of $3,000.

F45-
FOCUS PROFESSIONS GROUP FELLOWSHIPS
American Association of University Women

2201 North Dodge Street
Iowa City, IA 2243-4030
(319) 337-1716

INTEREST AREA: BUSINESS, LAW, MEDICINE
This program provides financial assistance to women who are under represented in one of following professions: business administration, law or medicine. Applicants must be U.S. citizens and must be an enrolled graduate student. The awards range from $5,000 to $9,500 for full time study, the number of award given each year varies.

F46-
GENERAL MOTORS FOUNDATION GRADUATE SCHOLARSHIP
Society of Women Engineers
120 Wall Street, 11th Floor
New York, NY 10005-3902
(212) 509-9577
e-mail: 71764.743@compuserve.com

INTEREST AREA: ENGINEERING
Financial assistance is provided to women who are in their first year of their master's degree program and are intending to develop a career in engineering. Applicants must be studying in one of the following engineering fields: mechanical, electrical, chemical, automotive or manufacturing. One award is given each year in the amount of $1,000.

F47-
GLOBAL CHANGE GRADUATE FELLOWSHIPS
Oak Ridge Institute for Science and Education
P.O. Box 117
Oak Ridge, TN 37831-0117
(800) 569-7749
E-mail: gfglobal@orau.gov

INTEREST AREA: GLOBAL CHANGE
Funds are available for graduate study or work experience in the following fields: atmospheric sciences, meteorology, ecology, ocean

sciences, biology and related scientific fields. Applicants must be enrolled in a master's or doctoral program. The number of awards varies each year. Each award provides for full payment of tuition and fees and a stipend of $14,000 per year.

F48-
HOWARD HUGES MEDICAL INSTITUTE PREDOCTORAL FELLOWSHIPS IN BIOLOGICAL SCIENCES
National Research Council
2101 Constitution Avenue
Washington, DC 20418
(202) 334-2872
E-mail: infofell@nas.edu

INTEREST AREA: BIOLOGICAL SCIENCES
Funding is provided to women students pursuing graduate studies in the fields of biological sciences. Each year approximately 80 awards are given, each with a stipends of $15,000, a cost of education allowance and $2,000 for health benefits, books, etc.

F49-
IADES FELLOWSHIP AWARD
International Alumnae of Delta Epsilon Sorority
8619 Pin Oak Drive
Springfield, VA 22153

INTEREST AREA: DEAF WOMEN GRADUATE STUDENTS
Funds are provided for female students studying at the graduate level and are deaf. Applicants do not need to be members of Delta Epsilon to apply. Candidates must have completed 12 or more units at the doctoral level of their studies. The number of awards varies each year, the amount awarded ranges between $500 and $1,000 each award.

F50-
INDIVIDUAL PREDOCTORAL NATIONAL RESEARCH SERVICE AWARDS FOR M.D./PH.D. FELLOWS
National Institutes of Health

Office of Scientific Affairs
Willco Building, Suite 409
6000 Executive Boulevard MSC 7003
Bethesda, MD 20892-7003
(301) 443-1890
E-mail: jv24p@nih.gov

INTEREST AREA: MENTAL HEALTH, DRUG OR ALCOHOL ABUSE/ADDICTION RESEARCH
Female students enrolled in an M.D.\Ph.D. program and plan a career in mental health, drug or alcohol abuse and addiction research may apply for financial assistance. Applicants must be U.S. citizens and planning a career in research. The number of awards varies each year, the annual stipend in $10,000.

F51-
JOHN AND MURIEL LANDIS SCHOLARSHIP AWARD
American Nuclear Society
555 North Kensington Avenue
LaGrange Park, IL 60525
(708) 352-6611

INTEREST AREA: NUCLEAR RELATED FIELDS
Financial assistance is offered to undergraduate or graduate students pursuing a career in nuclear science, nuclear engineering or a related field. Each year 8 awards are given in the amount of $3,000 each.

F52-
JULIA KIENE FELLOWSHIP IN ELECTRICAL ENERGY
Electrical Women's Round Table, Inc.
P.O. Box 292793
Nashville, TN 37229-2793
(615) 890-1272

INTEREST AREA: EDUCATION
Funds are available for women interested in graduate work in the field of electrical energy. The following fields are a few of the considering areas for this fellowship: communication, education, electric utilities,

engineering, marketing, radio and television. One award is given each year in the amount of $2,000.

F53-
KARLA SCHERER FOUNDATION SCHOLARSHIP
>Karla Scherer Foundation
>100 Renaissance Center, Suite 1680
>Detroit, MI 48243-1009
>(313) 259-4520

INTEREST AREA: BUSINESS
Financial assistance for women interested in careers in business. All levels of education are considered for this fellowship including re-entry women student. The number of awards varies each year and dollar amount varies according to the needs of the recipient.

F54-
LAURELS FUND ENDOWMENT FELLOWSHIPS
>Educational Foundation for Women in Accounting
>530 Church Street, Suite 700
>Nashville, TN 37219
>(615) 254-3687

INTEREST AREA: ACCOUNTING
This fund provides financial support to women studying accounting and working on their doctoral research. One award is given each year in the amount of $5,000.

F55-
M.A. CARTLAND SHACKFORD MEDICAL FELLOWSHIP
>Wellesley College
>Center for Work and Service
>106 Central Street
>Wellesley, MA 02181-8200
>(617) 283-2347

INTEREST AREA: MEDICAL FIELDS

Financial assistance is available to women graduate students pursuing a career in the medical field (excluding psychiatry) and are enrolled as a full time graduate student. One award is given each year in the amount of $3,500.

F56-
MAGNETIC FUSION ENERGY TECHNOLOGY FELLOWSHIP PROGRAM

Oak Ridge Institute for Science and Education
P.O. Box 117
Oak Ridge, TN 37831-0117
(800) 569-7749
E-mail: mfetfp@orau.gov

INTEREST AREA: MAGNETIC FUSION ENERGY TECHNOLOGY
Funding is providing for graduate study in the fields of physical sciences, mathematics or engineering. The number of awards given varies each year, each stipend is approximately $15,500 per year.
Oak Ridge Institute for Science and Education also offers fellowships through the Magnetic Fusion Science Fellowship Program. Each stipend is approximately $15,000 per year.

F57-
MATHEMATICAL SCIENCES POSTDOCTORAL RESEARCH FELLOWSHIPS

National Science Foundation
Division of Mathematical Sciences
4201 Wilson Boulevard, Room 1025
Arlington, VA 22230
(703) 306-1870
E-mail: msprf@nsf.gov

INTEREST AREA: MATHEMATICS
This fund provides financial assistance for postdoctoral research development and training in the field of mathematics. Candidates must be U.S. citizens, have a Ph.D. in a mathematical science and have not previously held any other postdoctoral fellowship from the National

Science Foundation. The yearly dollar amount is $66,000+, each year 30-40 awards are presented.

F58- MATHEMATICAL SCIENCES UNIVERSITY-INDUSTRY POSTDOCTORAL RESEARCH FELLOWSHIPS

National Science Foundation
Division of Mathematical Sciences
4201 Wilson Boulevard, Room 1025
Arlington, VA 22230
(703) 306-1870
E-mail: uicrp@nsf.gov

INTEREST AREA: MATHEMATICS
The fund provides financial assistance to women graduate students who are studying in the field of mathematics and wish to expand their field of interest through exposure to industrial environments. The award is for 2 years of study and research. Applicants must be U.S. citizens and have a Ph.D. in a mathematical science. The number of awards given each year varies, each award is approximately $111,000 for two years of study.

F59- MENTORED CLINICAL SCIENTIST DEVELOPMENT AWARDS

National Institutes of Health
Attn: Office of Extramural Research
Extramural Outreach and Information Resources Offices
6701 Rockledge Drive, Room 6207
MSC 7910
Bethesda, MD 20892-7910
(301) 435-0714
E-mail: asknih@odrockm1.od.nih.gov

INTEREST AREA: RESEARCH/CLINICAL STUDY
This fund provides financial assistance for a wide range of professional clinically trained researchers who wish to advance their career in research. Applicants must be U.S. citizens, have a clinical degree and

be committed to research within this program for 3-5 years. Several departments at NIH are involved in this fellowship fund, so the number of awards varies each year. Each award includes a yearly salary (varies with each department) and up to $20,000 per year for tuition, fees, books and other costs related to career development.

F60-
MERRITT-PUTNAM RESEARCH\CLINICAL TRAINING FELLOWSHIPS
Epilepsy Foundation of America
4351 Garden City Drive
Landover, MD 20785
(800) EFA-1000
E-mail: postmaster@efa.org

INTEREST AREA: EPILEPSY RESEARCH
Funds are available to women students who have received their M.D. degree and completed their residency training and wish to further their career in epilepsy research and clinical epilepsy work. The number of awards varies each year, the award amount is $40,000 per year.

F61-
MICROSOFT CORPORATION SCHOLARSHIPS
Society of Women Engineers
120 Wall Street, 11th Floor
New York, NY 10005-3902
(212) 509-9577
E-mail: 71764.743@compuserve.com

INTEREST AREA: COMPUTER SCIENCE
This fund provides financial assistance to women students at the undergraduate or graduate level of study in computer sciences or computer engineering. Each year ten awards are given out, each is $1,000.

F62-
NATIONAL LAWYERS GUILD SUMMER PROJECTS

National Lawyers Guild
126 University Place, Fourth Floor
New York, NY 10013
(212) 627-2656
E-mail: nfgno@igc.apc.org

INTEREST AREA: LAW
Funding is provided to female law students, legal workers and lawyers wanting to advance their careers in the field of civil rights and poverty law groups. Approximately 20 awards are given each year, each in the amount of $2,000.

F63-
NCAA POSTGRADUATE SCHOLARSHIP PROGRAM
National Collegiate Athletic Association
Attn: Director of Professional Development
6201 College Boulevard
Overland Park, KS 66211-2422
(913) 339-1906

INTEREST AREA: GRADUATE EDUCATION STUDENT-ATHLETES
Funds are available for students who are also athletes excelling in academics and sports and are in their final year of intercollegiate athletics competition. Applicants must have a grade point average of 3.0. Each year 154 awards are given, each is $5,000.

F64-
NCAA WOMEN'S ENHANCEMENT POSTGRADUATE SCHOLARSHIP PROGRAM
National Collegiate Athletic Association
6201 College Boulevard
Overland Park, KS 66221-2422
(913) 339-1906

INTEREST AREA: GRADUATE EDUCATION IN ATHLETICS
Funding is provided for women interested in graduate education in the field of athletics. Candidates must have been accepted in a NCAA

member institution's sports administration program, must also be U.S. citizens and be entering the first semester or term of their postgraduate studies. Ten awards are given each year in the amount of $6,000 each.

F65-
NPSC GRADUATE FELLOWSHIPS
National Physical Science Consortium
New Mexico State University
O'Loughlin House on University Boulevard
Box 30001, Dept 3NPS
Las Cruces, NM 88003-8001
(800) 952-4118
E-mail: npsc@nmsu.edu

INTEREST AREA: GRADUATE STUDY: ASTRONOMY, CHEMISTRY, COMPUTER SCIENCE, GEOLOGY, MATERIAL SCIENCES, MATHEMATICS, PHYSICS
Financial assistance is available to women pursuing graduate study in the above fields. Applicants must be U.S. citizens, earned a 3.0 GPA and be pursuing doctoral study in the above areas. The number of awards varies each year. The fellowship awards $12,000+ per year plus the cost of tuition and fees.

F66-
NSEP AREA AND LANGUAGE STUDIES DOCTORAL FELLOWSHIPS
Academy for Educational Development
1875 Connecticut Avenue, NW, Suite 900
Washington, DC 20009-1202
(202) 884-8285
E-mail: nsep@aed.org

INTEREST AREA: DOCTORAL STUDIES-LANGUAGES
Financial assistance is provided to women graduate students who are interested in developing expertise in the languages, cultures and area studies of countries not usually studied and considered critical to national security. Over 300 awards are given each year, the maximum yearly amount per award is $25,000. *The Academy for Educational*

Development also has a NSEP Graduate Enhancement Fellowships fund for above interest areas.

F67-
NSF GRADUATE FELLOWSHIPS
Oak Ridge Associated Universities
P.O. Box 3010
Oak Ridge, T37831-3010
(423) 241-4300
E-mail: nsfgrfp@orau.gov

INTEREST AREA: SCIENCES, MATHEMATICS, ENGINEERING
Financial assistance is provided to women who are working on a master's or doctoral degree in the field of sciences, mathematical sciences, computer and information science, chemistry, earth sciences, physics, social sciences, psychology, astronomy, life sciences or engineering. Applicants must be U.S. citizens and have completed at least 20 semester/30 quarter hours of study. Each year 850 awards are given, each award is $14,000 per year, plus $9,000 cost of education allowance.

F68-
NUCLEAR ENGINEERING AND HEALTH PHYSICS FELLOWSHIP PROGRAM
Oak Ridge Institute for Science and Education
P.O. Box 117
Oak Ridge, TN 37831-0117
(423) 576-9558
E-mail: nehpfp@orau.gov

INTEREST AREA: NUCLEAR SCIENCE, ENGINEERING, HEALTH PHYSICS
This fund provides funding for graduate study and research in the fields of nuclear science, engineering and/or health physics. Students may be working on a master's or doctoral degree. The number of awards varies each year, each award in $14,000.

F69-
OLIVE LYNN SALEMBIER SCHOLARSHIP
Society of Women Engineers
120 Wall Street, 11th Floor
New York, NY 10005-3902
(212) 509-9577
E-mail: 71764.743@compuserve.com

INTEREST AREA: ENGINEERING
Financial assistance is available to women who have been out of the engineering market for a minimum of 2 years and now wish to further their education to reenter the job market. Applicants may be either undergraduate or graduate students. One award is given each year in the amount of $2,000.

F70-
P.O.E. PROGRAM FOR CONTINUING EDUCATION
P.E.O. Sisterhood
3700 Grand Avenue
Des Moines, IA 50312-2899
(515) 255-3153

INTEREST AREA: GENERAL EDUCATION
Funds are available to women wanting to resume or continue their education. Applicants must be sponsored by a local chapter of the P.E.O. Sisterhood. The number of awards and the dollar amount given each year varies with the needs of the recipients.

F71-
POSTDOCTORAL FELLOWSHIP ON PEACE AND SECURITY IN A CHANGING WORLD
Social Science Research Council
810 Seventh Avenue
New York, NY 10019
(212) 377-2700

INTEREST AREA: RESEARCH: SECURITY WORLDWIDE

Funds are available to women doing postdoctoral research on the worldwide cultural, social, economic, military and political changes and the effects this has on security. Each year approximately 6 awards are given in the amount of up to $37,000 per year.

F72- POSTDOCTORAL RESEARCH FELLOWSHIPS IN BIOSCIENCES RELATED TO THE ENVIRONMENT

National Science Foundation
Division of Biological Infrastructure
4201 Wilson Boulevard, Room 615
Arlington, VA 22230
(703) 306-1469
E-mail: ckimsey@nsf.gov

INTEREST AREA: RESEARCH

Financial assistance is available for women studying at the doctoral level and engaged in research training on the mechanisms underlying and affecting interactions between organisms and their environment at several levels within the study of biology. Each year approximately 40 awards are given, each is $28,000+ per year.

F73- RENATE W. CHASMAN SCHOLARSHIP FOR WOMEN

Brookhaven Women in Science
Building 197C
P.O. Box 183
Upton, NY 11973-5000
(516) 344-7226

INTEREST AREA: SCIENCES

This fellowship provides funds to women who wish to resume their education in the fields of natural science, engineering or mathematics. Applicants must be U.S. citizens and be planning a career in one of the sciences. The annual award is $2,000, the number of awards given each year varies.

F74-
RITA DIMARTINO SCHOLARSHIP IN COMMUNICATIONS
MANA, A National Latina Organization
1725 K Street, NW, Suite 501
Washington, DC 20006
(202) 833-0060

INTEREST AREA: COMMUNICATIONS
Funds are available for Latina women continuing their undergraduate or graduate education in the field of communications. Applicants must be enrolled full time in an accredited college or university in the U.S. One award is given each year in the amount of $1,000.

F75-
RITA LEVINE MEMORIAL SCHOLARSHIP
American Mensa Education and Research Foundation
201 Main Street, Suite 1101
Fort Worth, TX 76102-3115
(817) 332-2600

INTEREST AREA: POSTSECONDARY EDUCATION
Financial assistance is provided for post-secondary education to women who wish to return to school after an absence of at least 7 years. Applicants must be and are intended to be enrolled in a degree program in an accredited U.S. school. One award is given each year, the amount varies from $200 to $1,000 according to the need of the applicant.

F76-
RUTH SATTER MEMORIAL AWARD
Association for Women in Science
1522 K Street, NW, Suite 820
Washington, DC 20005
(202) 408-8321
E-mail: awis@awis.org

INTEREST AREA: SCIENCES, Ph.D. PROGRAMS

Financial assistance is provided to reentry women working on a doctoral degree in the sciences. Applicants must have been away from their education for at least 3 or more years to raise a family. Applicants need to be enrolled in a physical science, life science, social science or engineering program. One award is given each year ranging from $500-$1,000.

F77-
SCHUYLER M. MEYER, JR. SCHOLARSHIP FUND
American Indian Science and Engineering Society
5661 Airport Boulevard
Boulder, CO 80301
(303) 939-0023
E-mail: ascholar@spot.colorado.edu

INTEREST AREA: GENERAL EDUCATION
Financial assistance is provided to American Indian women who are pursuing education at the undergraduate or graduate level and who are single parents, raising a minor child. The number of awards given each year varies, the dollar amount is approximately $1,000.

F78-
SELECTED PROFESSIONS FELLOWSHIPS IN SCIENCE AND TECHNOLOGY
American Association of University Women
2201 North Dodge Street
Iowa City, IA 52243-4030
(319) 337-1716

INTEREST AREA: ARCHITECTURE, COMPUTER SCIENCE, INFO SCIENCE, ENGINEERING MATHEMATICS, STATISTICS
Funds are provided to assist women entering their last year of training in the fields of architecture, computer science, information science, engineering, mathematics or statistics. Applicants must be U.S. citizens and be enrolled at an accredited U.S. institution. The number of awards varies, each award ranging from $5,000 to $9,000.

F79-
STAR GRADUATE ENVIRONMENTAL EDUCATION FELLOWSHIPS

Environmental Protection Agency
Attn: Office of Research and Development
National Center for Environmental Research and Quality Assurance
Waterside Mall, Room 2411
401 M Street, SW
Washington, DC 20460
(202) 260-3837

INTEREST AREA: ENVIRONMENTAL RESEARCH
Financial assistance is provided to graduate students pursuing degrees and careers in the field of environmental research. Each year 50-100 awards are given, each award is approximately $34,000 per year with additional funds available to cover costs for research expenses, tuition and fees.

F80-
STEPHEN BUFTON MEMORIAL EDUCATION FUND

American Business Women's Association
9100 Ward Parkway
P.O. Box 8728
Kansas City, MO 64114-0728
(816) 361-6621

INTEREST AREA: BUSINESS ADMINISTRATION
Funds are available for women undergraduate and graduate students studying in business administration. Each year this fund changes the field of education it supports. Applicants must be sponsored by a chapter of the American Business Women's Association. Each chapter awards one scholarship and one loan per year, the dollar amount varies; scholarships from $400-$800,, interest free loans from $100-$1,500.

F81-
SUPPLEMENTS TO PROMOTE REENTRY INTO BIOMEDICAL AND BEHAVIORAL RESEARCH CAREERS

National Institutes of Health
Attn: Office of Extramural Research
Extramural Outreach and Information Resources Office
6701 Rockledge Drive, Room 6207
MSC 7910
Bethesda, MD 20892-7910
(301) 435-0714
E-mail: asknih@odrockm1.od.nih.gov

INTEREST AREA: BIOMEDICAL AND BEHAVIORAL RESEARCH
Funds are provided in grant form for women re-entering a research career after having spent time caring for their children, parents or other family responsibilities. Candidates must have a doctoral degree (MD, DDS, Ph.D., OD, DVM or equivalent) to apply. The number of awards varies each year, each award is up to $50,000 per year.

F82-
SWS MINORITY SCHOLAR FUND
Sociologist for Women in Society
Department of Educational Policy Studies
310 South Sixth Street, EPS 360
P.O. Box 1678
Champaign, IL 61820
(217) 333-7658
E-mail: bmbarnet@uxicso.uiuc.edu

INTEREST AREA: SOCIOLOGY
Financial assistance is provided for women entering into graduate studies in sociology. One award is given each year in the amount of $2,500.

F83-
THANKS BE TO GRANDMOTHER WINIFRED FOUNDATION GRANTS
Thanks Be to Grandmother Winifred Foundation
P.O. Box 1449
Wainscott, NY 11975-1449

(516) 725-0323

INTEREST AREA: CREATIVE DEVELOPMENT OF OLDER WOMEN

This unusual fund provides financial assistance for women over the age of 54 and who are interested in developing projects, program or policies that empower and enrich themselves as well as other women. Funding for specific projects or improvements for talents or skills are encouraged. Each year approximately 30 awards are given, ranging from $500 to $5,000 each.

F84-
VETERANS' DEPENDENCY AND INDEMNITY COMPENSATION (DIC)

Department of Veterans Affairs
810 Vermont Avenue, NW
Washington, DC 20420
(202) 418-4343

INTEREST AREA: VETERANS FAMILIES

Financial assistance is available for the spouses, children and/or parents of deceased veterans who died of disabilities or other causes. Funds are available to the families of veterans who died on or after January 1, 1957. Contact the above office for the details on the monthly payments available.

F85-
VETERANS DEPENDENTS' EDUCATIONAL ASSISTANCE BENEFITS

Department of Veterans Affairs
810 Vermont Avenue, NW
Washington, DC 20420
(202) 418-4343

INTEREST AREA: VETERANS FAMILIES

Financial assistance for post-secondary education is available to the children and spouses of veterans whose deaths or disabilities were service related. Contact the above office for the benefits available.

F86-
WALTER BYERS POSTGRADUATE SCHOLARSHIP PROGRAM
    National Collegiate Athletic Association
    6201 College Boulevard
    Overland Park, KS 66211-2422
    (913) 339-1906

INTEREST AREA: STUDENT-ATHLETES
Financial assistance is provided to students who are also athletes and are in their senior year of competing at a recognized NCAA member institution. Applicants must have a GPA of 3.5 to apply. One award is given each year in the amount of $10,000.

F87-
WILDER PENFIELD RESEARCH\CLINICAL TRAINING FELLOWSHIPS
    Epilepsy Foundation of America
    Attn: Dept. of Research and Professional Education
    4351 Garden City Drive
    Landover, MD 20785
    (301) 459-3700
    E-mail: postmaster@efa.org

INTEREST AREA: EPILEPSY RESEARCH
Funds are available to researchers who have received their MD degree and are entering into a career of research and want to develop expertise in clinical epilepsy and/or epilepsy research. The number of awards varies each year, each award is $40,000 .

F88-
WILHELM-FRANKOWSKI MEDICAL EDUCATION SCHOLARSHIP
    American Medical Women's Association
    801 North Fairfax Street, Suite 400
    Alexandria, VA 22314-1767
    (703) 838-0500

INTEREST AREA: MEDICAL
Financial assistance is provided for women pursuing medical education and are members of the American Medical Women's Association. One award is given each year in the amount of $4,000.

F89-
WOMEN IN ENGINEERING AND COMPUTER AND INFORMATION SCIENCE
> Oak Ridge Associated Universities
> P.O. Box 3010
> Oak Ridge, TN 37831-3010
> (423) 241-4300
> E-mail: nsfgrfp@orau.gov

INTEREST AREA: ENGINEERING-COMPUTER SCIENCES
Funds are provided to encourage women student in continue their education at the graduate level in the fields of engineering and computer sciences. Each year approximately 90 awards are given, each is $14,000+.

F90-
WOMEN IN GEOGRAPHIC EDUCATION SCHOLARSHIP
> National Council for Geographic Education
> 16A Leonard Hall
> Indiana University of Pennsylvania
> Indiana, PA 15705
> (412) 357-6290

INTEREST AREA: GEOGRAPHIC EDUCATION
Financial assistance is provided for women pursuing a career in geographic education and entering post-secondary levels of education. Applicants must have a GPA of 3.0. The number of awards varies each year, each award is $300.

F91-
ZETA PHI BETA GENERAL GRADUATE FELLOWSHIPS
> Zeta Phi Beta Sorority, Inc.

1734 New Hampshire Avenue, NW
Washington, DC 20009
(202) 387-3103

INTEREST AREA: GENERAL EDUCATION
Financial assistance is available to graduate women studying at all levels and all areas of education. Applicants do not need to be members of Zeta Phi Beta to apply. The number of awards given each year varies, each award may be up to $2,500.

**F92-
ZONTA INTERNATIONAL AMELIA EARHART FELLOWSHIP AWARDS**
Zonta International
557 West Randolph Street
Chicago, IL 60661-2206
(312) 930-5848

INTEREST AREA: AEROSPACE SCIENCE-ENGINEERING
Funds are available to provide financial assistance to women doing graduate work in the field of aerospace, including scientific and engineering areas. Applicants must have a BA in science or engineering. Each year approximately 35 fellowships are given.

AWARDS

Awards are given in recognition for professional or personal accomplishments, professional contributions to a field of study or practice and for dedicated public service. Awards can be granted through competitions, prizes and honorarias, but do not include prizes or awards given on the basis of entering any contest. The awards listed are given based on recognized talent and dedication.

A1-
AAUW ACHIEVEMENT AWARD
American Association of University Women
Attn: Educational Foundation
1111 16th Street, NW
Washington, DC 20036-4873
(202) 785-7700
E-mail: foundation@mail.aauw.org

RECOGNITION AREA: SCHOLARLY OR PROFESSIONAL ACHIEVEMENTS
This award recognizes American women who are outstanding in scholarly or professional achievements. This award is given biannually and is a minimum of $5,000.

A2
AAUW FOUNDERS DISTINGUISHED SENIOR SCHOLAR AWARD
American Association of University Women
Attn: Educational Foundation
2201 North Dodge Street
Iowa City, IA 52243-4030
(319) 337-1716

RECOGNITION AREA: SCHOLARLY ACHIEVEMENTS
This award recognizes woman scholars in any field who have contributed exceptionally to their chosen profession. The award is presented annually and is $1,000.

A3-
AAUW RECOGNITION AWARD FOR EMERGING SCHOLARS
American Association of University Women
Attn: Educational Foundation
1111 16th Street, NW
Washington, DC 20036-4873
(202) 785-7700
E-mail: foundation@mail.aauw.org

RECOGNITION AREA: AMERICAN WOMEN FACULTY
This award is presented to young American women who are faculty members and have been recognized for their positive influence on other females in their field. The award is given annually and is $3,500.

A4-
ACS AWARD FOR ENCOURAGING WOMEN INTO CAREERS IN THE CHEMICAL SCIENCES
American Chemical Society
Attn: Awards Office
1155 16th Street, NW
Washington, DC 20036
(202) 872-4481

RECOGNITION AREA: WOMEN INFLUENCING CAREERS IN CHEMISTRY OR ENGINEERING
Any female professional working in a professional environment (academia, industry, government or independent facility) who significantly influences and encourages women to enter into a career in chemistry or engineering may be nominated for this award. The award is presented annually and is $5,000.

A5-
ALBERTA E. CROWE STAR OF TOMORROW AWARD
Young American Bowling Alliance
Attn: Scholarship Administrator
5301 South 76th Street
Greendale, WI 53129
(414) 423-3343

RECOGNITION AREA: OUTSTANDING WOMEN BOWLER
The fund provides for a $1,000 per year award to assist an outstanding female bowler who is enrolled in college in the United States. Applicant must be under the age of 22 and have a minimum bowling average of 175.

A6-
AMERICAN MOTHERS NATIONAL ART SCHOLARSHIP
>American Mothers, Inc.
>Waldorf-Astoria
>301 Park Avenue
>New York, NY 10022
>(212) 755-2539

RECOGNITION AREA: MOTHERS WITH ARTISTIC TALENT
Three categories of art are open for recognition to any mother living in the United States who shows artistic or creative talent. Areas of consideration are: sculpture, painting, and crafts. Each category has an award between $1,000 and $500.

A7-
AMERICAN MOTHERS NATIONAL VOCAL MUSIC SCHOLARSHIP
>American Mothers, Inc.
>Waldorf-Astoria
>301 Park Avenue
>New York, NY 10022
>(212) 755-2539

RECOGNITION AREA: MOTHERS AS MUSICIANS
Any mother living in the United States and pursuing a career in music, professional and well as non-professional, may enter to be recognized for her achievements including blending family and career. The annual award is $1,000.

A8-
AMERICA'S JUNIOR MISS
>American's Junior Miss
>P.O. Box 2786
>Mobile, AL 36652-2786
>(334)-438-3621

RECOGNITION AREA: OUTSTANDING YOUNG WOMEN

Any high school senior under the age of 19 prior to entry into the national finals may apply for this awards program which offers approximately $5 million in college scholarships. Candidates must be U.S. citizens.

A9-
AMERICA'S NATIONAL TEEN-AGER SCHOLARSHIP PROGRAM
>National Teen-Ager Scholarship Foundation
>4708 Mill Crossing West
>Colleyville, TX 76034

RECOGNITION AREA: OUTSTANDING YOUNG WOMEN
Awards for scholastic and leadership achievements of American teenagers ages 13 through 15 are available at local, regional and national levels. Over $5 million in cash, tuition scholarships and awards in available annually.

A10-
BORDEN AWARD
>American Association of Family and Consumer Sciences
>1555 King Street
>Alexandria, VA 22314
>(703) 706-4600

RECOGNITION AREA: NUTRITION RESEARCH
An annual award of $2,000 is given to any eligible home economist in the United States who has had her research on nutrition published in a professional journal.

A11-
COMMUNITY ACHIEVEMENT AWARD
>Future Homemakers of America, Inc.
>1910 Association Drive
>Reston, VA 22091-1584
>(703) 476-4900

RECOGNITION AREA: OUTSTANDING FUTURE HOMEMAKERS OF AMERICA
Awards are given to recognize outstanding women who meet community needs with service programs developed to impact the community positively. Awards are given at the state and national level and one grand winner. First prize is $1,500, four national winners each receive $500 and 45 state winners each receive $100.

A12-
CONTINUUM BOOK AWARD
> Continuum Publishing Group
> 370 Lexington Avenue
> New York, NY 10017-6503
> (212) 953-5858

RECOGNITION AREA: WOMEN WRITERS
Recognition is given to females who have completed outstanding writing in women's studies, psychology, literature, art, and religious studies. The award of $10,000 is given semi-annually and includes publication of the book.

A13-
ELEANOR ROOSEVELT FUND RESEARCH AND DEVELOPMENT AWARD
> American Association of University Women
> 1111 16th Street, NW
> Washington, DC 20036-4873
> (202) 785-7700

RECOGNITION AREA: PROVIDING EDUCATION FOR WOMEN
Awards between $2,000 and $5,000 are given to any professional women (teachers, directors, trainers, etc.) who demonstrates she and/or her organization offer educational equity for women.

A14-
FRONTRUNNER AWARD

Sara Lee Corporation
Three First National Plaza
Chicago, IL 60602-4260
(312) 726-2600

RECOGNITION AREA: OUTSTANDING WOMEN
Candidates for this award program must be American women who have made a major difference by influencing the fields of business, government, the arts or the humanities. The Sara Lee Corporation will contribute $25,000 in the name of 4 individual winners to a nonprofit women's organization of their choosing. The awards are given out annually.

A15-
ILLINOIS - NWSA MANUSCRIPT AWARD
National Women's Studies Association
7100 Baltimore Avenue, Suite 301
College Park, MD 20740
(301) 403-0525

RECOGNITION AREA: WOMEN WRITERS
This annual award of $1,000 is given to the outstanding female writer providing a book length manuscript on any subject in women's studies. The winner also received a contract for publication with the University of Illinois Press.

A16-
JANET M. GLASGOW ESSAY AWARD
American Medical Women's Association
801 North Fairfax Street, Suite 400
Alexandria, VA 22314-1767
(703) 838-0500

RECOGNITION AREA: WOMEN MEDICAL STUDENTS
This award is given annually to the outstanding female medical student who has written the best essay on any woman physician who has shown to be an outstanding role model for medical students. The award is $1,500.

A17-
JOAN KELLY MEMORIAL PRIZE IN WOMEN'S HISTORY
American Historical Association
400 A Street, SE
Washington, DC 20003-3889
(202) 544-2422
E-mail: aha@aha.msu.edu

RECOGNITION AREA: PUBLICATIONS - WOMEN'S HISTORY
The award of $1,000 is given annually for books written on women and their impact on history. Areas covered may include chronological history, geographical locations and any areas of feminist perspectives that includes an historic story line.

A18-
LERNER-SCOTT PRIZE
Organization of American Historians
112 North Bryan Street
Bloomington, IN 47408-4199
(812) 855-7311
E-mail: oah@indiana.edu

RECOGNITION AREA: DOCTORAL DISSERTATIONS
The annual prize is $1,000 and is awarded to the writer of an outstanding doctoral dissertation on women's history and was written during the previous academic year.

A19-
LETTERS SCHOLARSHIPS FOR MATURE WOMEN
National League of American Pen Women, Inc.
1300 17th Street, NW
Washington, DC 20036
(202) 785-1997

RECOGNITION AREA: WOMEN WRITERS

This award is granted biannually to an outstanding woman writer who is 35 years of age or older. The topic area is non restrictive. The award amounts vary each year.

A20-
LOREEN ARBUS FOCUS ON DISABILITY GRANT
Women in Film Foundation
6464 Sunset Boulevard, Suite 530
Los Angeles, CA 90028
(213) 463-6040

RECOGNITION AREA: FILMS: WOMEN & DISABILITIES
This annual award is $5,000 and is given to the video or film which best promotes the goals of Women in Film.

A21-
LOREEN ARBUS FOCUS ON DISCRIMINATION GRANT
Women in Film Foundation
6464 Sunset Boulevard, Suite 530
Los Angeles, CA 90028
(213) 463-6040

RECOGNITION AREA: FILM: WOMEN & DISCRIMINATION
Up to $10,000 is awarded annually for the best film or video on women and discrimination. Discrimination in any form is accepted: race, gender, age or religion.

A22-
MARIA GOEPPERT-MAYER AWARD
American Physical Society
One Physics Ellipse
College Park, MD 20740-3844
(301) 209-3668
E-mail: cole@aps.org

RECOGNITION AREA: WOMEN PHYSICISTS

The award of $2,500 plus $4,000 travel allowance is given annually to the outstanding woman physicist who is a U.S. citizen and is working in the field of physics.

A23-
MISS UNIVERSE
>Miss Universe, Inc.
>1801 Century Park East, Suite 2100
>Los Angeles, CA 90067
>(310) 553-2555

RECOGNITION AREA: WOMEN: BEAUTY
The most beautiful unmarried women are identified and rewarded annually with over $220,000 in cash and prizes for Miss Universe and over $150,000 in cash and prizes for Miss USA.

A24-
MS. NATIONAL SENIOR CITIZEN PAGEANT AWARDS
>Ms. National Senior Citizen Pageant, Inc.
>511 Fourth Avenue
>Joliet, IL 60433
>(815) 722-2952

RECOGNITION AREA: OLDER WOMEN
This annual award recognizes the talent, grace and energy of older women in the United States. Candidates must be at least 55 years of age. Winner receives $3,000 and a trip for two anywhere in the United States.

A25-
NATIONAL HISPANIC DESIGNERS MODEL SEARCH
>JC Penney Company, Inc.
>P.O. Box 10001
>Dallas, TX 75301-8105
>(214) 431-4182

RECOGNITION AREA: HISPANIC MODELS

Recognition is given to an outstanding Hispanic female between the ages of 16 and 22 who has a non professional modeling status. This annual award includes a $2,500 scholarship, $1,000 JC Penney wardrobe and gifts and merchandise.

A26-
NATIONAL TOP FEMALE "MATHLETE"
American Association of University Women
1111 16th Street, NW
Washington, DC 20036-4873
(202) 785-7700
E-mail: foundation@mail.aauw.org

RECOGNITION AREA: FEMALE MATHEMATICIAN
The award is a $3,000 scholarship given annually to the outstanding female mathematician.

A27-
OFF CENTER THEATER PRIZE
Off Center Theater
1010 North Mac Innes Place
Tampa, FL 33602-3720
(813) 222-1033

RECOGNITION AREA: PLAYS ABOUT/BY WOMEN
The award is granted to recognize an outstanding play by and about women and to be produced for the annual Women Playwright's Festival in Florida. The annual prize is $1,000.

A28-
PEN/JERARD FUND AWARD
PEN American Center
568 Broadway, Room 401
New York, NY 10012-3225
(212) 334-1660

RECOGNITION AREA: WOMEN WRITERS

This award is given to an outstanding American woman writer of nonfiction who has had at least one magazine article published in a national publication or major literary magazine. The award is $4,000 and is given every other year.

A29-
SAPPHO AWARD OF DISTINCTION
    Astraea National Lesbian Action Foundation
    116 East 16th Street, Seventh Floor
    New York, NY 10003
    (212) 529-8021
    E-mail: anlaf@aol.com

RECOGNITION AREA: LESBIAN WRITERS
The annual award of $5,000 is given to the outstanding lesbian writer in the United States. There is no limit on the topic area for submission to the Board.

A30-
SUAVE FAMILY MANAGER OF THE YEAR CONTEST
    Suave
    P.O. Box 8199
    Grand Rapids, MN 55745-8199

RECOGNITION AREA: WRITERS ON FAMILY MANAGEMENT
Applicants for this award must be 18 years of age or older and be U.S. residents. The award is given to recognize an outstanding essay on managing a family. Each year a grand prize is awarded for $10,000 and first prize is $2,500.

A31-
SUSAN SMITH BLACKBURN PRIZE
    Susan Smith Blackburn Prize, Inc.
    3239 Avalon Place
    Houston, TX 77019
    (713) 522-8529

RECOGNITION AREA: WOMEN WRITERS: THEATER
Recognition is given to women who have written an outstanding play for the English speaking theater. The annual award is $5,000 and $1,000 to the runner-up.

A32-
UNSUNG HEROINE AWARD
>Ladies Auxiliary of the Veterans of Foreign Wars
>c/o National Headquarters
>406 West 34th Street
>Kansas City, MO 64111
>(816) 561-8655

RECOGNITION AREA: AMERICAN WOMEN: HEROIC ACTS
American women who have shown they have overcome great adversities are eligible for this annual award. The award is $3,000.

A33-
WOMEN OF ENTERPRISE AWARDS
>Avon Products, Inc.
>9 West 57th Street
>New York, NY 10019
>(212) 546-6060

RECOGNITION AREA: WOMEN ENTREPRENEURS
This award recognizes women entrepreneurs who have overcome hardships and obstacles to be successful in their chosen business. The annual award is given to five outstanding women in the amount of $1,000 each and a trip to New York City, speaking engagements and national publicity.

A34-
YOUNG ARTIST AUDITIONS
>National Federation of Music Clubs
>1336 North Delaware Street
>Indianapolis, IN 46202-2481
>(317) 638-4003

RECOGNITION AREA: FEMALE MUSICIANS

Recognition is given to outstanding female vocalists between the ages of 23 and 35 years; or instrumentalists between 18 and 30. Competition is held in piano, string and voice. The biennial awards are $7,500 for first place and $1,250 for second place.

LOANS

Loan programs are funds which must be repaid, some loans are repaid with interest, usually low interest, and some loans are payable without interest. In some cases forgivable loans are available.

L1-
AAAA LOAN PROGRAM
Army Aviation Association of America Scholarship Foundation
49 Richmondville Avenue
Westport, CT 06880-2000
(203) 226-8184
E-mail: aaaa@quad-a.org

INTEREST AREA: EDUCATION
Interest free loans are available for post-secondary education to members of the AAAA or their dependents. The individual loan amount varies, usually no more than $1,000 per year. Each year at least 5 awards are given.

L2-
AIR FORCE AID SOCIETY VOCATIONAL/TECHNICAL PROGRAM
Air Force Aid Society
1745 Jefferson Davis Highway, Suite 202
Arlington, VA 22202-3410
(703) 607-3072

INTEREST AREA: VOCATIONAL/TECHNICAL EDUCATION
Interest free loans are available to dependents of Air Force personnel for vocational/technical education. The number of loans varies each year, with each loan being a maximum of $1,000 per year.

L3-
AMERICAN BUSINESS WOMEN'S ASSOCIATION LOAN PROGRAM
American Business Women's Association
9100 Wart Parkway
P.O. Box 8728
Kansas City, MO 64114-0728
(819) 361-6621

INTEREST AREA: EDUCATION LOANS
Interest free loans of over $600,000 annually are available through the over 2,000 chapters of the ABWA in the United States. Applicants must be enrolled as freshmen or sophomores in college and do not need to be members of ABWA to apply. Annual number of awards and dollar amounts vary each year.

L4-
ARMED FORCES BENEFIT ASSOCIATION PARENT LOANS FOR UNDERGRADUATE STUDENTS (PLUS) PROGRAM
>Armed Forces Benefit Association
>AFBA Building
>909 North Washington Street
>Alexandria, VA 22314-1556
>(703) 549-4455

INTEREST AREA: EDUCATION
Financial assistance is available to members of the Armed Forces Benefit Association to support their own or their dependents' education. Funds are to be used for undergraduate education. Applicants must be U.S. citizens. Loan interest rates varies, not to exceed 10 percent. The number and dollar amount of the loans varies each year.

L5-
ARMED FORCES BENEFIT ASSOCIATION STAFFORD LOAN PROGRAM
>Armed Forces Benefit Association
>AFBA Building
>909 North Washington Street
>Alexandria, VA 22314-1556
>(703) 549-4455

INTEREST AREA: POSTSECONDARY EDUCATION
Financial assistance is available to members of the AFBA, their spouses, dependent children and not remarried widow(er)s and have AFBA insurance coverage. Yearly undergraduate loans may not exceed $2,600 for the first 2 years and not exceed $4,000 for the next 3

years. Yearly graduate loans may not exceed $7,500 for 5 years. Interest is paid on the loan by the federal government while the student is enrolled and for a short time after graduation. When the student begins payment of the loan, interest rates vary, but do not exceed 9 percent. The number of awards given each year varies.

L6-
ARMY EMERGENCY RELIEF LOANS & GRANTS
Army Emergency Relief
200 Stovall Street
Alexandria, VA 22332-0600
(703) 428-0000

INTEREST AREA: GENERAL
Financial assistance is available for veterans, military personnel and their dependents. Each year approximately 70,000+ individuals receive financial support through this program which annually has awarded over $25 million dollars. Funds are distributed as interest free loan or grants or a combination of both and can be used for basic needs, emergency fund needs and much more.

L7-
BPW LOAN FUND FOR WOMEN IN ENGINEERING STUDIES
Business and Professional Women's Foundation
2012 Massachusetts Avenue, NW
Washington, DC 20036-1070
(202) 293-1200

INTEREST AREA: ENGINEERING DEGREE
Financial assistance is available to women studying for an engineering degree and in their last two years of study in an accredited engineering program at the undergraduate or graduate level. Each year approximately 15 to 25 loans are given, each not to exceed $5,000. Interest of 7 percent per annum begins immediately after program or degree completion.

L8-
BPW/SEARS-ROEBUCK LOAN FUND
FOR WOMEN IN GRADUATE BUSINESS STUDIES
Business and Professional Women's Foundation
2012 Massachusetts Avenue, NW
Washington, DC 20036-1070
(202) 293-1200

INTEREST AREA: GRADUATE BUSINESS EDUCATION
Women enrolled in a graduate business program or studying graduate level course work at a school accredited by the American Assembly of Collegiate Schools of Business may apply for a loan. Each year over $75,000 is available, loans range between $500 and $2,500 per academic year. Interest at 7 percent per annum begins after program or degree completion.

L9-
DOT SHORT TERM LENDING PROGRAM
Department of Transportation
Attn: Office of Small and Disadvantaged Business Utilization
400 Seventh Street, SW, Room 9410
Washington, DC 20590
(202) 366-2852

INTEREST AREA: SHORT TERM WORKING CAPITAL
Any Disadvantaged Business Enterprises (DBE), Minority Business Enterprises(MBE) or Women-Owned Business Enterprises(WBE) who have transportation related contracts and are in need of short term working capital for the projects may apply. Most loans range from $100,000 to $200,000 with a maximum of $500,000 repayable within 1 year of receiving the loan. The number of annual loans varies each year with the fund having approximately $20 million available each year.

L10-
EDUCATIONAL LOANS FOR SPOUSES OF VETERANS
Department of Veteran Affairs
810 Vermont Avenue, NW
Washington, DC 20420

(202) 418-4343

INTEREST AREA: POSTSECONDARY EDUCATION
Funds are available for post-secondary education to spouses of veterans whose death or permanent and total disabilities were service-connected. Each loan is approximately $2,500 per year, the number of loans given each year varies.

L11-
E.K. WISE LOAN PROGRAM
American Occupational Therapy Association
4720 Montgomery Lane
P.O. Box 31220
Bethesda, MD 20824-1220
(301) 652-2682

INTEREST AREA: EDUCATION-OCCUPATIONAL THERAPY
Women studying for a degree in occupational therapy and enrolled in a graduate program or a post professional graduate program may apply. The number of loans awarded each year varies, each loan is approximately $5,000.

L12-
GILLETTE HAYDEN MEMORIAL FOUNDATION LOAN PROGRAM
American Association of Women Dentists
401 North Michigan Avenue
Chicago, IL 60611-4267
(312) 527-6757
E-mail: aawd@sba.com

INTEREST AREA: DENTAL STUDIES
Low interest loans are available to women dental students who are juniors, seniors or graduate students and in financial need. Each year up to 6 loans are granted, each is $2,000. Interest begins at 8 percent one month after graduation.

L13-
KNIGHTS OF COLUMBUS STUDENT LOAN PROGRAM
Knights of Columbus
P.O. Box 1670
New Haven, CT 06507-0901
(203) 772-2130

INTEREST AREA: EDUCATION
Educational loans are available to members and relatives of the Knights of Columbus, members of the Catholic clergy and members of Columbian Squires. Applicants must be enrolled as a student and be a U.S. citizen. The amount available each year varies from freshman to senior year ($2,600 to $5,500) the interest rate never exceeds 9 percent and the loan must be repaid within 10 years.

L14-
MEDICAL EDUCATION LOAN PROGRAM
American Medical Women's Association
801 North Fairfax Street, Suite 400
Alexandria, VA 22314-1767
(703) 838-0500

INTEREST AREA: MEDICAL EDUCATION
Loans are available to women students enrolled in an accredited medical school in the United States. Applicants must be student members of the American Medical Women's Association and be U.S. citizens. The number of loans given each year varies, loan amounts do not exceed $4,000 per year. Loans are payable 1 year after graduation at an interest rate of 10 percent.

L15-
NAFE PRIVATE RESERVE LOAN PROGRAM
National Association for Female Executives, Inc.
30 Irvine Place, 5th Floor
New York, NY 10003
(212) 477-2200

INTEREST AREA: BUSINESS LOANS

Funds are available to any member of NAFE in the form of a loan. Individual loans range up to $35,000 with interest at 7.9 percent over the prime rate. The number of yearly loans varies.

L16-
NATIONAL ASSOCIATION OF BUSINESS OWNERS/WELLS FARGO BUSINESS LOANS

Wells Fargo Bank
Attn: Business Director Division
P.O. Box 720310
San Jose, CA 95172-0310
(800) 359-3557

INTEREST AREA: WOMEN OWNED BUSINESSES
Through this program over $1 billion per year has been designated for loans to female business owners   Applicants must be female business owners, have good personal and business credit records, have been in business for at least 2 years, have a profitable business and have not declared bankruptcy in the past 10 years. A variable interest rate applies to the loans.

L17-
NATIONAL RESEARCH SERVICE AWARD INDIVIDUAL FELLOWSHIPS IN HEALTH SERVICES RESEARCH

Agency for Health Care Policy and Research
Attn: NRSA Project Officer
Executive Office Center, Suite 501
2101 East Jefferson Street
Rockville, MD 20852
(301) 594-1362

INTEREST AREA: ACADEMIC TRAINING/RESEARCH
Funds are available for training in applying quantitative research methods to systematic analysis and evaluation of health services. Applicants must be U.S. citizens and have a Ph.D. M.D., D.O., D.D.S. , D.V.M. or equivalent doctoral degree. Research and training must be focused on successful health care market reform, evaluation of health care plans, effective management by health care providers and several

other related areas of health care. The loans range from $20,000 to $32,000 and are based on the experience of the applicant.

L18-
NATIONAL RESEARCH SERVICE AWARD SENIOR FELLOWSHIPS

> National Institutes of Health
> Attn: Office of Extramural Research
> Extramural Outreach and Information Resources Office
> 6701 Rockledge Drive, Room 6207
> MSC 7910
> Bethesda, MD 20892-7910
> (301) 435-0714
> E-mail: asknih@odrockm1.od.nih.gov

INTEREST AREA: RESEARCH TRAINING
Funds are available to provide research training for scientists wanting to change the direction of their research career. Applicants must have a Ph.D., D.D.S., D.M.D. or equivalent degree and have at least 7 years of research experience. Loans are in the form of salary and may not exceed $32,000 per year.

L19-
NATIONAL RESEARCH SERVICE AWARDS FOR INDIVIDUAL POSTDOCTORAL FELLOWS

> National Institutes of Health
> Attn: Office of Extramural Research
> Extramural Outreach and Information Resources Office
> 6701 Rockledge Drive, Room 6207
> MSC 7910
> Bethesda, MD 20892-7910
> (301) 435-0714
> E-mail: asknih@odrockm1.od.nih.gov

INTEREST AREA: BIOMEDICAL OR BEHAVIORAL RESEARCH TRAINING
Funds are provided for postdoctoral biomedical or behavioral research training. Applicants must be U.S. citizens and hold a degree in one the

following: Ph.D., M.D. D.O., D.D.S., D.V.M. or the equivalent doctoral degree from an accredited domestic or foreign institution. The loan is in the form of an annual salary and is based upon the years of research experience. Over 700 loans have been made annually through this program.

L20-
NAVAJO NATION VETERANS PERSONAL LOANS
Navajo Nation
Department of Veteran Affairs
P.O. Box 430
Window Rock, AZ 86515
(520) 871-6413

INTEREST AREA: NAVAJO INDIANS

Any member of the Navajo Nation who served in the U.S. armed forces and was discharged, but not under dishonorable conditions, may apply for a loan. Applications are also received from God Star Mothers and surviving spouses of any Navajo veteran. Loans range from $200 to $3,000 with a payable interest rate at 9 percent. Each loan is for a maximum of 36 months.

L21-
NIH UNDERGRADUATE SCHOLARSHIP PROGRAM FOR INDIVIDUALS FROM DISADVANTAGED BACKGROUNDS
National Institutes of Health
Attn: Loan Repayment and Scholarship Programs
Federal Building, Room 604
7550 Wisconsin Avenue, MSC 9015
Bethesda, MD 20892-9015
(800) 528-7689
E-mail: kk10b@nih.gov

INTEREST AREA: EDUCATION-LIFE SCIENCES

Funds are available to students from disadvantaged backgrounds who wish to pursue undergraduate education in the field of biomedical research. Each year up to 15 loans are granted, each not to exceed $20,000.

L22-
OPTION 4 EDUCATION LOAN PROGRAM
American Legion
P.O. Box 1055
Indianapolis, IN 46206
(317) 630-1200

INTEREST AREA: EDUCATION
Funds are available for education for members of the American Legion, American Legion Auxiliary, Sons of the American Legion, participants in the American Legion Auxiliary Girls State Program or America Legion baseball programs. Applicants can borrow from $2,000-$15,000 per academic year, not to exceed a total of $75,000. Loan re-pay may include a 15 year payment plan.

L23-
P.E.O. EDUCATIONAL LOAN FUND
P.E.O. Sisterhood
3700 Grand Avenue
Des Moines, IA 50312-2899
(515) 255-3153

INTEREST AREA: EDUCATION
Low interest loans are available for women wishing to continue their education beyond high school. Applicants must be sponsored by a local chapter of the P.E.O. Sisterhood. The loan amounts vary according to individual needs.

L24-
SBA MICROLOAN PROGRAM
Small Business Administration
Attn: Office of Women's Business Ownership
409 Third Street, SW
Washington, DC 20416
(800) 8-ASK-SBA

INTEREST AREA: SMALL BUSINESS ASSISTANCE
The SBA makes funds available to nonprofit organizations for the purpose of lending these funds to any small business needing small loans. Applicants the SBA assist include women, minority entrepreneurs and small businesses. Loans range from $100 to $25,000 and average $10,000. Interest cannot be higher than 4 percent over the New York prime rate.

L25-
STEPHEN BUFTON MEMORIAL EDUCATION FUND
American Business Women's Association
9100 Ward Parkway
P.O. Box 8728
Kansas City, MO 64114-0728
(816) 361-6621

INTEREST AREA: EDUCATION
Women students majoring in any course study and in their junior or senior years in college or graduate school may apply. Candidates must be sponsored by a chapter of the ABWA. Each year a different subject area is chosen and financially chosen. Interest free loans range from $100 to $1,500.

L26-
VA HOME LOAN GUARANTIES
Department of Veterans Affairs
810 Vermont Avenue, NW
Washington, DC 20420
(202) 418-4343

INTEREST AREA: HOME PURCHASE
Funds are available to assist veterans and their not-remarried surviving spouses to purchase a residence. The Department of Veterans Affairs does not lend money. A commercial lender provides the loan, the VA will guarantee payment on loans for the purchase of homes, farm homes, condos, and refinancing of existing loans under certain conditions.

L27-
WOMEN'S PREQUALIFICATION PILOT LOAN PROGRAM
Small Business Administration
Office of Women's Business Ownership
409 Third Street, SW
Washington, DC 20416
(800) 8-ASK-SBA

INTEREST AREA: BUSINESS LOANS
The purpose of this program is to provide a quick turnaround to a nonprofit intermediary for loan requests of $250,000 or less to women owned and operated businesses. Applicants must meet the SBA requirements. The maximum interest rate is Wall Street Journal prime plus 2.5 percent and up. The intermediary assists the applicant in locating a competitive lender.

L28
WOMEN'S WORLD BANKING LOAN PROGRAM
Women's World Banking
8 West 40th Street
New York, NY 10018
(212) 768-8513
E-mail: wwb@igc.apc.org

INTEREST AREA: WOMEN BUSINESS LOANS
The purpose of this loan program is to guarantee loans for women's businesses which need funding to start or expand an existing business. Loan guarantees can range from $5,000 to over $1 million.

BUSINESS

This section offers several excellent resources for the women wanting to start a business or expand an existing business. Over the past few years, the federal government has greatly increased the funds available to minority and women owned businesses. Your chances of receiving funding for a business are very good with this expansion of funding services.

How To Apply For A Loan

Understanding The Loan Application Process

Having a relationship with a banker or lender that works well is a valuable tool in today's society. As is the case in any other relationship, understanding and the capacity to communicate with your banker is highly important and desirable. In fact, developing a high level of comfort and trust in this important relationship has become a necessity for surviving in our fast-paced economy. That's true for nearly every working woman – whether she is an employee or the owner of her own business.

Sometimes, however, searching for a special relationship with a bank or other lending institution can be one of a woman's greatest frustrations. The information contained in this section is designed to assist you in making the initial contact and developing the critical working relationship. It details the essentials of your initial approach, what you need to do prior to your first meeting, and how to implement the initial loan application. It also includes information for building a solid working relationship.

Specific topics have been included with the intent of developing a step-by-step guide for making an application for a loan. Business owners will find information and suggestions to help you research and design a business plan, prepare a loan proposal, obtain a loan commitment and successfully negotiate the terms of a loan. Thus, the information in this section can be used to build upon and improve a current banking relationship, if you have one, or to find a bank or other lending institution if you do not.

Much of the information in this section also applies to the process of getting a scholarship, grant, fellowship, or other kinds of financial assistance.

Suggestions For The Initial Approach

Start with a common sense approach to the first meeting with a banker. In a way, the initial contact with a banker is very similar to the initial approach for a job application. Some suggestions for this initial approach follow.

A. Remember, loaning money is a lending institution's primary function.

Keep clearly in mind that a *bank or lending institution's business is lending money.* If lending institutions are unable to circulate their money and earn interest on it, they would quickly go out of business.

By requesting a loan, you are doing him or her as great a business service as the service you are expecting from them. You are peers in this relationship. If you are not treated as a peer, work with a banker who will not intimidate you.

B. Document your financial plan and know exactly what you want.

If possible, prepare as many of the documents as you can in advance of the interview. Forms for a statement of financial condition and a loan application can often be obtained from a bank prior to the initial interview. By completing them in advance, you can more easily facilitate the initial interview. Realize, there will always be additional documents required by your banker. She will explain what she needs and why it is needed as the interview progresses. As the need for these documents arise, ask any questions which come to mind, and arrange to call her if questions come up later that you can't answer.

Information you have prepared for an initial meeting, should be concise and easy to read. Do not bring huge volumes of information to "sell your banker." Just provide general information which can be easily evaluated and discussed.

C. Project an attitude of confidence.

Carry yourself erect, walk erect and sit erect; answer questions directly, with confidence, in a moderate tone of voice.

As mentioned above, talking to an individual representing a financial institution is much like having an interview with a prospective employer. Remember that no one knows the nature of your situation better than you do. It is important to convey your request to your banker in as clear and concise a way possible.

D. Wear conservative clothing.

Take care in how you dress for this initial meeting. A plain dress or business suit is highly recommended. Do not use excessive makeup or wear heavy, glaring jewelry. Simple jewelry, such as a strand of pearls or a gold necklace, is always acceptable. Also, leave the perfume at home. Even the most expensive of perfumes can be offensive. You want to leave a positive impression, don't risk that important impression on perfume.

E. Leave the children at home.

If you have children, do not take them to the initial interview. Few things are more distracting to a banker than to have children in a financial interview (even if they are well behaved).

F. Be prepared to verbally respond to the following questions:

What is the requested loan for?

How will it be repaid?

What collateral can be used to guarantee the loan?

All this information is contained in the loan application that will later be submitted to the institution; however, bankers nearly always ask these questions in order to determine how an individual will respond to them.

Making A Loan Application

Any lending institution will require a great deal of information about you prior to making its decision to loan you money. In this context, be as familiar with the nature of your employer's business as possible. Be certain of the length of time you have been employed. Know the amount of your earnings including medical benefits and other benefits that may be available from your employment.

If you have additional sources of income, be able to explain what these sources are, how much income they generate and when and how you receive this income. If you have rental properties, you will need copies of your leases and other pertinent documents for your banker's review. Remember your banker will tell you what additional documents are required at the time of the initial interview.

In preparing the paperwork necessary for any loan application, it is important to look at your paperwork objectively. Remember that the individual reviewing this information rarely knows anything about you. If you are missing certain records or financial information, or if you are "not good with numbers," seek help from a professional. A good bookkeeping or accounting service can be of great value in developing the kind of records that are necessary for a loan application.

Remember that commercial banks are <u>cash flow</u> lenders; they look to the amount of cash flowing to you (or into your business) to determine your capability to repay a potential loan. With this in mind, as you structure your financial information, carefully consider every source of cash flow available to you. This includes what you are owed and by whom, the probability of collecting it, and any income from leases, mortgages or other sources of immediate cash if you have any of these.

If you are attempting to get a business loan, always try to develop as complete and detailed a picture of your business as possible. Consider all the records available to you including receivables, payables, leases for equipment, furniture, fixtures, inventory, real estate owned, vehicles owned or leased and other items of value. If you need help with the preparation of these documents, seek the help of a professional. It is better to spend a small amount of money with a professional who knows how to tailor a loan application, than to develop a plan yourself that could be inaccurate.

Professional companies, proficient in developing financial information for loan applications can be very helpful. You can find them by consulting a certified public accountant. Often your banker can recommend consultants or services that can be of great assistance and sometimes they can be found by simply looking in the yellow pages of your telephone directory.

In addition, several books in the business section of your local library or in a bookstore can guide you in developing the financial information required for a business loan.

Once you have updated your financial statements, business plan and other financial records, keep them current on a monthly basis. Consider hiring an accounting service or utilizing a good accounting program on your computer to help you with this important task.

Evaluating Your Credit Worthiness

To evaluate your credit worthiness or the credit worthiness of your business, a lending institution's first step will be to review your past financial performance. First and foremost your banker wants to know whether you or your company have successfully repaid loans granted to you (or your company) in the past. A bank or financial institution will always evaluate you **based on the strengths and weaknesses of your past credit history.**

If you do not have a previous credit history, it's usually necessary to start by borrowing as small amount and repaying it promptly on exactly the terms and conditions that the loan agreement specifies. If this procedure is followed, usually a lender will raise the amount you can borrow the next time you need a loan.

Structuring A Loan Agreement

Ask your banker to work with you in creating a repayment plan that is comfortable for both you and the lending institution. This is always a very important part of the loan agreement.

You may be asked to place a lien on your home or any other assets that you may own as security for your loan. This is a frequent practice of lending institutions and they are not singling you out to do anything extra ordinary or special.

Finding The Banking Institution That Is Right For You

Many women have bank accounts and have had at least some basic dealings with banks. As was noted previously, it is important to remember that banks are commercial institutions anxious to create new accounts and they compete with each other for loan business. If you do not now have a bank, interview representatives at several banks or lending institutions. By interviewing more than one, you can better establish which bank you believe will meet your banking needs.

Then approach the bank you have selected with a clear understanding of the kind of financial arrangements you want to work out. You will also want to determine how the bank or lending institution can help you find solutions to your financial needs and problems.

Developing A Long Term Relationship

When an individual or business obtains a loan they enter into a partnership with the lending institution making the loan. To make this partnership strong and reliable both parties need to build on the trust that has been initially established in granting the loan. Here are some simple techniques for developing this relationship:

- Ask your banker for her thoughts on building and making a good working relationship between the two of you.
- Arrange to maintain regular contact with your banker, even if this is informal. This contact can range from periodic telephone calls to more comprehensive monthly conferences and a complete financial review.
- Make yourself accessible to your banker. Be sure to call her occasionally and be in contact with her periodically just to "bring her up to date." Remember to return calls from your banker promptly.
- Ask your banker about her institution's participation in government loan programs. Usually a bank can provide a large number of pamphlets and other information about government loans in which they participate. This information may be of great financial value to you.
- Schedule at least semiannual appointments with your banker, to bring her up to date on your employment situation or the progress of your business.

If these techniques are followed, you can expect that your banker will show an interest in you, your employment or your business and this will expedite the business (and interpersonal) relationship between the two of you.

If you feel you need to increase the amount of money you have borrowed sometime in the future, give your banker a written memo that factually and concisely highlights recent events in your employment or business. This update will give her a quick, easy reference to your current financial situation or the current state of affairs of your business. It also provides an ongoing record of your employment and/or business progress.

If Problems Develop

If a problem should develop in your employment or your business which affects your capacity to repay your loan, it is important that you contact your banker or financial institution immediately. Inform your banker immediately if you feel there may be a loan default. This helps avoid your loan becoming delinquent as well as possibly eroding the confidence and trust already established in your banking relationship.

If a problem develops, contacting your banker immediately will establish a heightened level of trust; she will recognize the integrity of your action. Your early contact allows her to establish and work with suggested strategies to stabilize your loan account. If you follow these suggestions when a problem your partnership with the bank will remain intact and the foundation of trust is increased by your honest and quick response to the problem.

Banking is a service business. You, the customer, should feel that you are receiving the kind of service that you truly deserve. Remember the degree of cooperation, integrity and trust that develops between you and your banker is a vital ingredient in making the lending partnership successful. As a member of this partnership you should *give* your full cooperation and expect to *receive* the full cooperation from your banker. If you both know what to expect from each other and make every effort to fulfill your obligations, the relationship between you and your banker will flourish and grow stronger.

The bond of trust that develops and is established will lay the groundwork for an ever increasing degree of mutual respect and borrowing power, and will enable you to conduct your banking business productively, reasonably and without costly delays.

Documents Required For A Business Loan

1. If you are applying for a business loan, the following documents are generally required:
2. A current profit and loss statement and balance sheet for existing businesses or a pro forma statement for new businesses.
3. A realistic projected cash flow and profit and loss statement for one year (monthly breakdown).
4. A current personal financial statement of the proprietor, or each partner or stockholder owning 20 percent or more of the corporate stock.
5. An itemized use of proceeds.

6. Collateral with an estimate of current market value and liens against the collateral.
7. A business plan including resumes of the principals.
8. A schedule of business debt, aging of accounts receivable and accounts payable.
9. Personal and business tax returns for the past three years.
10. Copy of lease (if property is to be leased)
11. Any contracts or agreements pertinent to the applicant.
12. A current business plan.

PREPARING A BUSINESS PLAN

Developing a business plan is widely considered the most important thing you do before going into business. For a startup company, the business plan is an assessment tool. As you develop all the points of the business plan, you will have to continually reaffirm the viability of the business idea.

The business plan is the blueprint or road map for your business. A thoroughly researched and well thought-out plan will clarify your goals, focus your energy, give direction to your work and help you gauge your progress.

It is a tool for raising capital, and must be presented to any banker when approaching a lending institution or investor(s) for capital. To obtain a loan or attract investors, you will need to present a cohesive picture of your business and the management team. It explains why the business will succeed and how you intend to repay the bank or investors.

To get started writing a business plan, it is important to understand the concepts of business planning. Writing an outline may help you avoid overlooking important points.

Here are general points you need to ask and answer to begin the planning process. Not all points will apply to you, especially if you have a small startup company, however, it's important to carefully consider each one:

The Business

- Describe the business, including history, legal structure, major products or services, the management team, and personnel.
- Clarify the company goals for sales, new product development, growth, etc.

Products and/or Services

- Describe all the products and services the company offers.
- Explain what makes these products/services better than the competition.
- Outline the cost and profit of each product/service and describe the break-even point.
- Describe opportunities to improve on existing product/service line(s).
- Include any patents, trademarks or proprietary features.

Industry

- Describe the size, maturity and competitive nature of your industry.
- Describe any barriers to entry and growth.
- Describe the effect of economic swings upon your industry.
- Describe the overall financial position and performance of your industry.

- Explain what role, if any, government regulations have on your industry.

Location
- Consider the importance of location to your business in terms of customer access, distribution of goods, zoning, etc.

Marketing Analysis
- Describe the product emphasis necessary to penetrate target markets.
- Explain the difference between your product and that of your competitors.
- Describe what distribution channels will be used.
- Explain the type and number of sales staff and sales support staff needed.
- Explain the type of service you plan to offer.
- Outline the pricing scheme in light of your competition and your product.
- Explain the company credit policy for customers.
- Outline the advertising plan including the amount budgeted for the plan.

Operations
- Describe the outline and schedule of all business activities.
- Describe the hours and days of operation.
- List the equipment and supplies needed.

- List suppliers of equipment and materials necessary for operation.
- List inventory storage and maintenance.

Management and Organization
- List current and anticipated organizational structure for your business (sole proprietorship, partnership or corporation)
- List the personal history of the principals (e.g. age, education, industry experience, business affiliations) and their role in daily operations.
- List the percent interest or stock that each principal holds.
- Describe the succession plan in case of the loss of key personnel.
- List professional resources (e.g., attorney, accountant) available to the business.

Personnel
- Describe current staffing and expected turnover.
- Describe the need for permanent employees and independent contractors.
- Describe personnel needs 1-3 years into the future including the skills that will be needed.
- Describe the compensation package including salary, insurance, opportunities for advancement, profit sharing.
- Describe personnel policies including performance evaluation, hiring and firing practices.

Finance

- List the total funds needed by your business for the next three years.
- List financing being sought from a lending institution or investors. If seeking debt financing, describe the loan amount, interest and the anticipated method of making payments; if seeking equity finance, describe the method of compensating the investor, e.g. buy back, public offering, dividends, etc..
- Describe specifically how borrowed or invested funds will be used.
- Describe the collateral that can be offered.
- Explain methods of financial reporting you will use.

Marketing

Nothing is more important than knowing your market. The most innovative product or idea in the world won't make money if its inventor can't find customers for it. The biggest part of your planning efforts needs to go into a market study: Who are you going to sell to and how are you going to get them to buy?

Cash Flow

At its most basic, cash flow is the cycle of turning sales into cash that in turn pays the cost of doing business and, hopefully, returns a profit. Note that cash flow is not the same as profit. A business with good cash flow may not show profits, while a business can be showing profits and be illiquid because it has insufficient cash to pay its debts. Remember, cash, not profits, pays the bills.

To do a cash flow projection you must understand the movement of cash through a business operation. You need to know starting cash, cash payments during the period (usually one month) and cash receipts. The difference between starting and ending cash represents the change in cash flow. If payments during the period exceed receipts (cash receipts, not credit sales) then the business has less working capital. Conversely, if receipts exceed payments, then working capital has increased.

Breakeven Point

The breakeven point is that level of sales that covers the fixed and variable costs of providing your product or service. You must know your actual costs of doing business. Your fixed costs, (rent, utilities, insurance, etc.) remain constant regardless of your sales. Your variable costs (cost of goods, sales commissions) increase with sales.

It's extremely important to accurately identify all your costs, know the sales level needed to break even and be reasonably sure of meeting or exceeding that sales figure. Without this knowledge, you might be embarking on a losing venture.

Financial Statements and Projections

In financial terms, these documents reflect the business' historical, (if applicable), and future performance, profitability and cash flow.

A cash flow projection will reflect your company's credit and collection policies, trade credit and other financing activities and purchase or disposal of fixed assets.

The process of putting into financial terms the strategies detailed in the business plan will provide valuable insight as to whether you will be able to reach your goals and objectives. It will also be a key indicator of the amount of outside financing needed to support execution of the strategy.

Grasping the terms and concepts used for financial projections and accounting systems can be very confusing, especially to the inexperienced owner of a business startup. It is advisable to consult one of the many books that have been written specifically about small business accounting systems, cash flow projections and bookkeeping.

Profit and Loss Statements

Also known as an income statement, this reflects the company's expenses and earnings, usually on a monthly or quarterly basis, projected over three years; include historical income statements, if it's an existing business.

A balance sheet shows the assets and liabilities of the company on a given date; include projected quarterly income and expenses for the next three years.

Financing Your Business Start Up

More the 80% of new entrepreneurs start their business without any commercial loans or debt financing. Although the SBA does make some loans to start a business, they represent less than 20% of the SBA's entire loan portfolio. Lenders and investors prefer to finance a business with a track record and a plan for growth based on experience in the industry.

Banks are often hesitant to make small (under $50,000) commercial loans because they are not particularly cost-effective. So if you are just starting out and need $25,000 to set up shop and fill your first orders, where does that leave you?

You can use this valuable directory to locate financial resources for business ventures. Also, you may want to fill out the *Request For Funding* application located in the back of this directory. For a nominal fee, we will search out the most current financial resources specific to your individual requirements.

USE THIS SPACE TO MAKE NOTES

BUSINESS DEVELOPMENT

The business section includes financial resources from federal, state, local, private and capital venture funds. This section covers financial assistance for all aspects of business development, including locating funds, guidance from professionals, planning and development services and much more.

B1- ADRIAN DOMINICAN SISTERS ALTERNATIVE INVESTMENT FUND

Adrian Dominican Sisters
1257 East Sienna Heights Drive
Adrian, MI 49221
(517) 265-5135

INTEREST AREA: ECONOMIC JUSTICE

The purpose of this fund is to support organizations interested in supporting economic justice, particularly to women and the poor by making investments and loans. Candidates must be non-profit community-based enterprises demonstrating a commitment to advancing social justice for women and the poor. Individuals or for-profit corporations are not considered for loans or investments. The number of awards varies each year and range from $30,000 to $50,000 per year. Interest charged on loans ranges between 1 percent and market rate.

B2- BUSINESS LOANS FOR 8(a) PROGRAM PARTICIPANTS

Director, Loan Policy and Procedures Branch
Small Business Administration
409 Third Street, SW
Washington, DC 20416
(202) 205-7510

INTEREST AREA: BUSINESS LOANS

This fund provides direct and guaranteed loans to small business contractors receiving assistance under the subsection of 7(j) 10 and section 8 (a) of the Small Business Act, who are unable to obtain financing on reasonable terms in the private credit marketplace. Candidates must demonstrate an ability to repay loans granted. Financial assistance is in forms of low interest loans with estimated annual funds available in the amount of $4,900,000.

B3- LYNN CAMPBELL MEMORIAL FUND

Astraea National Lesbian Action Foundation
666 Broadway, Suite 520
New York, NY 10012
(212) 529-8021

INTEREST AREA: WOMENS PROJECTS
This fund provides support financially for women's projects in community organizations or projects serving as a resource for community organizations. Applications are accepted from individuals and/or organizations. The number of awards varies each year and the amount awarded varies depending upon the scope of the project.

B4-
CHURCH WOMEN UNITED'S INTERCONTINENTAL GRANTS
Church Women United
475 Riverside Drive, Room 812
New York, NY 10115
(212) 870-2347

INTEREST AREA: ECONOMIC/SOCIAL
The purpose of this fund is to provide funding for projects by and for women sponsored by nonprofit organizations from any country. Priority is given to programs in two areas 1) Economic alternative for women in poverty, 2) Health care; study of ethical dilemmas of current health care system and the interrelations of health, environment and women. Each year approximately 20 awards are given ranging from $500 to $2,500.

B5-
DEPARTMENT OF AGRICULTURE
Rural Business Enterprise Grant Program
Bonnie S. Justice
12th and Independence Avenue, SW
Room 2245 South Ag. Box 1521
Washington, DC 20250
(202) 720-1490

INTEREST AREA: RURAL BUSINESS
Financial assistance is provided through grants to public or nonprofit agencies to provide loans and/or technical assistance to for-profit enterprises with the intent of creating jobs for rural residents. Contact the above office for information on specific program guidelines.

B6-
DEPARTMENT OF AGRICULTURE
> Intermediary Relending Program
> 12th and Independence Avenue, SW
> Room 2245
> Washington, DC 20250
> (202) 690-4100

INTEREST AREA: RURAL BUSINESS
Funds are available in the form of loans to public or private non-profit organizations, which in turn lend the money to rural businesses. Contact the above office for information on applications. The interest rate to the intermediaries is one percent, with repayment terms of up to 30 years.

B7-
DEPARTMENT OF COMMERCE
> Economic Adjustment Division
> 14th and Constitution Avenue, NW
> Room 7327
> Washington, DC, 20230
> (202) 482-2659

INTEREST AREA: BUSINESS LOANS
The purpose of this fund is to help areas overcome specific capital market gaps and to encourage greater private sector participation in economic development activities. For information on application requirements, contact the above office. Each year several loans are given, the amounts vary according to need.

B8-
DEPARTMENT OF TRANSPORTATION SMALL BUSINESS INNOVATION RESEARCH GRANTS

Department of Transportation
Attn: Office of Small and Disadvantaged Business Utilization
400 Seventh Street, SW, Room 9410
Washington, DC 20590
(202) 366-2852

INTEREST AREA: RESEARCH FUNDS
The Dept. of Transportation offers financial support to small businesses having technological experience to contribute to the research and development mission of the Dept. of Transportation and other related agencies. Preference is given to women-owned small businesses and to socially and economically disadvantaged small business concerns. The number of awards varies each year. Support is offered in 2 phases. Phase 1 may not exceed $50,000, Phase 2 may not exceed $250,000.

B9-
DOT SHORT TERM LENDING PROGRAM

Department of Transportation
Attn: Office of Small and Disadvantaged Business Utilization
Minority Business Resource Center
400 Seventh Street, SW, Room 9410
Washington, DC 20590
(202) 366-2852

INTEREST AREA: BUSINESS LOANS
The Dept of Transportation provides short-term working capital to Disadvantaged Business Enterprise (DBE) firms owned by minorities and women. Some long-term capital is available for transportation related projects. Only certified DBEs are eligible to apply. To be certified as a Disadvantaged Business Enterprise, a firm must meet 3 basic qualifications. 1. It must be owned and controlled by the socially disadvantaged. 2. It must be owned and controlled by the economically disadvantaged. 3. It must be a small business as defined in Section 3 of the Small Business Act. The number of awards varies each year and the amount loaned varies, the average loan is approximately $180,000,

with a maximum of $500,000. Interest is charged at the current New York Prime Rate.

B10-
ECONOMIC INJURY DISASTER LOANS
Office of Disaster Assistance
Small Business Administration
409 Third Street, SW
Washington, DC 20416
(202) 502-6734

INTEREST AREA: DISASTER FUNDS
The purpose of this fund is to provide assistance to businesses in economic struggle as a result of certain Presidential, SBA, and/or Department of Agriculture disaster declarations. Contact the above office for specific information. Assistance is in the form of loans with estimated annual funds of $108,000,000.

B11-
ENTREPRENEUR GRANT CONTEST
Working Women Magazine
Attn: Anne Nelson
230 Park Avenue
New York, NY 10169
(212) 551-9497

INTEREST AREA: WOMEN OWNED BUSINESSES
This fund is provided to reward outstanding small businesses owned or managed by women. Candidates must be women who own or manage a small business. One award is given each year. The award is $25,000 worth of computer equipment to be used in their business.

B12-
GLOBAL FUND FOR WOMEN GRANTS
Global Fund for Women
2480 Sand Hill Road, Suite 100
Menlo Park, CA 94025-6941

(415) 854-0420

INTEREST AREA: WOMEN'S ADVANCEMENT
This fund provides money to organizations committed to improving women's roles in society. Primary interest areas for application are women's rights, communications, communications technology and economic development. Organizations not normally funded by traditional granting organizations are favored, however, no grants are awarded to individuals or groups based and working solely in the United States or groups headed and managed by men. Approximately 80 grants are given each year ranging from $500 to $10,000.

B13-
LOCAL DEVELOPMENT COMPANY LOANS
Office of Economic Development
Small Business Administration
409 Third Street, SW, Room 720
Washington, DC 20416
(202) 205-6485

INTEREST AREA: BUSINESS LOANS
This fund provides federal loans for long-term financing to small businesses located in local communities. Applicants must be local development companies. Financial assistance is in the form of loan guarantees. Estimate of annual funds available is $34,718,000.

Although the following lender is for Los Angeles women only, we have included this for your information and we suggest you contact the Los Angeles Women's Entrepreneurial Fund and other listed organizations for information regarding similar projects in your area.

B14-
LOS ANGELES WOMEN'S ENTREPRENEURIAL FUND
California Community Foundation
606 South Olive Street, Suite 2400
Los Angeles, CA 90014-1526
(212) 413-4042

INTEREST AREA: BUSINESS LOANS
Funds are provided as small loans to women-owned businesses in the Los Angeles area to re-establish or expand their business enterprises. Applicants must have legal status in the U.S., have lived in Los Angeles Country for 6 months or more, meet income requirements, plan to use funds exclusively for business purposes and be able to work with a sponsoring agency or technical assistance provider. Application is made through one of the following support organizations:

American Woman's Economic Development Corporation (AWED)
301 East Ocean Boulevard, #1010
Long Beach, CA 90802

Central American Refugee Center (CARE-CEN)
668 South Bonnie Brae Street
Los Angeles, CA 90057

Coalition for Women's Economic Development (CWED)
315 West 9th Street, #408
Los Angeles, CA, 90015

Korean American Inter-Agency Council (KAIAC)
610 South Harvard Street, Suite 220
Los Angeles, CA 90005

New Economics for Women (NEW)
6100 Wilshire Boulevard, #810
Los Angeles, CA 90048

The number of awards varies each year, with loans ranging from $1,000 to $15,000 and being offered in two phases. Phase 1) awards are approximately $35,000, Phase 2) awards are approximately $10,000.

B15-
MANAGEMENT AND TECHNICAL ASSISTANCE FOR SOCIALLY AND ECONOMICALLY DISADVANTAGED BUSINESSES

Associate Administrator for Minority Small Business and
Capital Ownership Development
409 Third Street, SW
Washington, DC 20416
(202) 205-6423

INTEREST AREA: DISADVANTAGED BUSINESSES
The purpose of this fund is to provide management and technical assistance to existing or potential businesses. Applicants must be economically and socially disadvantaged or located in areas of high concentration of unemployment. Financial assistance is in the form of grants with estimated annual funds available in the amount of $8,040,000.

B16-
MEDICARE AND MEDICAID SMALL BUSINESS INNOVATION RESEARCH GRANTS
Health Care Financing Administration
Attn: Office of Research and Demonstrations
2226 Oak Meadows Building
6325 Security Boulevard
Baltimore, MD 21207-5187
(410) 966-6645

INTEREST AREA: BUSINESS LOAN
The purpose of this fund is to offer financial aid to small businesses having technological experience to contribute to the research and development mission of the Dept. of Transportation and other related agencies. This program encourages women and socially and economically disadvantaged business people to participate in small business support for federal research and development needs. The number of awards varies each year. There are 2 phases to the financial support offered. Phase 1) awards are usually $35,000, Phase 2) awards are usually $10,000.

B17-
NAFE LOANS-BY-MAIL PROGRAM
National Association for Female Executives, Inc.

30 Irvine Place, 5th Floor
New York, NY, 10003
(212) 477-2200

INTEREST AREA: BUSINESS LOAN
This program provides financial assistance to females in the form of a loan. Loans are given only to members of the National Association for Female Executives, Inc. (NAFE). The number of awards varies each year and the interest is 7.9 percent over the prime rate. NAFE lends up to $21,000,000 each year. Individual loans can be up to $35,000. Once a credit line is established, members can borrow on their signature alone and pay interest only on the amount borrowed.

B18-
NAFE VENTURE CAPITAL FUND
National Association for Female Executives, Inc.
30 Irvine Place, 5th Floor
New York, NY 10003
(212) 477-2200

INTEREST AREA: BUSINESS GROWTH
This fund provides capital to start new ventures or to help an existing business grow. Applicants must be NAFE members to apply and must represent women-owned businesses. The number of awards varies each year. This is not a loan, rather a capital venture investment. Minimum investment in each business is $5,000, maximum is $50,000. A percentage of profits is owed NAFE if business succeeds. If the business fails, the recipient owes nothing.

B19-
NATIONAL ASSOCIATION OF GOVERNMENT GUARANTEED LENDERS (NAGGL)
P.O. Box 332
Stillwater, OK 74076-0332
(405) 377-4022

INTEREST AREA: BUSINESS LOANS

The purpose of this fund is to represent financial institutions and small business lenders who participate in SBA guaranteed lending and secondary market programs. For application information and financial assistance available contact the above location.

B20-
NEW WOMEN, NEW BUSINESS CONTEST
New Women
215 Lexington Avenue
New York, NY 10016

INTEREST AREA: NEW BUSINESS VENTURES
This fund provides monies for women for start-up businesses. Participants may enter more than one business idea, provided each proposal is postmarked separately. Applicants must be 18 years of age and supply a brief outline of the new business idea. Contact New Women for description of outline requirements. Three awards are given each year. First prize is $25,000, second prize is $15,000, third prize is $10,000.

B21-
NIH SMALL BUSINESS TECHNOLOGY TRANSFER GRANTS
National Institutes of Health
Attn: Division of Research Grants
Westwood Building, Room 449
Bethesda, MD 20892
(301) 594-7248

INTEREST AREA: BUSINESS GROWTH
The purpose of this fund is to encourage participation of women owned businesses and socially and economically disadvantaged small businesses in technological and scientific fields. The small business must apply in collaboration with a nonprofit research institution. Preference is given to women owned small businesses. There are two phases. The first phase has a limit of $100,000. In the second phase, up to $500,000 is available depending upon the results of the first phase research and commercial merit.

B22-
PUBLIC HEALTH SERVICE SMALL BUSINESS INNOVATIONS RESEARCH PROGRAM
Public Health Service
Attn: Solicitation Office
13687 Baltimore Avenue
Laurel, MD 20707
(301) 206-9385

INTEREST AREA: BUSINESS GROWTH
The purpose of this fund is to encourage participation of women owned businesses and socially and economically disadvantaged small businesses in federal research and development projects. Small businesses must meet the program definition of "Small Business". Preference is given to women-owned small businesses. Grants are offered by the Public Health Service, National Institutes of Health, Centers for Disease Control and Prevention and Food and Drug Administration. Approximately 700 awards each year are made by NIH, 6-9 by CDC and 2 by FDA. There are two phases to the grants. Phase 1 do not exceed $100,000. Phase 2 do not exceed $750,000.

B23-
RIVIERA FINANCE
1171 Homestead Road, Suite 250
Santa Clara, CA 95050
(408) 248-8828

INTEREST AREA: BUSINESS LOANS
This fund provides monies for women owned businesses. Preference is given to start-up companies with small to medium size credit needs, companies whose profit and loss or balance sheets may not be acceptable to banks and companies whose credit needs are such that other financial firms find them too burdensome.

B24-
SMALL BUSINESS ADMINISTRATION MINI-LOAN PROGRAM

Office of Women's Business Ownership
Small Business Administration
409 Third Street, SW
Washington, DC 20416
(202) 205-6673

INTEREST AREA: BUSINESS LOANS
The purpose of this loan program is to guarantee loans for small businesses in the United States. Preference is given to women-owned businesses, but all small businesses are eligible for these guaranteed loans. The number of awards varies each year. Loans up to $50,000 can be guaranteed through this program.

B25-
SMALL BUSINESS INNOVATION RESEARCH (SBIR PROGRAM)
SBIR Coordinator
Office of Grants and Program Systems
Cooperative State Research Service
U.S. Department of Agriculture
Room 323, Aerospace Bldg.
14th and Independence Ave., SW
Washington, DC 20250-2200
(202) 401-6852

INTEREST AREA: BUSINESS GROWTH
The purpose of this fund is to advance technological innovation in the private sector, strengthen the role of small businesses in merging business with federal research. Assistance is in the form of grants with estimated annual funds of approximately $5,600,500.

B26-
SMALL BUSINESS INNOVATION RESEARCH (SBIR PROGRAM)
Grants Management Officer
National Institutes of Drug Abuse
Alcohol, Drug Abuse and Mental Health Administration
Public Health Service

U.S. Department of Health and Human Services
Room 8A-54, Parklawn Bldg.
5600 Fishers Lane
Rockville, MD 20857
(301) 443-6710

INTEREST AREA: BUSINESS
The purpose of this fund is to advance technological innovations and promote ventures with small businesses to meet research needs in the areas of alcohol, drug and mental health research. Financial assistance is available in the form of grants with estimated annual funds of $9,997,000.

B27-
SMALL BUSINESS INVESTMENT COMPANIES
409 Third St., NW
Washington, DC 20418
(202) 205-6512

INTEREST AREA: VENTURE CAPITAL
Funds are provided by privately organized and privately managed investment firms in partnership with the government to provide venture capital to small independent businesses both new and already established. Two types of SBICs provide monies; the original SBIC and MESBICs (Minority Enterprise Small Business Investment Companies) which specifically target the needs of entrepreneurs denied the opportunity to own and operate a business due to social or economic disadvantage. Type of assistance includes loans and loan guarantees. Estimate of annual funds available is $263,000,000.

B28-
SMALL BUSINESS LOANS
Director, Loan Policy and Procedures Branch
Small Business Administration
409 3rd Street, SW
Washington, DC 20416
(202) 205-7510

INTEREST AREA: BUSINESS LOANS
The purpose of this fund is to provide guaranteed loans to small businesses which are unable to obtain financing in the private credit marketplace. Applicants must be able to prove they can repay loans. The estimate of annual funds available is $5,133,000,000. Types of assistance include loan guarantees.

B29-
SPECIAL LOANS FOR NATIONAL HEALTH SERVICE CORPS MEMBERS TO ENTER PRIVATE PRACTICE
>Director, National Health Service Corps
>Health Resources and Services Administration
>Public Health Service
>U.S. Department of Health and Human Services
>Parklawn Bldg., Room 7A039
>5600 Fishers Lane
>Rockville, MD 20857
>(301) 443-2900

INTEREST AREA: BUSINESS LOAN
Funds are available to assist in establishing private practices in a health manpower shortage area. Applicants must be members of the National Health Service Corps. Assistance is in the form of loans. Contact the office above for estimated annual funds available.

B30-
WOMEN'S BUSINESS OWNERSHIP ASSISTANCE
>Small Business Administration
>Office of Women's Business Ownership
>409 Third Street, SW
>Washington, DC 20416
>(202) 205-6673

INTEREST AREA: BUSINESS LOANS
The purpose of this fund is to promote financial interest of small business concerns owned and controlled by women and to remove any discriminatory barriers encountered by women business owners applying for capital funds and other needed financial assistance for

business growth and development. Must be women owned or women controlled businesses to apply. Assistance is in the form of grants with estimated annual funds available in the amount of $1,267,000.

B31-
WOMEN'S BUSINESS OWNERSHIP PROJECT GRANTS
Office of Women's Business Ownership
Small Business Administration
409 Third Street, SW
Washington, DC 20416
(202) 205-6673

INTEREST AREA: BUSINESS LOANS
This fund provides counseling on all phases of business development including location of capital sources for women-owned businesses. Nonprofit organizations, for profit organizations, and state or local government agencies may also apply. The number of awards varies each year ranging from $150,000,000 to $30,000.

B32-
WOMEN, INC.
1401 21st Street, Suite 310
Sacramento, CA 95814
1-800-930-3993

INTEREST AREA: BUSINESS LOANS
This fund provides over $3,000,000 for women owned businesses. Women, Inc. teamed up with The Money Store Investment Corporation to provide financial assistance for business development, business expansion and all aspects of business growth. Loans average between $25,000 and $150,000.

B33-
WOMEN'S WORLD BANKING LOAN PROGRAM
Women's World Banking
8 West 40th Street
New York, NY 10018
(212) 768-8513

INTEREST AREA: BUSINESS LOANS

The purpose of this loan program is to guarantee loans for women's businesses. Applicants must be women who need funding to start or expand a business. This organization provides financial assistance to women in several countries including third world countries. The number of awards varies each year ranging from $1,000,000 to $5,000.

SBA Demonstration Programs

The U.S. Small Business Administration co-funds 19 Demonstration Centers in the United States. These centers offer programs to assist women wishing to start up or expand small businesses. The service at these centers is unique since counseling is one on one only. All help is offered by women for women. As non-profit centers, funding is a combination of private and public funds. In addition to any of the offices located in your area, contact the main Office of Women's Business Ownership in Washington, D.C. for general resource for women's business contracts.

Main Office for U.S. Small Business Administration's Office of Women's Business Ownership:

OFFICE OF WOMEN'S BUSINESS OWNERSHIP
409 Third Street, SW
Washington, DC 20418
202- 205-6673

AMERICAN WOMAN'S ECONOMIC DEVELOPMENT CORPORATION (AWED)
301 E. Ocean Blvd., Suite 1010
Long Beach, CA 90802
213-983-3747

WEST COMPANY
Parent Organization to WEST Co. in Fort Bragg, CA
413 North State Street
Ukiah, CA 95482
707-462-2348

WEST Company
A Women's Economic Self Sufficiency Training Program
333 C N. Franklin St
Fort Bragg, CA 95437
707-964-7571

WOMEN'S INITIATIVE
Parent Organization To WISE in Oakland, CA
Executive Director
450 Mission Street, Suite 402
San Francisco, CA 94102
415-247-9473

WISE Oakland
Project Director
519 17th Street, Suite 520
Oakland, CA 94612
510-208-9473

WOMEN BUSINESS OWNERS CORPORATION
18 Encanta Drive
Rolling Hills Estates, CA 90274
310-530-0582

BUSINESS CENTER FOR WOMEN (BCW)
571 Galapago Street
Denver, CO 80204
303-573-1302

AMERICAN WOMAN'S ECONOMIC DEVELOPMENT CORPORATION (AWED)
2445 M St., NW. Room 490
P.O. Box 65644
Washington, DC 20035
202-857-0091

YMCA OF GREATER ATLANTA
957 N. Highland Avenue, NE
Atlanta, GA 30306
404-872-4747

WOMEN'S BUSINESS DEVELOPMENT CENTER (WBDC)
8 South Michigan Avenue, Suite 400
Chicago, IL 60603
312-853-3477

WOMEN'S BUSINESS DEVELOPMENT CENTER
SBDC/Joliet Junior College
214 Ottawa, 3rd Floor
Joliet, IL 60431
815-727-6544, ext. 1312

WOMEN'S BUSINESS DEVELOPMENT CENTER
Kankakee Community College
4 Dearborn Square
Kankakee, IL 60901
815-933-0375

WOMEN BUSINESS OWNERS ADVOCACY PROGRAM
SBDC/Rock Valley College
1220 Rock Street
Rockford, IL 61101
815-968-4087

WOMEN'S ECONOMIC VENTURE ENTERPRISE
229 16th Street
Rock Island, IL 61201
309-788-9793

INDIANA REGIONAL MINORITY SUPPLIER DEVELOPMENT COUNCIL, INC.
300 E. Fall Creek Parkway, N.D.
P.O. Box 44801
Indianapolis, IN 46244-0801
317-923-2110

EXCEL!

Women Business Owners Development Team
200 Renaissance Center, Suite 1600
Detroit, MI 48243
313-396-3576

EXCEL!
Women Business Owners Development Team
200 Ottawa NW, Suite 900
Grand Rapids, MI 49504
616-458-4783

BI-COUNTRY COMMUNITY ACTION PROGRAMS, INC.
P.O. Box 579
Bomidji, MN 56601
218-851-4631

NAWBO OF ST. LOUIS
911 Washington Ave., Suite 140
St. Louis, MO 63101
314-621-6162

WOMEN'S ECONOMIC SELF-SUFFICIENCY TEAM (WESST CORP)
414 Silver Southwest
Albuquerque, NM 87102
505-848-4760

WESST CORP. TAOS, NM
Taos County Economic Development Corporation
P.O. Box 1389
Taos, NM 87571
505-758-1161

AMERICAN WOMAN'S ECONOMIC DEVELOPMENT CORPORATION (AWED)
(Parent Organization to AWED Washington, DC and AWED CT)
641 Lexington Ave., 9th Floor
New York, NY 10022
212-688-1900

MINORITY FEMALE ENTREPRENEURSHIP PROGRAM

37 North High Street
Columbus, OH 43215-3065
614-225-6910

WOMEN ENTREPRENEURS INC.
525 Vine Street 3rd Floor
Cincinnati, OH 45202
513-684-0700

WOMEN'S ECONOMIC ASSISTANCE VENTURES
105 West North College
P.O. Box 512
Yellow Springs, OH 45387
513-767-2667

WOMEN'S ENTREPRENEURIAL GROWTH ORGAN.
58 W. Center Street
P.O. Box 544
Akron, OH 44309
216-535-9346

WOMEN'S BUSINESS RESOURCE PROGRAM/OHIO UNIVERSITY
Director
One President Street
Athens, OH 45701
614-593-0474

CLEVELAND WOMEN'S CONSORTIUM
1979 East 56th Street
Cleveland, OH 44199
216-881-8146

CENTER FOR WOMEN'S BUSINESS ENTERPRISE (CWBE) AUSTIN SITE
301 Congress Avenue, Suite 100
Austin, TX 78701
512-476-7501

CENTER FOR WOMEN'S BUSINESS ENTERPRISE
1200 Smith St.

2800 Citicorp Bldg.
Houston, TX 77002
713-658-0300

CENTER FOR WOMEN'S BUSINESS ENTERPRISE
800 Interstate Bank Tower
Dallas, TX 75202
214-855-7300

SOUTHWEST RESOURCE DEVELOPMENT
8700 Crownhill
Suite 700
San Antonio, TX 78209
512-828-9034

CENTER FOR WOMEN'S BUSINESS ENTERPIESE
8023 Vantage Drive, Suite 600
San Antonio, TX 78230
512-377-2100

WOMEN'S BUSINESS INITIATIVE CORPORATION (WBIC)
1020 N. Broadway
Milwaukee, WI 53202
414-277-7004

WISCONSIN WOMEN ENTREPRENEURS, INC.
Project Manager
2830 North 48th Street
Milwaukee, WI 53210
(414) 873-0687

National Association of Women Business Advocates

Supportive mentors can be a major key to success for anyone new to the entrepreneurial world. The Office of Women's Business Ownership of the Small Business Administration provides this state-by-state list of mentors essential to the development of women-owned businesses in their states. If you own a business or are thinking about starting one, contact the NSWBA office nearest to you for advice, information and referrals.

ARIZONA
Governor's Office of Women's Services
1700 West Washington, Suite 420
Phoenix, AZ 85007
(602) 542-1755

U.S. Small Business Administrator
2005 North Central Ave., 5th Floor
Phoenix, AZ 85004
(602) 379-3737

ARKANSAS
Money Magic, Inc.
2923 Imperial Valley Drive
Little Rock, AR 72212
(501) 277-6644

CALIFORNIA
Office of Small and Minority Business
Dept. of General Services
1808 14th St., Room 100
Sacramento, CA 95814
(916)-322-5060

Entrepreneurial Woman
2392 Morse Avenue
Irvine, CA 92714
(714) 261-2325

COLORADO
Women's Business Program
Office of Business Development
1625 Broadway, Suite 1710
Denver, CO 80202
(303) 892-3840

Assistant Regional Admin. for Public Affairs and Communications
U.S. Small Business Administration
999 18th St., Suite 701
Denver, CO 80202
(303) 892-3840

CONNECTICUT
Director of Public Relations
Connecticut Mutual Life Insurance Co.
140 Garden St., MS-G-26
Hartford, CT 06154
(800) 234-2865

DISTRICT OF COLUMBIA
Head of the AA/OWBO
Small Business Administration
409 Third Street, SW
Washington, DC 20416
(202) 205-6673

ILLINOIS
Women's Business Ownership Coordinator
U.S. Small Business Administration
230 South Dearborn St., Suite 510
Chicago, IL 60604
(312) 353-4252

Women Business Advocate Dept. of Commerce and Community Affairs
100 West Randolph, Suite 3-400
Chicago, IL 60601
(312) 814-6111

INDIANA
Government Marketing Assistance Group
Indiana Dept. of Commerce
1 North Capitol St., Suite 700
Indianapolis, IN 46204
(317) 232-3393

LOUISIANA
Louisiana Dept. of Economic Development
Division of Minority and Women's Business Enterprise
P.O. Box 94185
Baton Rouge, LA 70804
(405) 841-5242

MICHIGAN
WBO Services
MI Department of Commerce
4th Floor Law Bldg., P.O. Box 30225
Lansing, MI 48909-7504
(517) 335-1835

MINNESOTA
SBDC - Winona State University
P.O. Box 5838
Winona, MN 55987
(507) 334-3965

NEVADA
Office of Small Business
State of Nevada
2501 East Sahara #304
Las Vegas, NV 89158
(702) 486-4506

OHIO
Women's Business Resource Program
Ohio Department of Development
77 South High Street, 28th Floor
Columbus, OH 43215
(614) 466-4945

Women Small Business Division
Department of Commerce
6601 Broadway Extension
Oklahoma City, OK 73116
(405) 841-5242

OREGON
The Foundation for Women Owned Businesses
5031 East Foothills Rd.

Lake Oswego, OR 97034
(503) 790-7672

PENNSYLVANIA
Bureau of Women's Business Development
Department of Commerce
462 Forum Building
Harrisburg, PA 17120
(717) 787-3339

VIRGINIA
P.O. Box 3604
Lynchburg, VA 24503
(804) 528-9424

WISCONSIN
Women Business Services
Department of Development
123 West Washington Avenue
P.O. Box 7970
Madison, WI 53707
(608) 266-0593

Herrewood Associates
4101 Pennington
Racine, WI 53404
(414) 554-8301

For more information on resources for women's businesses, contact:

OFFICE OF WOMEN'S BUSINESS OWNERSHIP
409 Third Street, SW
Washington, DC 20416
(202) 205-6673

National Score Women's Business Ownership Coordinators

SCORE, the Service Corps of Retired Executives, has a special division focused on women-owned businesses. At little or no cost to you, you can make use of the lessons that professional, entrepreneurs and business people have learned. These services are valuable to any business women. Below you will find the contact information for the Women's Business Ownership coordinator in your area.

Region I
Aline Lotter
41 Brook Street
Manchester, NH 03104
(603) 668-5166

Region II
Vacant

Region III
Beatrice Checket
907 Sextant Way
Annapolis, MD 21401
(410) 266-8754

Region IV
Julie Mullane
141 Green Heron Court

Daytona Beach, FL 32119
(904) 788-5350

Region V
Gwen Arnold
1923 Sheffield Drive
Ypsilanti, MI 48198
(313) 483-1121

SBA Personnel
OWBO SCORE Liaison
Small Business Administration
409 Third, St., SW, 6th Floor
Washington, DC 20416
(202) 205-6673

Region VI
Doris Bentley
222 Amelia Street
Lafayette, LA 70506
(318) 232-2970

Region VII
Betty Finnell
7640 N. Lucerne Court
Kansas City, MO 64151
(816) 741-5997

Region VIII
Ms. Bernie Zieler
1020 Burlington Avenue
Billings, MT 59102
(406) 259-1779

Region IX
Betty Williamson
525 East St. Louis #406
Las Vegas, NV 89104
(702) 734-6211

Region X
Diana White
N. 617 Helena
Spokane, WA 99202
(509) 534-9001

For more information on SCORE, contact:

National Score Office
409 Third Street, SW, Suite 5900
Washington, DC 20024

For more information on resources for women-owned businesses, contact:

Office of Women's Business Ownership
Small Business Administration
409 Third Street, SW, 6th Floor
Washington, DC 20416
(202) 205-6673

Venture Capital Clubs

Venture Capital Clubs are located throughout the United States and are an excellent contact for the business woman who may not want to secure federal or state money for her business ventures. Venture capital investors are willing to invest in new and expanding business ventures for a percentage of the equity.

Venture Capital Clubs welcome entrepreneurs and encourage presentation of ideas and business plans to potential investors. We have also listed Venture Capital Associations who publish directories of venture capital contacts and Small Business Investment Companies. Contact each club or association to clarify your business needs and their potential interest in your company.

We also provide a state by state list of over 500 venture capital clubs which can be obtained by contacting us at www.stressresource.com.

The National Venture Capital Association
1655 N. Fort Meyer Dr., Suite 700
Arlington, VA 22209
703-351-5269

The association publishes a directory of their membership that includes names, addresses, phone numbers, fax numbers and contact person.

The members include venture capital organizations, individual investors and financiers interested in investing in innovative new companies.

National Association of Investment Companies
1111 14th St. NW, Suite 700
Washington, DC 20005
202-289-4336

The association publishes a directory of Small Business Investment Companies and describes the investment preferences of each company.

National Association of Small Business Investment Companies
1199 N. Fairfax St., Room 200
Alexandria, VA 22314
703-683-1601

This association also publishes a directory of their membership listing over 300 small business investment companies.

Technology Capital Network
201 Vassar Street
Cambridge, MA 02139
617-253-7163

The association was in the process of publishing a directory of their membership at the time of this printing.

The International Venture Capital Institute
P.O. Box 1333
Stamford, CT 06904

Contact the Institute for their directory of members.

Association of Venture Capital Clubs
265 East 100 South, Suite 300
P.O. Box 3358
Salt Lake City, UT 84111
801-364-1100

Contact the association for their directory of members.

VENTURE CAPITAL CLUBS

ALABAMA
For AL, LA, MO, TX
Birmingham Venture Club   205-323-5461

Mobile Venture Club   205-433-6951

ALASKA
Alaska Pacific Venture Club   907-563-3993

ARIZONA
Arizona Ventures   602-254-8560

ARKANSAS
Venture Resources Inc.   501-375-2004

CALIFORNIA
For CA, OR, WA
Orange Coast Venture Group   714-855-0652

Community Entrepreneurs Organization   415-435-4461

San Diego Venture Group   619-595-0284

COLORADO
Rockies Venture Club, Inc.   303-831-4174

CONNECTICUT
For CT, MA, MI, NJ, NY, IN, OH, PA, DC
Connecticut Venture Capital Fund   203-677-0183

DISTRICT OF COLUMBIA
Baltimore-Washing Venture Group   301-405-2144

FLORIDA
Gold Coast Venture Capital Club   561-997-6594

For FL, GA, TN. KY
Gold Coast Venture Capital Club   561-488-4505

For FL, GA, TN, KY
Florida Venture Group   407-365-5374

HAWAII
Hawaii Venture Capital Association   808-526-1277

IDAHO
Rocky Mountain Venture Group   208-526-1277

Treasure Valley Venture Capital Forum   208-385-1640

IOWA
Iowa City Development   319-354-3939

ILLINOIS
Madison Dearborn Partners   312-732-5400

INDIANA
Venture Club of Indiana   317-253-1244

KENTUCKY
Kentucky Investment Capital Network   502-564-7140

Mountain Ventures Inc.   606-864-5175

LOUISIANA
For AL, LA, MO, TX
Louisiana Seed Capital Corporation   504-383-1508

For AL, LA, MO, TX
Greater New Orleans Venture Capital Club   800-949-7890

MARYLAND
Mid Atlantic Venture Association   410-560-2000

MASSACHUSETTS
Venture Capital Fund of New England　　617-439-4646

UTAH
For CO, MT, UT, NM, ID, AZ
Mountain West Venture Group　　801-364-5300

Utah Ventures　　801-583-4105

VERMONT
Vermont Venture Network　　802-658-7830

VIRGINIA
Richmond Venture Capital Club　　804-560-7000

WASHINGTON
For CA, OR, WA
Northwest Venture Group　　206-746-1973

WEST VIRGINIA
Enterprise Venture Capital Company　　304-872-3000

WISCONSIN
Wisconsin Venture Network　　414-278-7070

Venture Capital Funders Licensed by SBA

Small Business Investment Companies (SBIC) was formed across the United States in 1960 to provide venture capital funds. These businesses and organizations are privately owned and all operate on a for profit basis. The federal license they each hold allows the affiliated companies to pool their financial resources with borrowed money from the government, providing small businesses with financing based on equity securities or long term debt.

The list of SBIC's grows each year and within the next two to three years over *$6 billion* in funding is expected to be available for small businesses through SBIC's . Since 1960 these organizations have provided financing for over 75,000 companies including Apple Computer, Staples, and Federal Express.

To obtain a **current list** contact the Associate Administrator for Investment, U.S. Small Business Administration, Washington, DC 20416, 202-205-6510.

The U.S. Small Business Association Office of Women's Business Ownership

The Small Business Administration, Office of Women's Business Ownership is the only federal agency assigned to specifically assist in the development and growth of women business ownership. Women are starting businesses at twice the rate of all businesses and having the SBA address the special needs of this business-growth group, benefits the overall economic well-being of the nation.

The Office of Women's Business Ownership (OWBO) provides support in the form of assistance and/or training in business development. Included in the program is technical assistance, aid in locating access to credit and capital, access to marketing opportunities and access to federal contracts.

We have listed these U.S. SBA representatives alphabetically according to states. The name of the present representative is also listed at the beginning of each location. The OWBO locations are changing continually. To receive the most up-to-date list of Women's Business Centers contact the SBA,

Office of Women's Business Ownership, 409 Third Street, SW 4th Floor, Washington, D.C. 20416, 202-205-6673.

ALABAMA
Business Development Specialist, SBA
2121 8th Avenue, Suite 200
Birmingham, AL 35203
205-731-1334

Business Development Specialist, SBA
1301 Azalea Rd., Suite 201A
Mobile, AL 36693
334-660-2725

ALASKA
Small Business Administration WBOR
Federal Building #67
222 West 8th Avenue
Anchorage, AK 99513
907-271-4022

ARIZONA
Small Business Administration
2828 N. Center Avenue, Suite 800
Phoenix, AZ 85004
602-640-2316

Self Employment Loan Fund, Inc.
201 North Central Avenue
Phoenix, AZ 85073
602-340-8834

ARKANSAS
Business Development Specialist SBA
2120 Riverfront, Suite 100
Little Rock, AK 72202
501-324-5871

CALIFORNIA
WBO Representative SBA
2719 N. Air Fresno Drive, Suite 107
Fresno, CA 93727
209-487-5791

Business Development Specialist SBA
330 N. Brand Blvd., Suite 1200
Glendale, CA 91203
818-552-3215

Loan Specialist SBA
660 J Street, Suite 215
Sacramento, CA 95814
916-498-6426

WBO Representative SBA
455 Market Street, 6th Floor
San Francisco, CA 94105
415-744-8491

U. S. Small Business Administration
550 W. C Street, Suite 550
San Diego, CA 92188
619-557-7250

WBOR - SBA
200 W. Santa Ana Blvd., Suite 700
Santa Ana, CA 92703
714-950-7420

Women's Initiative for Self Employment
450 Mission Street, Suite 402
San Francisco, CA 94105
415-247-9473

Spanish Site
1398 Valencia Street
San Francisco, CA 94110
415-826-5090

Oakland Site
11611 Telegraph Ave., Suite 702
Oakland, CA 94612
510-451-3415

WEST Company - Ukiah Office
367 North State Street, Suite 201
Ukiah, CA 95482
707-468-3555

WEST Company - Fort Bragg Office
306 East Redwood Avenue, Suite 2
Fort Bragg, CA 95437
707-964-7571

COLORADO
Small Business Administration
721 19th Street
Denver, CO 80202
303-844-3461

Mi Casa Resource Center for Women, Inc.
571 Galapago Street
Denver, CO 80204
(303) 573-1302

Mi Casa Career Development and Business Center for Women
700 Knox Court
Denver, CO 80204
303-573-0333

CONNECTICUT
SBA
330 Main Street, 2nd Floor
Hartford, CT 06106
203-240-4842

DELAWARE
Program Assistant SBA

One Rodney Square, Suite 412
920 North King Street
Wilmington, DE 19801
302-573-6380

DISTRICT OF COLUMBIA
U. S. Small Business Administration
1110 Vermont Ave., NW
Washington, DC 20005
202-606-4000

National Women's Business Center
1250 24th Street, NW, Suite 350
Washington, DC 20037
202-466-0544

FLORIDA
Business Management Specialist SBA
1320 S. Dixie Hwy., Suite 501
Coral Gables, FL 33146
305-536-5833

SBA
7825 Bay Meadows Way, Suite 100B
Jacksonville, FL 32256-7504
904-443-1900

Women's Business Development Center
10555 West Flagler Street, Room 2612
Miami, FL 33174
305-348-3951

GEORGIA
Loan Officer, SBA
1720 Peachtree Street, NW, 6th Floor
Atlanta, GA 30309
404-347-4147

Women's Economic Development Agency
675 Ponce de Leon Avenue

Atlanta, GA 30308
404-853-7680

HAWAII
WBOR, SBA
30 Ala Moana, Room 2213
P.O. Box 50207
Honolulu, HI 96850-4981
808-541-2990

IDAHO
Business Management Specialist, SBA
1020 Main Street, Suite 290
Boise, ID 83720
208-334-9079

ILLINOIS
U.S. SBA
500 W. Madison Street, Suite 1250
Chicago, IL 60606
312-353-4528

U. S. SBA
511 W. Capitol Street, Suite 302
Springfield, IL 62704
217-492-4416

Women's Business Development Center
8 South Michigan Avenue, Suite 400
Chicago, IL 312-853-3477

IOWA
U.S. SBA
215 4th Avenue, SE
Cedar Rapids, IA 52401
319-362-6405

Business Development Specialist SBA
210 Walnut Street, Room 749
Des Moines, IA 50309

515-284-4761

KANSAS
SBA
100 East English, Suite 510
Wichita, KS 67202
316-269-6273

KENTUCKY
Business Development Specialist SBA
600 Dr. Martin Luther King, Jr. Place, Room 188
Louisville, KY 40202
502-582-5971

LOUISIANA
Business Development Specialist, SBA
365 Canal Street, Suite 3100
New Orleans, LA 70130
504-589-6685

Women Entrepreneurs for Economic Development, Inc.
1683 North Claiborne Avenue, Suite 101
New Orleans, LA 70116
504-947-1555

Southeast Louisiana Black Chamber of Commerce
Women's Business Center
2714 Canal Street, Suite 302
New Orleans, LA 70119
504-822-2202

MAINE
WBO Representative SBA
40 Western Avenue, Room 512
Augusta, ME 04330
207-622-8242

Coastal Enterprises, Inc.
Women's Business Development Program
P.O. Box 268

Wiscasset, ME 04578
207-882-7552

Coastal Enterprises, Inc.
Women's Business Development Program
7 North Chestnut Street
Augusta, ME 04330
207-621-0245

MARYLAND
Business Development Specialist SBA
10 South Howard Street
Baltimore, MD 21201
410-962-6195

SCORE
907 Sextant Way
Anapolis, MD 21401
410-366-8746

Women Entrepreneurs of Baltimore, Inc.
28 East Ostend Street
Baltimore, MD 21230
410-727-4921

MASSACHUSETTS
U.S. SBA
10 Causeway St., Room 265
Boston, MA 02222
617-565-5588

U.S. SBA
1441 Main Street, Room 410
Springfield, MA 01103
413-785-0268

Center for Women & Enterprise, Inc.
45 Broomfield Street, 6th Floor
Boston, MA 02108
617-423-3001

MICHIGAN
Business Development Specialist SBA
477 Michigan Avenue
Detroit, MI 48226
313-226-6075

Women's Initiative for Self Employment
C/o Center for Empowerment and Economic Development
2002 Hogback Road, Suite 12
Ann Arbor, MI 48105
313-677-1400

Grand Rapids Opportunities for Women
25 Sheldon SE, Suite 210
Grand Rapids, MI 49503
616-458-3404

MINNESOTA
SBA
100 N. 6th Street
Minneapolis, MN 55403
612-370-2324

Women in New Development
2715 15th Street NW
Benudji, MN 56601
218-751-4631

MISSOURI
Business Development Specialist, SBA
323 West 8th, 5th Floor
Kansas City, MO 64105
816-374-6762

Business Development Specialist SBA
911 Walnut Street, 13th Floor
Kansas City, MO 64106
816-426-3608

Public Affairs Specialist SBA
815 Olive Street, Suite 242
St. Louis, MO 63101
314-539-6600

National Assoc. of Women's Business Owners
7165 Delmar, Suite 204
St. Louis, MO 63130
314-863-0046

Business Development Specialist SBA
620 South Glenstone, Suite 110
Springfield, MO 65802
417-864-7670

MISSISSIPPI
SBA
One Government Plaza
13th Street
Gulfport, MS 39501
601-863-4449

SBA
101 West Capitol Street, Suite 400
Jackson, MS 39201
601-985-5342

Mississippi Women's Economic Entrepreneurial Project
106 West Green Street
Mound Bauou, MS 38762
601-741-3342

MONTANA
Business Development Specialist SBA
301 S. Park Avenue, Room 334
Helena, MT 59626
406-441-1081

Montana Women's Capital Fund
302 North Last Chance Gulch, Suite 400

P.O. Box 271
Helena, MT 59624

NEBRASKA
Loan Officer, SBA
11145 Mill Valley Road
Omaha, NB 68154

NEVADA
ADD Business Development SBA
301 East Steward, Box 7527
Downtown Station
Las Vegas, NV 89125
702-388-6611

Nevada Self Employment Trust
116 E. 7th Street, Suite 3
Carson City, NV 89704
702-841-1420

1600 East Desert Inn Road, Suite 209E
Las Vegas, NV 89109
702-734-3555

NEW HAMPSHIRE
Business Development Assistant SBA
Stewart Nelson Plaza, 2nd Floor
143 N. Main Street
Concord, NH 03301
603-225-1400

Women's Business Center, Inc.
150 Greenleaf Avenue, Unit 4
Portsmouth, NH 03801
603-430-2892

NEW JERSEY
Economic Development Specialist SBA
Two Gateway Center, 4th Floor
Newark, NJ 07102

201-645-2434

New Jersey NAWBO Excel
225 Hamilton Street
Bound Brook, NJ 08805
732-560-9607

NEW MEXICO
SBA
625 Silver SW, Room 320
Albuquerque, NM 87102
505-766-1879

Women's Economic Self Sufficiency Team
414 Silver Southwest
Albuquerque, NM 87102
505-241-4760

WESST Corp
500 West Main
Framington, NM 87401
505-522-3707

WESST Corp
200 West First, Suite 324
Roswell, NM 88201
505-624-9850

WESST Corp
Box 5007 NDCBU
Taos, NM 87571
505-751-1575

NEW YORK
Business Development Technician SBA
111 W. Huron Street, Room 1311
Buffalo, NY 14202
716-551-5670

SBA

Elmira Savings Bank Building
333 West Water Street
Elmira, NY 14901
607-734-8142

Business Development Specialist SBA
35 Pinelawn Road, Room 207W
Melville, NY 11747
516-454-0753

SBA
26 Federal Plaza, Room 3100
New York, NY 10278
212-264-1482

Business Development Specialist SBA
Federal Building
100 State Street
Rochester, NY 14614
716-263-6700

District Director SBA
100 S. Clinton Street
Syracuse, NY 13261
315-448-0428

SCORE
431 Woodland Land
Webster, NY 14580
716-671-4550

American Women's Economic Development Corp.
71 Vanderbilt Avenue, Suite 320
New York, NY 10169
212-692-9100

Women's Venture Fund, Inc.
45 John Street, Room 1009
New York, NY 10038
212-732-7500

NORTH CAROLINA
Business Development Specialist SBA
200 North College Street, Suite A2015
Charlotte, NC 28202
704-344-6587

NORTH DAKOTA
Business Development Specialist SBA
657 2nd Avenue North, Room 219
P.O. Box 3088
Fargo, ND 58102
701-239-5131

Women's Business Institute
320 North Fifth Street, Suite 203
Fargo, ND 58107
701-235-6488

OHIO
SBA
525 Vine Street, Room 870
Cincinnati, OH 45202
513-684-6907

Business Development Specialist SBA
1111 Superior Avenue, Suite 630
Cleveland, OH 44114
216-522-4180 ext. 128

Business Development Specialist SBA
Two Nationwide Plaza, Suite 1400
Columbus, OH 43215
614-469-6860 ext. 274

Ohio Women's Business Resource Network
77 South High Street, 28th Floor
Columbus, OH 43215
614-466-2682

WOMEN & Women's Network, Inc.
526 South Main Street, Suite 235
Akron, OH 44311
330-379-9280

Women's Business Resource Program of Southeastern Ohio
20 East Circle Drive, Suite 155
Technology and Enterprise Bldg.
Athens, OH 45701
614-593-1797

Pyramid Career Services
2400 Cleveland Avenue North
Canton, OH 44709
330-453-3767

Women Entrepreneurs, Inc.
36 East 4th Street, Suite 925
Cincinnati, OH 45202
513-684-0700

Glenville, Development Corp. Micro Enterprise Program
10640 St. Clair Avenue
Cleveland, OH 44108
216-851-8724

Greater Columbus Women's Business Development Center
Women's Business Enterprises Certification Program
3360 E. Livingston Ave., Suite 2B
Columbus, OH 43227
614-238-6081

Women's Development Center
42101 Griswold Road
Elyria, OH 44035
440-324-3688

Women's Entrepreneurial Network
3565 Havenhurst Road
Toledo, OH 43614

419-381-7555

OKLAHOMA
Business Development Specialist SBA
210 Park Avenue
Oklahoma City, OK 73102
405-231-4301

Women's Business Center
Working Women's Money University
234 Quadrum Drive
Oklahoma City, OK 73108
405-942-8257

OREGON
SBA
1515 SW 5TH Avenue, Suite 1050
Portland, OR 97207
503-326-5101

Southern Oregon Women's Access to Credit
33 North Central, Suite 209
Medford, OR 97501
541-779-3992

ONABEN – A Native American Business Network
520 Southwest 6th Avenue, Suite 930
Portland, OR 97204
503-243-5015

PENNSYLVANIA
Business Development Specialist SBA
475 Allendale Road, Suite 201
King of Prussia, PA 19406
215-962-3800

SBA
960 Penn Avenue, 5th Floor
Pittsburgh, PA 15222
412-644-5441

Women's Business Development Center
1315 Walnut Street, Suite 1116
Philadelphia, PA 19107
215-790-9232

PUERTO RICO
Women's Business Institute
Univeersidad Del Sagrado Corazon
P.O. Box 12383
San Juan, Puerto Rico 00914
787-728-1515

RHODE ISLAND
SBA
380 Westminster Street Fifth Floor
Providence, RI 02903
401-528-4688

SOUTH CAROLINA
Business Development Specialist SBA
1835 Assembly Street, Room 358
Columbia, SC 29201
803-253-3360

Center for Women Entrepreneurs
Columbia College of South Carolina
1301 Columbia College Drive
Columbia, SC 29203
803-786-3582

SOUTH DAKOTA
Business Development Specialist SBA
110 S. Phillips Avenue, Suite 200
Sioux Falls, SD 57104
605-330-4231

Watertown Area Career Learning Center
The Entrepreneur Network for Women
100 South Maple

P.O. Box 81
Watertown, SD 57201
605-882-5080

TENNESSEE
SBA
50 Vantage Way, Suite 201
Nashville, TN 37228
615-736-5881

The National Association for Women Business Owners
P.O. Box 292283
Nashville, TN 37229
615-248-3474

TEXAS
SBA
10737 Gateway West, Suite 320
El Paso, TX 79925
915-540-5154

U.S. Business Administration
4300 Amon Carter Blvd., Suite 114
Fort Worth, TX 76155
817-885-6504

Business Development Specialist SBA
222 E. Van Buren Street, Suite 500
Harlingen, TX 78550
210-427-8533

SBA
5400 Griggs Road
Houston, TX 77021
713-643-8193

Business Development Technician SBA
1611 10th Street, Suite 200
Lubbock, TX 79401
806-743-7462

Business Development Specialist SBA
727 East Durango, Room A527
North Star Executive Center
San Antonio, TX 78206
210-472-5900

Texas Center for Women's Business Enterprise
Two Commodore Plaza, 13th Floor
206 East 9th Street
Austin, TX 78701
512-261-8525

North Texas Women's Business Development Center Inc.
1402 Corinth Street, Suite 1536
Dallas, TX 75215
214-428-1177

North Texas Women's Business Development Center Inc.
Online Women's Business Center
1402 Corinth Street, Suite 209
Dallas, TX 75215
214-565-0447
http://www.onlinewbc.org

UTAH
Business Development Specialist SBA
Federal Building
125 South State Street
Salt Lake City, UT 84138
801-524-6831

Women's Business Center at the Chamber
Salt Lake Area Chamber of Commerce
175 East 400 South, Suite 600
Salt Lake City, UT 84111
801-328-5051

VERMONT
Business Development Specialist SBA

87 State Street, Room 205
Montpelier, VT 05601
802-828-4422

VIRGINIA
SBA
1504 Santa Rosa Road
Suite 200
Richmond, VA 23229
804-771-2765

WASHINGTON
SBA
1200 Sixth Avenue, Suite 1700
Seattle, WA 98101
206-553-7310

SBA
1020 W. Riverside Avenue
Spokane, WA 99201
509-353-2800

SBA
617 N. Helena
Spokane, WA 99202
509-534-9001

ONABEN – A Native American Business Network
520 Southwest 6th Avenue, Suite 930
Portland, OR 97204
503-243-5015

ONABEN – A Native American Business Network
3201 Broadway, Suite C
Everett, WA 98201
425-339-6226

WEST VIRGINIA
Business Development Technician SBA
168 West Main Street

P.O. Box 1608
Clarksburg, WV 26302
304-623-5631

West Virginia Micro-Business Center
601 Delaware Avenue
Charleston, WV 25302
304-345-1298

WISCONSIN
SBA
212 E. Washington Avenue, Room 213
Madison, WI 53703
608-264-5516

SBA
310 West Wisconsin Avenue
Milwaukee, WI 53203
414-297-3941

Wisconsin Women's Business Initiative Corp.
1915 North Dr. Martin Luther King J. Drive
Milwaukee, WI 53212
414-372-2070

WWBIC – Madison Office
16 North Carroll Street 7th Floor
Madison, WI 53703
608-257-7409

WYOMING
Business Development Specialist SBA
100 East B Street, Room 4001
Casper, WY 82602
307-261-6500

Small Business Development Centers

Small Business Development Centers are located in over 700 offices across the United States and offer many valuable business services. The first time entrepreneur as well as the established business woman has access to services offered by highly skilled professionals. The professionals provide consultations for free or for very low cost. These programs are funded by the Federal Government and are one of the best places to find support for your business ventures.

If you are looking for help in business development, help in starting a business or expanding an existing business, you will find the support here Services provided include how to write a business plan, how to protect your invention or artistic creation with trademark or copy write filing, how to create and implement a marketing plan, working with professionals such as attorneys, accountants, bankers, how to obtain financing for your business and much more.

Businesses who use these services across the country give the SBDC's very high ratings. An independent study was conducted to determine the impact these services were having on local business entrepreneurs. The survey stated that those businesses using the services averaged a 400% greater grow rate than other businesses in their area.

We have listed the Lead Centers for each state instead of all 700 offices. Contact the Lead Office in your state and ask for the SBDC address closest to your location.

Small Business Development Centers

ALABAMA
LEAD CENTER
Office of State Director, Alabama Small Business Development Consortium
University of Alabama at Birmingham
1717 11th Avenue S., Suite 419
Birmingham, AL 35294-7645
205-934-7260

ALASKA
LEAD CENTER
University of Alaska SBDC
430 West 7th Avenue, Suite 110
Anchorage, AK 99501
907-274-7232

ARIZONA
LEAD CENTER
Arizona SBDC
9215 N. Black Canyon Highway
Phoenix, AZ 85021
602-943-9818

ARKANSAS
LEAD CENTER

Arkansas SBDC University of Arkansas at Little Rock
Little Rock Technology Center Building
100 S. Main, Suite 401
Little Rock, AR 72201
501-324-9043

CALIFORNIA
LEAD CENTER
California SBDC California Dept. of Commerce
Office of Small Business
801 K St., Suite 1700 Sacramento, CA 95814
916-322-3502

COLORADO
LEAD CENTER
Colorado SBDC Office of Economic Development
1625 Broadway
Denver, CO 80202
303-892-3809

CONNECTICUT
LEAD CENTER
Connecticut SBDC University of Connecticut
School of Business Administration
2 Bourn Place, U-94
Storrs, CT 06260
806-486-4135

DELAWARE
LEAD CENTER
Delaware SBDC University of Delaware
Purnell Hall, Suite 005
Newark, DE 19716
302-831-1555

DISTRICT OF COLUMBIA
LEAD CENTER
District of Columbia SBDC Howard University
6th and Fairmont St., NW

Washington, DC 20059
202-806-1550

FLORIDA
LEAD CENTER
Florida SBDC University of West Florida
Downtown Center
19 W. Garden Street, Suite 300
Pensacola, FL 32501
904-444-2060

GEORGIA
LEAD CENTER
Georgia SBDC University of Georgia
Chicopee Complex
1180 East Broad Street
Athens, GA 30602
706-542-6762

HAWAII
LEAD CENTER
Hawaii SBDC University of Hawaii at Hilo
200 W. Kawili Street
Hilo, HI 96720
808-933-3515

IDAHO
LEAD CENTER
Idaho SBDC Boise State University
College of Business
1910 University Drive
Boise, ID 83725
208-385-1640

ILLINOIS
LEAD CENTER
Illinois SBDC Network
Dept. of Commerce and Community Affairs
620 East Adams Street
Springfield, IL 62701

217-524-5856

INDIANA
LEAD CENTER
Indiana SBDC Economic Development Council
One N. Capitol
Indianapolis, IN 46204
317-264-6871

IOWA
LEAD CENTER
Iowa Small Business Development Center
Iowa State University
College of Business Administration
Chamblynn Bldg.
137 Lynn Avenue
Ames, IA 50010
515-292-6351

KANSAS
LEAD CENTER
Kansas SBDC Wichita State University
1845 Fairmount
Wichita, KS 67260
316-689-3647

KENTUCKY
LEAD CENTER
Kentucky SBDC University of Kentucky
Center for Business Development
College of Business and Economics
225 Business and Economics Bldg.
Lexington, KY 40506
606-257-7668

LOUISIANA
LEAD CENTER
Louisiana SBDC
Northeast Louisiana University
Adm. 2-57

Monroe, LA 71209
318-342-5510

MAINE
LEAD CENTER
Maine SBDC University of Southern Main
96 Falmouth St. P.O. Box 9300
Portland, ME 04101
207-780-4420

MARYLAND
LEAD CENTER
Small Business Development Center
1420 N. Charles St.
Baltimore, MD 21202
410-837-4141

MASSACHUSETTS
LEAD CENTER
Massachusetts SBDC, University of Massachusetts
205 School of Management
Amherst, MA 01003
413-545-6301

MICHIGAN
LEAD CENTER
Michigan SBDC
2727 Second Avenue
Detroit, MI 48201
313-964-1798

MINNESOTA
LEAD CENTER
Minnesota SBDC, Dept. of Trade and Economic Development
500 Metro Square
121 7th Place E.
St. Paul, MN 55101
612-297-5770

MISSISSIPPI
LEAD CENTER
Mississippi SBDC, University of Miss.
Old Chemistry Bldg.
University, MS 38677
601-232-5001

MISSOURI
LEAD CENTER
Missouri SBDC, University of Missouri
Suite 300, University Place
Columbia, MO 65211
573-882-0344

MONTANA
LEAD CENTER
Montana SBDC, Dept, of Commerce
1424 Ninth Avenue
Helena, MT 59620
406-444-4780

NEBRASKA
LEAD CENTER
Nebraska SBDC, Omaha Business and Tech Center.
2505 N. 24th St.
Omaha, NE 68110
402-595-3511

NEVADA
LEAD CENTER
Nevada SBDC, University of Nevada at Reno
College of Business Administration
Room 411, Business Bldg.
Reno, NV 89577
702-784-1717

NEW HAMPSHIRE
LEAD CENTER
New Hampshire SBDC, University of New Hampshire
108 McConnell Hall

Durham, NH 03824
603-862-2200

NEW JERSEY
LEAD CENTER
New Jersey SBDC
Rutgers Graduate School of Management
University Heights
180 University Avenue
Newark, NJ 07102
201-648-5950

NEW MEXICO
LEAD CENTER
New Mexico SBDC Santa Fe Community College
P.O. Box 4187
Santa Fe, NM 87502
505-438-1362

NEW YORK
LEAD CENTER
New York SBDC
State University of New York
State University Plaza, S-523
Albany, NY 12246
518-465-5398

NORTH CAROLINA
LEAD CENTER
North Carolina SBDC University of North Carolina
333 Fayette St. Mall, Suite 1150
Raleigh, NC 27601
919-715-7272

NORTH DAKOTA
LEAD CENTER
North Dakota SBDC
University of North Dakota
118 Gamble Hall, Box 7308
Grand Forks, ND 58202

701-777-3700

OHIO
LEAD CENTER
Ohio SBDC Dept. of Development
77 S High St., 28th Floor
Columbus, OH 43226
614-466-2480

OKLAHOMA
LEAD CENTER
Oklahoma SBDC Network
Southeastern Oklahoma State University
517 University
Durant, OK 74701
405-924-0277

OREGON
LEAD CENTER
Oregon SBDC
44 W. Broadway, Suite 501
Eugene, OR 97401
503-726-2250

PENNSYLVANIA
LEAD CENTER
Pennsylvania SBDC, University of Pennsylvania
The Wharton School
409 Vance Hall
Philadelphia, PA 19104
215-898-4861

RHODE ISLAND
LEAD CENTER
Rhode Island SBDC, Bryant College
1150 Douglas Pike
Smithfield, RI 02917
401-232-6416

SOUTH CAROLINA
LEAD CENTER
South Carolina SBDC, University of South Carolina

College of Business Administration
Columbia, SC 29208
803-777-4907

SOUTH DAKOTA
LEAD CENTER
South Dakota SBDC, University of South Dakota
414 East Clark
Vermillion, SD 57069
605-677-5498

TENNESSEE
LEAD CENTER
Tennessee SBDC, Memphis State University
South Campus (Gatwell Rd.)
Building #1
Memphis, TN 38152
901-678-2500

TEXAS
LEAD CENTER
North Texas SBDC, Dallas County Community College
1402 Corinth Street
Dallas, TX 75215
214-860-5831

UTAH
LEAD CENTER
Utah SBDC University of Utah
102 West 500 South
Salt Lake City, UT 84101
801-581-7905

Southern Utah University SBDC
351 West Center

Cedar City, UT 84720
801-586-5400

VERMONT
LEAD CENTER
Vermont SBDC, Vermont Tech, College
P.O. Box 422
Randolph, VT 05060
802-727-9101

VIRGINIA
LEAD CENTER
Virginia SBDC
901 E. Byrd St., Suite 1800
Richmond, VA 23219
804-371-8253

WASHINGTON
LEAD CENTER
Washington SBDC, Washington State University
501 Johnson Tower
Pullman, WA 99164
509-335-1576

WEST VIRGINIA
LEAD CENTER
West Virginia SBDC
West Virginia Development Office
950 Kanawha Blvd.
Charleston, WV 25301
304-558-2960

WISCONSIN
LEAD CENTER
Wisconsin SBDC, University of Wisconsin
432 N. Lake St., Room 423
Madison, WI 53706
608-263-7794

WYOMING
LEAD CENTER

Wyoming SBDC
111 West 2nd St., Suite 416
Casper, WY 82601
800-348-5207

GENERAL WELFARE

General Welfare sources are listed in alphabetical order and include various grants, loans and other services provided for emergency short term and long term funding. Funds are provided to individuals for personal, living and/or medical expenses.

GW1-
DOROTHY AMES TRUST
    c/o Key Trust Co. of Maine
    Key Trust Co.,
    35 State Street
    Albany, NY 12207

LOAN SUPPORT: HEARING IMPAIRED
This trust offers grants to the hearing impaired only. Applicants must be children and be in need of financial assistance for hearing aids or other personal needs. Grants vary according to need.

GW2-
ARMY EMERGENCY RELIEF LOANS/GRANTS
    Army Emergency Relief
    200 Stovall Street
    Alexandria, VA 22332-06600
    (703) 960-9382

LOAN SUPPORT: MILITARY/VETERANS
Veterans, military personnel and/or their dependents may apply for financial assistance. Applicants may apply for financial assistance when regular pay is delayed or stolen. Funds are to be used for food, rent or utilities, emergency needs, funeral expenses, medical or dental expenses. Each year over $25,000,000 is available in interest free loans or grants.

GW3-
ADOLPH AND ESTHER GOTTLIEB FOUNDATION, INC.
    380 West Broadway
    New York, NY 10012
    (212) 226-0581

LOAN SUPPORT: PAINTERS/SCULPTORS
The purpose of this fund is to provide financial assistance to professional sculptors, painters or printmakers in need of financial assistance due to an unexpected, catastrophic event in their life. Grant categories are divided into two programs: Applicants with 20 years +

in their art, and applicants with at least 10 years in their profession. Grant amounts vary according to need. Average is $2,000 each.

GW4-
THE AMERICAN SOCIETY OF JOURNALISTS AND AUTHORS CHARITABLE TRUST
1501 Broadway, Suite 302
New York, NY 10036
(212) 997-0947

LOAN SUPPORT: FREELANCE WRITERS
Professional freelance writers who are experiencing financial difficulties in their career may apply. Applicants who are 60 years of age or older and apply will be given first consideration for financial assistance. Grants average $2,000 each.

GW5-
ARTISTS FELLOWSHIP, INC.
c/o Salmagundi Club
47 Fifth Avenue
New York, NY 10003

LOAN SUPPORT: VISUAL ARTISTS
Financial assistance is available to American professional visual artists and their families for relief of financial burdens due to disability, age or bereavement. Grants have ranged from over $8,000 to $500 each.

GW6-
THE BAGBY FOUNDATION FOR THE MUSICAL ARTS, INC.
501 Fifth Avenue, Suite 1401
New York, NY 10017
(212) 986-6094

LOAN SUPPORT: MUSICIANS
Financial assistance is provided for individuals who have supported the field of music and are in need of financial assistance. Grants are given

for pension and/or emergency aid. Dollar amounts vary according to need and range from $4,000 to $500.

GW7-
THE BILL BALDWIN FUND, INC.
P.O. Box 388
Troy, NY 12181-0388
(518)252-8420

LOAN SUPPORT: PUBLISHING INDUSTRY
This fund provides financial assistance to females who are presently employed by or are retired from the publishing or periodical distribution industry. Annual grant amounts vary according to need. Average individual grant is $2,000.

GW8-
BIBLE STUDENTS AID FOUNDATION
c/o PNC Bank, Kentucky, Inc.
Citizens Plaza
Louisville, KY 40296

LOAN SUPPORT: BIBLE STUDY STUDENTS
This program provides emergency funds for Bible students who show a need for financial assistance with personal, medical or living expenses. Annual awards vary according to need and have reached as high as $6,000 for a individual grant.

GW9
BLUE STAR MOTHERS REHABILITATION PROGRAM
Blue Star Mothers of America
C/o Bessie Davis
1815 Potomac, Apt. 6
Lansing, MI 48910

LOAN SUPPORT: VETERANS OR BLUE STAR MOTHERS
The purpose of this fund is to provide financial assistance to veterans or Blue Star Mothers who are in need of emergency funds for personal,

medical or living expenses. The number of awards varies each year according to need.

GW10-
BROADCASTERS FOUNDATION INC.
296 Old Church Road
Greenwich, CT 06830

LOAN SUPPORT: BROADCAST INDUSTRY
The foundation provides financial assistance to needy members of the broadcast industry and their families. Annual grants to individuals vary according to need.

GW11-
ELLA LYMON CABOT TRUST, INC.
109 Rockland Street
Holliston, MA 01746

LOAN SUPPORT: GENERAL INTEREST
This program is very unique. Grants are given to individuals whose projects are founded in personal significance and will offer a positive contribution to other people. No grants are given for scholarships or fellowships which are a regular part of their academic study. Two grants are given each year often in the range of $7,000 to $12,000 each.

GW12-
CARNEGIE FUND FOR AUTHORS
One Old Country Road
Carle Place, NY 11514
(516) 764-8899

LOAN SUPPORT: WRITERS
This fund provides emergency financial assistance to writers who have a need as a result of illness or injury to self, spouse or dependent child or some other personal misfortune. Candidates must have published commercially at least one book and have received reader acceptance

for the publication. Number of awards and dollar amount of awards varies according to need.

GW13-
THE CB TRUST
8201 Preston Rd., Suite 600
Dallas, TX 75225
(214) 890-8000

LOAN SUPPORT: NFL PLAYERS & FAMILY
Financial assistance is provided for players and coaches, including their spouses, who have been or are now on the active roster of a football team who is a member of the National Football League. Use of funds is not limited to emergency need. Amounts vary according to need, ranging from $25,000 to $3,000.

GW14-
CHURCH WOMEN UNITED'S INTERCONTINENTAL GRANTS
Church Women United
475 Riverside Drive, Room 812
New York, NY 10115
(212) 870-2347

LOAN SUPPORT: AID FOR WOMEN
The purpose of this program is to provide funding for projects that assist women in two areas: economic alternatives for women in poverty and health care for women. The funds are distributed through a nonprofit organization to the individual. Annual awards vary according to need. Average range is $1,500.

GW15-
COAL MINERS BLACK LUNG BENEFITS
Division of Coal Mine Workers Compensation
U.S. Department of Labor
ESA/OWCP/DCMWC
200 Constitution Avenue, NW

Washington, DC 20210
(202) 523-8347

LOAN SUPPORT: COAL MINERS
This fund provides financial aid to coal miners who are disabled because of black lung disease. Funds are available to present or former coal miners, including their surviving dependents, orphaned children and totally dependent parents, brothers and sisters. The number of awards varies each year. Benefits are paid monthly and amounts vary.

GW16-
THE CORRESPONDENTS FUND
c/o Rosenman & Cohen
575 Madison Avenue
New York, NY 10022-2511

LOAN SUPPORT: BROADCAST INDUSTRY
The purpose of this fund is to provide financial assistance to men and women in the field of broadcasting. Grants are available to men and women and their spouses and children who have served in the U.S. press, television, radio, news, film and other U.S. organizations within or outside the U.S. or who have served the foreign press or other foreign news organizations. Use of funds is limited to emergency relief aid, average annual individual amounts range from $5,000 to less than $800.

GW17-
THE CULTURAL SOCIETY, INC.
200 West 19th Street
Panama City, FL 32405

LOAN SUPPORT: MUSLIMS
Financial assistance is available as welfare funds to any needy Muslims. Annual grants are given throughout the year and average $1,300.

GW18-
DEATH GRATUITY FOR MILITARY PERSONNEL
Department of Veterans Affairs
810 Vermont Avenue, NW
Washington, DC 20420
(202) 233-4000 800-827-1000

LOAN SUPPORT: MILITARY

The purpose of this fund it to provide a death gratuity for the surviving spouses and dependents of military personnel. Applicants must be dependents of military personnel who died of any cause in active service or within 120 days after leaving active duty from specified causes related to service. This is a 1-time payment of $6,000.

GW19-
DISTRICT LODGE NO. 3, SONS OF NORWAY CHARITABLE TRUST
c/o Robert J. Regevir
274 Bay Ridge Parkway
Staten Island, NY 10314

LOAN SUPPORT: NORWEGIANS

The purpose of this fund is to provide grants to needy individuals of Norwegian descent. Funds are not limited to emergency needs. Grants to individuals are provided throughout the year and average $1,500.

GW20-
EAGLES MEMORIAL FOUNDATION, INC.
4710 14th Street West
Bradenton, FL 34207

LOAN SUPPORT: CHILDREN OF EAGLES

This fund provides grants to children of decreased Eagle servicemen and women, law officers and fire fighters for dental, medical and hospital expenses. No benefits are available for illnesses caused by drug or alcohol abuse. Individual amounts vary according to need.

GW21-
ECONOMIC JUSTICE FOR WOMEN GRANTS
Rockefeller Family Fund
1290 Avenue of the Americas
New York, NY 10104
(212) 373-4252

LOAN SUPPORT: WOMEN'S RIGHTS
This fund provides financial assistance for projects that support the economic aspects of women's rights. Eligible to apply are tax-exempt organizations engaged in educational and charitable activities seeking to provide women with equitable opportunities in employment, education and welfare. The number of awards varies each year, average is 15 each year ranging from $15,000 to $30,000 plus.

GW22-
FANNIE E. RIPPEL FOUNDATION GRANTS
Fannie E. Rippel Foundation
P.O. Box 569
Annandale, NJ 08801-0569
(908) 735-0990

LOAN SUPPORT: ELDERLY WOMEN
The fund provides assistance to corporations, organizations, associations, institutions or societies that maintain relief and care of aged women. The grants are awarded to organizations and not individuals. Over $3 million in grants is awarded each year, ranging from $250,000, to $4,000.

GW23-
FORD FOUNDATION GRANTS
Ford Foundation
320 East 43rd Street
New York, NY 10017
(212) 573-5141

LOAN SUPPORT: GENERAL PUBLIC

The purpose of this program is to provide financial assistance for programs addressing the needs of women who suffer economic, social and cultural deprivation. Programs confronting issues for Blacks, Hispanics, Native Americans, poor women and other disadvantaged groups are important considerations for the Foundation. The number of awards varies each year. Average grants are between $50,000 and $200,000.

GW24-
VINCENT GAFFNEY FOUNDATION
>c/o American State Bank & Trust Co.
>P.O. Box 1446
>Williston, ND 58802-1446
>(701) 774-4121

LOAN SUPPORT: CHILDREN
The purpose of this program is to provide financial assistance for the health and welfare of any needy children under the age of 18. Funds are used for medical, living or emergency needs. The number and dollar amount of grants varies with need.

GW25-
GI LOANS
>Department of Veterans Affairs
>810 Vermont Avenue, NW
>Washington, DC 20420
>(800) 827-1000

LOAN SUPPORT: VETERANS
This program provides financial assistance to disabled and other veterans or their not remarried surviving spouses in the purchase of residences. The actual loan comes from a commercial lender. The DVA will guarantee payment on loans for the purchase of homes, farm homes, condominium units or refinancing of existing loans.

GW26-
JOSEPH S. AND CAROLINE GRUSS GEMILATH CHESED FUND
1650 56th Street
Brooklyn, NY 11204
(718) 871-2500

LOAN SUPPORT: GENERAL
Financial assistance is provided for needy individuals and may be used for personal, medical, living or emergency needs. Number and dollar amount of awards varies according to need.

GW27-
THE GEOFFREY FOUNDATION, INC.
P.O. Box 1112
Kennebunkport, ME 04046

LOAN SUPPORT: HEARING IMPAIRED
Financial assistance is provided in the form of grants to severely to profoundly hearing impaired individuals who use auditory expression as their primary mode of communication. Applicants must be United States residents and attending post-secondary or high school in the United States. Individual grants average $750, the number of grants varies each year with need.

GW28-
HOECHST MARION ROUSSEL INDIGENT PATIENT PROGRAM
c/o Samples Dept., K2-M1216
P.O. Box 9950
Kansas City, MO 64134-0950

LOAN SUPPORT: GENERAL-MEDICAL NEED
Financial support is available for payment of prescription drugs to individuals who are in need of continual drug therapy and fall below the federal poverty level for assistance. The program supplies the necessary drug therapy, no monies are given. Recipients may continue

indefinitely in the program providing they are still in severe financial and medical need.

The following agency limits their funds to residents of Illinois. However, we suggest you contact the Department of Veterans' Affairs in your state for information on similar programs.

GW29-
ILLINOIS BURIAL BENEFITS FOR INDIGENT VETERANS
Illinois Department of Veterans' Affairs
P.O. Box 19432
833 South Spring Street
Springfield, IL 62794-9432

LOAN SUPPORT: BURIAL - VETERANS
The purpose of this fund is to provide an allowance for the burial of indigent veterans and certain members of their family. Applicants must have charge of the burial of indigent veterans, their fathers, mothers, spouses, surviving spouses or minor children. The one time benefit is $600.

GW30-
ITALIAN-AMERICAN COMMUNITY SERVICES AGENCY
678 Green Street
San Francisco, CA 94133-3896

LOAN SUPPORT: GENERAL - WELFARE
Financial assistance is provided for indigent individuals, including senior citizens who are in need of aid for personal, medical, living or emergency expenses. Grant amounts vary according to need.

GW31-
JOCKEY CLUB FOUNDATION
40 East 52nd Street
New York, NY 10022

LOAN SUPPORT: JOCKEYS

The purpose of this fund is to provide financial assistance to needy persons legitimately connected with the thoroughbred breeding and racing industry. The number of grants varies each year with need and range from $22,000 to $250.

GW32-
JOHN EDGAR THOMSON FOUNDATION AID
John Edgar Thomson Foundation
The Rittenhouse Claridge
201 South 18th Street, Suite 318
Philadelphia, PA 19103
(215) 545-6083

LOAN SUPPORT: RAILROAD EMPLOYEES/FAMILY
The purpose of this fund is to provide financial assistance to daughters of railroad employees who died while in the employ of a railroad in the United States. Candidates must live in the home of surviving parent. 100 or more grants are given each year. Monthly payments may be available from infancy up to 22 years of age.

GW33-
LEROY C. MERRITT HUMANITARIAN FUND AWARD
LeRoy C. Merritt Humanitarian Fund
Attn: Secretary
50 East Huron Street
Chicago, IL 60611
(312) 944-6780

LOAN SUPPORT: LIBRARIANS
This fund provides financial support to librarians facing discrimination on basis of their race, sex, or other factors. The number of awards varies each year.

GW34-
LONGSHORE AND HARBOR WORKERS' COMPENSATION PROGRAM
Department of Labor

Attn: Employment Standards Administration
Office of Workers' Compensation Programs
Division of Longshore and Harbor Workers' Compensation
200 Constitution Avenue, NW
Washington, DC 20210
(202) 219-8721

LOAN SUPPORT: LONGSHORE/HARBOR WORKERS
The fund provides benefits to any maritime workers who are disabled or were killed due to employment injuries. The compensation for disability is based on a percentage of the employee's average weekly wage. The number of and dollar amount of individual financial benefits varies according to need. Over 84,000 workers and survivors have received more than $630 million per year in compensation and medical benefits from this program.

GW35-
MINNESOTA WOMEN'S FUND GRANT PROGRAM
Minnesota Women's Fund
A200 Foshay Tower
821 Marquette Avenue
Minneapolis, MN 55402
(612) 337-5010

LOAN SUPPORT: WOMEN, GENERAL AID
The purpose of this fund is to address the causes of discrimination against women and girls and to create fundamental change so women and girls are able to have equality in society. The following applicants are encouraged to apply: informal groups of women, emerging grassroots groups or organizations and formal nonprofit organizations. 40 or more grants are given each year totaling $225,000, ranging from $15,000 to $500.

GW36-
MONEY FOR WOMEN/BARBARA DEMING MEMORIAL FUND, INC.
P.O. Box 40-1043

Brooklyn, NY 11240-1043

LOAN SUPPORT: WOMEN ARTISTS
This program provides funds in the form of grants to individual feminists who are active artists in the fields of visual art, fiction, poetry, nonfiction, music and photography. Number of grants varies according to need, each grant averaging $750.

GW37-
MUSICIANS FOUNDATION, INC.
875 Sixth Avenue, Suite 2303
New York, NY 10001
(212) 239-9137

LOAN SUPPORT: MUSICIANS
Emergency funds are available to professional musicians and their families for use in personal, medical, living or emergency expenses. Grants to individuals total $100,000 with the average amount of $3,000.

GW38-
NATIONAL NETWORK OF ABORTION FUNDS GRANTS AND LOANS
National Network of Abortion Funds
c/o CLPP
Hampshire College
Amherst, MA 01002-5001
(413) 582-5645

LOAN SUPPORT: MEDICAL FUNDS
The purpose of this fund is to provide financial assistance to low income women who are seeking to terminate an unwanted pregnancy. Member organizations provide the loans and/or grants-in-aid. There are individual funds to provide assistance for related needs. There are usually over 6,000 individual awards given each year, the dollar amount varies according to need.

GW39-
NAVAJO NATION VETERAN'S BURIAL FUNDS
Navajo Nation
Attention: Department of Veteran Affairs
P.O. Box 430
Window Rock, AZ 86515
(520) 871-6413

LOAN SUPPORT: VETERANS
This program provides a burial allowance for indigent Navajo veterans and their dependents. Candidates must have served in the U.S. armed forces and been discharged under other than dishonorable conditions. The one time benefit is $350.

GW40-
NAVAJO NATION VETERAN'S HOUSING ASSISTANCE
Navajo Nation
Attention: Department of Veteran Affairs
P.O. Box 430
Window Rock, AZ 86515
(520) 871-6413

LOAN SUPPORT: VETERANS
Financial assistance is provided to Navajo veterans who need assistance to purchase a home. The program offers financial support to indigent members of the Navajo Nation who served in the U.S. armed forces during any period and who are discharged under other than dishonorable conditions. The amount of the grant depends on the availability of funds.

The following fund is limited to the state of Nebraska. However, we suggest you contact your local Department of Veterans' Affairs for similar programs within your state.

GW41-
NEBRASKA VETERANS' AID FUND
Department of Veterans' Affairs
301 Centennial Mall, South

P.O. Box 95083
Lincoln, NE 68509-5083
(402) 471-2458

LOAN SUPPORT: EMERGENCY
Financial assistance is provided to assist veterans, their spouses and dependents in time of temporary emergency need. Applicants must be veterans who served in wartime, their spouses or their dependent children. The amount of aid awarded varied depending upon the needs of the recipient.

GW42-
NETZACH FOUNDATION
c/o Eisner & Lubin
250 Park Avenue
New York, NY 10177

LOAN SUPPORT: RELIGIOUS/GENERAL WELFARE
This fund provides financial assistance to individuals for religious and literary tutoring and for general welfare needs. Students must be studying in the United States to apply. Annual grants and dollar amounts vary according to need.

GW43-
NEW YORK SOCIETY FOR THE RELIEF OF WIDOWS & ORPHANS OF MEDICAL MEN
O'Conner, Davies & Co.
60 East 42nd Street
New York, NY 10165

LOAN SUPPORT: MEDICAL PROFESSION - FAMILY
The purpose of this fund is to provide financial assistance for widows and orphans of physicians. Financial assistance is provided in the form of annuities. The number and dollar amount of grants varies according to need.

GW44-
NFL ALUMNI FOUNDATION FUND
c/o Sigmund M. Hyman
P.O. Box 248
Stevenson, MD 21153-0248
(410) 486-5454

LOAN SUPPORT: NFL DISABLED MEMBER
The purpose of this fund is to provide financial relief to physically or mentally disabled former National Football League alumni, including grants for death benefits and medical expenses. Relief assistance is provided to alumni prior to 1959. Ten grants to individuals have been given totaling $50,000, individual range is $12,000, to $140.

GW45-
NONSERVICE-CONNECTED DEATH PENSION
Department of Veterans Affairs
810 Vermont Avenue, NW
Washington, DC 20420
(202) 233-4000   800-827-1000

LOAN SUPPORT: VETERANS BENEFITS
The fund provides pensions to disabled and other spouses and children of decreased eligible veterans who have died of disabilities or other nonservice-connected causes. Contact the Department of Veterans Affairs for specific information. Amounts vary according to individual needs and are payable monthly.

The following 5 programs are limited to the state providing funds. However, we suggest you contact your state departments requesting information on similar programs.

GW46-
NEW HAMPSHIRE PROPERTY TAX CREDIT FOR DISABLE VETERANS
New Hampshire Department of Revenue
Administration
61 South Spring Street

P.O. Box 457
Concord, NH 03302-0457
(603) 271-2687

LOAN SUPPORT: VETERANS
This fund provides property tax credits in New Hampshire to disabled veterans or their surviving spouses. Applicants must be U.S. citizens, veterans and totally and permanently disabled from a service-connected injury. The number of awards varies each year. Amounts vary according to the needs of the applicant.

GW47-
NEW JERSEY DISABLED VETERANS PENSION
New Jersey Department of Military and Veterans' Affairs
Attn: Public Information Officer
Eggert Crossing Road, CN 340
Trenton, NJ 08625-0340
(800) 624-0508

LOAN SUPPORT: VETERANS
The purpose of this fund is to supplement the compensation benefits paid by the U.S. Department of Veterans Affairs to veterans or their surviving spouses. Applicants must be receiving VA compensation benefits for 100 percent disability or be a surviving spouse of disabled veteran. The number of awards varies each year. Benefits are paid for the life of the veteran or spouse in the amount of $750 per year.

GW48-
NEW JERSEY PROPERTY TAX EXEMPTION FOR DISABLED VETERANS OR SURVIVING SPOUSES
New Jersey Division of Taxation
Attn: Taxpayer Information Services
50 Barrack Street, CN 269
Trenton, NJ 08646-0269
(609) 292-6400

LOAN SUPPORT: VETERANS

The purpose of this fund is to provide certain exemptions from real estate taxes to disabled New Jersey veterans and certain of their widow(er)s. Applicants must have completed at least 90 days of service in the armed forces and identified as totally and permanently disabled as a result of service-connected conditions. The number of awards varies each year. A 100% exemption from locally-levied real estate taxes is provided.

GW49-
NEW JERSEY PROPERTY TAX DEDUCTION FOR VETERANS OR SURVIVING SPOUSES

New Jersey Division of Taxation
Attn: Taxpayer Information Services
50 Barrack Street, CN 269
Trenton, NJ 08646-0269
(609) 292-6400

LOAN SUPPORT: VETERANS

This program provides a deduction from property taxes paid by New Jersey veterans or their surviving spouses. Contact the Division of Taxation for specific requirements. The number of awards varies each year. Qualified veterans and surviving widow(er)s may deduct $50 each year from taxes due on their real or personal property.

GW50-
TENNESSEE PROPERTY TAX RELIEF FOR DISABLED VETERANS AND THEIR SPOUSES.

Tennessee Department of Veterans Affairs
215 8th Avenue North
Nashville, TN 37203-3583
(615) 741-2931

LOAN SUPPORT: VETERANS

This fund provides property tax relief for disabled veterans and their spouses. Applicants must be severely disabled veterans or their surviving not remarried spouses. The number of awards varies each year.

GW51-
NURSES HOUSE, INC.
350 Hudson Street
New York, NY 10014
(212) 645-9685

LOAN SUPPORT: NURSES
The purpose of this fund it to provide short-term assistance to ill and indigent registered nurses in the U.S. Applicants must be in need of financial assistance to help meet basic living expenses. Costs of medical care and education are not funded. Annual grants to individuals total $55,000, each individual grant averaging $850.

GW52-
THE OSTBERG FOUNDATION, INC.
278 Fountain Road
Englewood, NJ 07631

LOAN SUPPORT: ELDERLY AND ILL
Financial assistance is provided to any elderly and ill women for personal, medical, living or emergency expenses. Applications are accepted throughout the year and range from $4,000 to $200.

GW53-
PEARLE VISION FOUNDATION
2534 Royal Lane
Dallas, TX 75229
(972) 277-5993

LOAN SUPPORT: GENERAL WELFARE
This fund provides financial assistance to any United States resident who needs and cannot afford eye surgery, treatment and/or low vision equipment. Grants are not given for routine eye exams or eyeglasses. Applications are accepted 4 times a year. Grant amounts vary according to need.

GW54-
W.L. PEGRAM EVANGELISTIC ASSOCIATION, INC.
14709 East 17th Avenue
Spokane, WA 99037

LOAN SUPPORT: MINISTERS
This fund provides financial assistance to retired ministers for emergency aid to cover living expenses. The amount of each grant varies according to need.

GW55-
PRECIOUS MOMENTS FOUNDATION
P.O. Box 802
Carthage, MO 64836

LOAN SUPPORT: GENERAL WELFARE
Financial assistance in the form of grants is provided to financially needy United States citizens. Applicants may use the financial aid to provide for their general welfare. The number and dollar amount of the annual grants varies according to need.

GW56-
THE PRESSER FOUNDATION
Presser Place
Bryn Mawr, PA 19010
(610) 525-4797

LOAN SUPPORT: MUSIC TEACHERS
The purpose of this fund is to provide care and housing of retired music teachers who during their career have encouraged musical appreciation and education. Annual number and dollar amount of grants varies with need.

GW57-
RAILROAD RETIREMENT DISABILITY ANNUITY
Railroad Retirement Board
844 North Rush Street

Chicago, IL 60611-2092
(312) 751-4500

LOAN SUPPORT: RAILROAD WORKERS FAMILY
This program provides an annuity to railroad workers with disabilities and provides for their families. Contact the Railroad Retirement Board for the requirements for application for the two types of disability considerations.

GW58-
REIMBURSEMENT OF BURIAL EXPENSES
Department of Veterans Affairs
810 Vermont Avenue, NW
Washington, DC 20420
800-827-1000

LOAN SUPPORT: VETERAN BURIAL
This fund provides reimbursement of burial expenses for wartime and certain other peacetime veterans. Survivors are eligible for reimbursement if the veteran was entitled to receive pension or compensation at the time of death. Up to $300 is available for the burial expenses. Other financial aid is available for additional expenses related to the burial costs.

GW59-
REINSTATED ENTITLEMENT PROGRAM FOR SURVIVORS (REPS)
Department of Veterans Affairs
810 Vermont Avenue, NW
Washington, DC 20420
(202) 233-4000

LOAN SUPPORT: VETERANS
The purpose of this fund is to provide benefits to disabled and other survivors of certain decreased veterans. Survivors of deceased veterans who died of service-connected causes incurred or aggravated prior to August 13, 1981 are eligible for these benefits. The number of awards varies each year.

GW60-
RIVENDELL STEWARDS' TRUST
P.O. Box 3037
Santa Barbara, CA 93130

LOAN SUPPORT: GENERAL
Financial assistance is provided for those women who are financially needy and work within the Christian church in the United States. There is no restriction on the use of the funds granted. Amounts vary each year with need.

GW61-
SCOTS' CHARITABLE SOCIETY
32 Elgin Road
Pocasset, MA 02559-2032

LOAN SUPPORT: SCOTTISH DESCENT
Welfare relief is provided to individuals of verifiable Scottish descent. Funds may be used for medical, living or emergency needs. Annual awards vary according to need, each individual grant averaging $1,600.

GW62-
SEQUOIA TRUST FUND
555 California Street, 36th Floor
San Francisco, CA 94104
(415) 393-8552

LOAN SUPPORT: GENERAL WELFARE
The purpose of this fund is to provide financial assistance to needy people who, by their special talents have given great pleasure to others. Assistance is only for special and unusual medical expenses. Grants to individuals have totaled $33,000, average being between $22,000 and $3,000.

GW63-
SCHOLARSHIPS FOR CHILDREN OF AMERICAN MILITARY PERSONNEL

6282 Santa Ynez
Huntington Beach, CA 92647
(213) 934-2288

LOAN SUPPORT: MILITARY FAMILIES
The purpose of this fund is to award scholarships to children whose parent(s) served in the military forces including children of astronauts killed in space shuttle. Parent must have served in military forces in Southeast Asia or Iraq and was missing-in-action, killed-in-action, or a prisoner-of-war. Amounts and number of annual awards vary, the average award being $3,700.

GW64-
SOCIAL SECURITY DISABILITY INSURANCE BENEFITS (SSDI)
Social Security Administration
6401 Security Boulevard
Baltimore, MD 21234
(410) 594-1234

LOAN SUPPORT: GENERAL WELFARE
This fund provides monthly benefits to workers and their families if the worker becomes disabled or blind. Applicants must have earned a sufficient number of social security credits in a recent period. Call the Social Security Administration for more information. Currently about 3.5 million adults receive SSDI benefits.

GW65-
SPECIAL SUPPLEMENTAL FOOD PROGRAM FOR WOMEN, INFANTS AND CHILDREN
Food and Nutrition Service
Supplemental Food Programs Division
Department of Agriculture
3101 Park Center Drive
Alexandria, VA 22303
(703) 305-2286

LOAN SUPPORT: WOMEN, CHILDREN

The purpose of this financial assistance program is to assist low-income pregnant, postpartum and breast-feeding women, infants and children to improve and maintain their nutritional status during critical times of growth and development. Candidates must be low income and be determined by a physician, nutritionist, nurse or other health official to be at nutritional risk because of inadequate income. Grants are available to the 50 states, vouchers are redeemable to local approved grocery stores.

GW66-
ST. BENEDICT'S CHARITABLE SOCIETY
1663 Bristol Pike
Bensalem, PA 19020
(215) 244-9900

LOAN SUPPORT: GENERAL WELFARE
The fund provides relief assistance to aged, needy women who need assistance for basic living, medical and funeral expenses. Contact St. Benedict's Charitable Society for any restrictions.

GW67-
STEEPLECHASE FUND
400 Fair Hill Drive
Elkton, MD 21921

LOAN SUPPORT: JOCKEYS/FAMILY
Financial assistance is provided in the form of grants for relief assistance for injured jockeys and needy widows of jockeys. Funds may be used for personal, medical, living or emergency expenses. The number and dollar amount of awards varies according to need.

GW68-
TAX FORGIVENESS FOR DISABLED VETERANS
Internal Revenue Service
Service Headquarters
1111 Constitution Avenue, NW
Washington, DC 20224

(202) TAX-FORM

LOAN SUPPORT: VETERANS
This program provides financial assistance to veterans and their surviving spouses or estates for tax relief. Applicants must be military members who die as a result of wounds or injuries incurred after 1979 in terroristic or military actions outside the U.S. The number of awards varies each year, this is a one time benefit.

GW69-
DOROTHY H. THEIS MEMORIAL TRUST
> 400 Essex Drive
> Sierra Vista, AZ, 85635-4746

LOAN SUPPORT: CANCER PATIENTS
The purpose of this fund is to provide grants to seriously ill cancer patients. Monies are to be used to provide visitation by family members or for travel expenses where necessary for treatment or diagnosis. Number of and dollar amount of grants varies according to need.

GW70-
ANNIE RENSSELAER TINKER MEMORIAL FUND
> 369 Lexington Ave., 7th Floor
> New York, NY 10017

LOAN SUPPORT: GENERAL WELFARE
Financial assistance is available in the form of monthly grant assistance to financially needy retired person who are living independently. Contact the Fund for more information of application. Grants vary according to need.

GW71-
VETERANS' DEPENDENCY AND INDEMNITY COMPENSATION (DIC)
> Department of Veterans Affairs
> 810 Vermont Avenue, NW

Washington, DC 20420
(800) 827-1000

LOAN SUPPORT: VETERANS
The purpose of this fund is to provide financial support for the spouses, children, and/or parents of deceased veterans who died of disabilities or other causes. Benefits must be for veterans who died on or after January 1, 1957 and cause of death must be related to line of duty while on active duty or training. The number of awards varies each year. Monthly payments continue for the life of the surviving spouse, provided remarriage does not occur or parent and until unmarried children reach age 18.

GW72-
VETERANS DEPENDENTS' EDUCATIONAL ASSISTANCE BENEFITS
Department of Veterans Affairs
810 Vermont Avenue, NW
Washington, DC 20420
(202) 418-4343 800-827-1000

LOAN SUPPORT: VETERANS CHILDREN/SPOUSES
This fund provides financial assistance to children and spouses of veterans in the form of post-secondary educational support on a monthly basis. Requirements for application should be obtained from the Dept. of Veteran Affairs. Monthly benefits for this program are $404 for full time students and lesser amounts for part time training.

GW73-
THE WEINGLASS FOUNDATION, INC.
Two Hopkins Plaza, No. 802
Baltimore, MD 21201

LOAN SUPPORT: GENERAL WELFARE
Financial assistance is provided in the form of grants to individuals who are in need of support for medical treatment and related expenses. The number of and dollar amount of grants varies according to need.

GW74-
WELFARE TRUST FUND OF THE TWENTY-FIVE YEAR CLUB OF I.D., INC.

c/o The Bank of New York, Tax Department
One Wall Street, 28th Floor
New York, NY 10286

LOAN SUPPORT: JOURNALISM DISTRIBUTION

Financial assistance is provided is the form of grants for those "aged, infirmed or otherwise needy persons" who are connected with the independent distribution of magazines, small-sized books or newspapers. The dollar amount and number of grants varies with need.

GW75-
WORLD BOXING COUNCIL - FRIENDLY HAND FOUNDATION

9501 SW 65th Street
Miami, FL 33173-2209

LOAN SUPPORT: BOXERS

Financial assistance is provided in the form of grants for medical and emergency assistance to any former boxer who has professional standings. The average grant is $2,200 and the number of awards varies according to need.

ARTS & CULTURE

This section highlights resources for women in the arts and cultural fields. The resources are listed for visual artists, performing artiest, writers, and other artistic fields. The resources are available for all levels of education and professional training. Entries are arranged alphabetically by sponsoring foundation or program title.

Each listing includes the purpose of the financial assistance and eligibility. To receive detailed information on the amounts available, exact program description, application deadlines and other information, contact each lending institution directly. Also check the General Welfare section for welfare assistance and emergency aid available to artists for personal, living and/or medical expenses.

AC1-
THE AMERICAN SOCIETY OF JOURNALISTS AND AUTHORS CHARITABLE TRUST
1501 Broadway, Suite 12907
New York, NY 10036
(212) 997-0947

LOAN SUPPORT: FREE LANCE WRITERS
The purpose of this fund is to provide assistance to professional free lance writers in need of support. Free lance writers must be 60 years of age or older, disabled or dealing with an extraordinary professional crisis. Five grants are awarded each year to individuals ranging from $2,300 to $1,500.

AC2-
ARTISTS FELLOWSHIP, INC.
C/o Salmagundi Club Sport
47 Fifth Avenue
New York, NY 10003

LOAN SUPPORT: VISUAL ARTISTS
This fund provides emergency financial assistance to American professional visual artists and their families. Funds are available for relief from financial distress due to disability, age or bereavement. Each year over 28 grants are awarded to individuals totaling $65,000.

AC3-
ART MATTERS, INC.
131 West 24th Street
New York, NY 10011
(212) 929-7190

LOAN SUPPORT: ARTISTS
Financial support is provided for projects and fellowships to individuals in the arts. Candidates may apply for support in the following areas: fine arts, film and performance art. AMI does not fund publications, music or art studies of any kind. Each year over 100 grants are awarded to individuals totaling over $375,500.

AC4-
ARTISTS' BOOK PRODUCTION GRANTS
Women's Studio Workshop
P.O. Box 489
Resendale, NY 12472
(914) 658-9133

LOAN SUPPORT: ARTIST
Financial support is provided to help artists with the publication of their book works and who work independently in their own studies. These funds are not to be used for re-issuing previously published material or as partial funding for a larger project. Funds available up to $750 to cover production of new book works.

AC5-
ARTIST' BOOK RESIDENCY GRANTS
Women's Studio Workshop
P.O. Box 489
Rosendale, NY 12472
(914) 658-9133

LOAN SUPPORT: BOOK ARTISTS
The purpose of this fund is to provide financial assistance and a residency to women book artists. Financial assistance is for new books in an edition of at least 100 copies. Monies per artist include $1,800, plus a $450 materials grant and housing while in residence. Number of grants available per year is not known.

AC6-
THE BAGBY FOUNDATION FOR THE MUSICAL ARTS, INC.
501 Fifth Avenue
Suite 1401
New York, NY 10017
(212) 986-6094

LOAN SUPPORT: RETIRED MUSICIANS
This fund provides financial assistance to aged artists who have contributed to the world of music and are in need of financial support. Annually grants are awarded to individuals totaling $43,000.

AC7-
FRANK HUNTINGON BEEBE FUND FOR MUSICIANS
C/o Welch & Forbes
45 School Street
Boston, MA 02108
(617) 523-1635

LOAN SUPPORT: MUSICIANS/PAINTERS
Financial assistance is provided in the form of scholarships for studying abroad for young, talented and deserving musicians and painters. Annually ten grants are awarded to individuals totaling $50,000.

AC8-
BELLAGIO CENTER RESIENCY
Rockefeller Foundation
1133 Avenue of the Americans
New York, NY 10036
(212) 869-8500

LOAN SUPPORT: ARTISTS
This fund provides support to individuals looking for a place to engage in creative activities at the Bellagio Study and Conference Center on Lake Como in northern Italy. Scholars in any discipline, writers, composers and women and minorities are encouraged to apply. Monies are not given, however participants receive free room and board for 5 week residency. The annual number of awards varies, usually 2-3 per residency periods.

AC9-
JAMES HUBERT BLAKE TRUST
C/o Beldock, Levine & Hoffman

99 Park Avenue, Suite 1600
New York, NY 10016
(212) 490-0400

LOAN SUPPORT: MUSICIANS
This fund provides music scholarships, particularly for students interested in traditional American ragtime music. Twelve grants to individuals are given each year totaling $52,000.

AC10-
BROADCASTERS FOUNDATION, INC.
320 West 57th Street
New York, NY 10019
(212) 586-2000

LOAN SUPPORT: BROADCASTERS
Funds are provided in the form of financial assistance to members of the broadcast industry and their families. Completion of formal application is required. Annually seven grants are awarded to individuals totaling $14,400.

AC11-
BUNTING FELLOWSHIP PROGRAM
Mary Ingraham Bunting Institute
Attn: Fellowships Office
Radcliffe College
34 Concord Avenue
Cambridge, MA 02138
(617) 495-8212

LOAN SUPPORT: ARTISTS, POETS, WRITERS
This fund provides financial support for women pursuing independent study in academic or professional fields, in creative writing or the arts. Candidates must be women scholars, professionals, creative writers, poets, visual and performing artists or musicians at various levels of career development. The fellowship residence year is at the Bunting Institute with access to resources at Radcliffe College and Harvard University. Fellowships include a stipend of $30,000 per year, office

or studio space and access to campus facilities. The annual number of awards varies, generally 4-9 each year.

AC12-
CARNEGIE FUND FOR AUTHORS
330 Sunrise Highway
Rockville Center, NY 11570

LOAN SUPPORT: WRITERS
Financial assistance for emergencies is provided to needy writers who have commercially published at least one book of reasonable length and have received reader acceptance. Applicants must have suffered a financial emergency as a result of illness or injury to self, spouse or dependent child or some other misfortune placing applicant in substantial need. Each year 23 grants are awarded to individuals totaling $18,000.

AC13-
DIRECTING WORKSHOP FOR WOMEN
American Film Institute
2021 North Western Avenue
Los Angeles, CA 90027
(213) 856-7721

LOAN SUPPORT: DIRECTORS
Funds are available to help women acquire skills necessary to become film and television directors. Funds are provided to develop the opportunity for professional women to produce, write, cast, rehearse, edit and/or direct narrative videotape projects. Applicants should be professional women with considerable experience in television, film, video or the dramatic arts and who have not yet had the opportunity to direct dramatic films or television. Applicants chosen are given $5,000 per project to direct a 30 minute video tape. The institute provides production equipment and editing facilities.

AC14-
DOG WRITERS EDUCATIONAL TRUST

2508 Teal Road
Washington Depot, CT 06794

LOAN SUPPORT: JOUNALISM/VETERINARY MEDICINE
Scholarships are awarded to students with a background in dog activity and are planning on attending a U.S. college or university. Applicants must plan to major in journalism or veterinary medicine. Ten grants are given each year, each is $1,000.

AC15-
FRANCES SHAW FELLOWSHIP
Ragdale Foundation
1260 North Green Bay Road
Lake Forest, IL 60045
(847) 234-1063

LOAN SUPPORT: WOMEN WRITERS
Funds are available to women who started writing seriously after the age of 55. Candidates must submit 10 poems or 20 pages of prose to apply. The fund pays for travel expenses and room and board at Ragdale for 2 months or longer. Each year up to 150 artists are awarded this opportunity to do their artistic work in a quiet environment with other writers and artists.

AC16-
THE FREEDOM FORUM
1101 Wilson Boulevard
Arlington, VA 22209
(703) 528-0800

LOAN SUPPORT: JOURNALISM
The purpose of this scholarship fund is to provide financial assistance for journalists. Scholarships are for undergraduate and graduate journalism students. There are three programs available. Contact the Foundation for further information on each program and how to apply. The total grants to individuals in over $770,000.

AC17-
FUND FOR INVESTIGATIVE JOURNALISM, INC.
1755 Massachusetts Avenue, NW No 423
Washington, DC 20036
(202) 462-1844

LOAN SUPPORT: JOURNALISM
Financial assistance is provided in the form of grants to journalists doing investigative stories who have a statement of intent to publish from a suitable outlet. Each year over 26 grants are awarded to individuals totaling $35,000.

AC18-
GLADYS C. ANDERSON MEMORIAL SCHOLARSHIP
American Foundation for the Blind
11 Penn Plaza, Suite 300
New York, NY 10001
(212) 502-7600

LOAN SUPPORT: MUSIC
The scholarship fund provides financial assistance to legally blind undergraduate women studying religious or classical music. Applicants must be U.S. citizens and have been accepted in a college or university program in religious or classical music.

AC19-
GLADYS STONE WRIGHT MEMORIAL SCHOLARSHIP
Women Band Directors National Association
C/o Gladys S. Wright
345 Overlook Drive
West Lafayette, IN 47906-1219

LOAN SUPPORT: MUSIC EDUCATION
If you are a female student majoring in music education with the intent of becoming an active band director, you are eligible for their annual award of $300.

AC20-
ADOLPH AND ESTHER GOTTLIEB FOUNDATION, INC.
380 West Broadway
New York, NY 10012
(212) 226-0581

LOAN SUPPORT: PAINTERS, SCULPTORS, PRINTMAKERS
Financial support is provided in the form of grants for painters, sculptors and printmakers. Emergency assistance funds are available as a result of an unexpected, catastrophic event. Applicants have two categories; at least 20 years in a mature phase of their art and applicants who have at least 10 years in a mature phase of their art. Each year over 45 grants are awarded to individuals totaling $361,00.

AC21-
JOHN SIMON GUGGENHEIM MEMORIAL FOUNDATION
90 Park Avenue
New York, NY 10016
(212) 687-4470

LOAN SUPPORT: ARTISTS
This fund provides fellowships to published authors, exhibited artists, researchers and others in the arts, humanities, social services and sciences. Candidates are asked to show evidence of achievement through publication or exhibition and, if applying in the arts, submit examples of work. Annually over 178 grants are awarded to individuals totaling $4,472,000.

AC22-
FANNIE LOU HAMER AWARD
Money for women/Barbara Deming Memorial Fund, Inc.
P.O. Box 40-1043
Brooklyn, NY 11240

LOAN SUPPORT: ARTISTS
Financial assistance is provided to women in the arts who are working to combat racism or celebrate women of color through educational or artistic projects. The Fund does not give educational assistance,

monies for personal study or loans, monies for dissertation or research projects, grants for group projects, business ventures or emergency funds. One grant is awarded each year for $1,000.

AC23-
HEDGEBROOK RESIDENCIES
Hedgebrook
2197 East Millman Road
Langley, WA 98620
(360) 321-4786

LOAN SUPPORT: WOMEN WRITERS
Financial support is provided for this program which offers a supportive and nurturing environment for women writers. Applicants must be U.S. citizens and do not need to have been previously published. Funds cover room and board, residencies range from 1 week to 3 months.

AC24-
INSTRUMENTAL MUSIC GRANTS
Alpha Delta Kappa
1615 West 92nd Street
Kansas City, MO 64114
(816) 363-5525

LOAN SUPPORT: MUSICIANS
Funding is provided for women musicians who are in graduate school or are in midcareer. A $5,000 grant and a $3,000 alternate grant are awarded every other year. The categories for the award change every two years.

AC25-
MYRNA M. JOHNSON MEMORIAL TRUST SCHOLARSHIP FUND
1515 Charleston Avenue
Mattoon, IL 61938

LOAN SUPPORT: MUSIC, ART
This program offers financial assistance to students who want to develop a career in music, art or nursing. Each year several awards are given averaging $800 per scholarship.

AC26-
JOHN ANSON KITTREDGE EDUCATIONAL FUND
C/o Key Trust Company of Maine
P.O. Box 1054
Augusta, ME 04330

LOAN SUPPORT: ARTISTS
Funds are provided in the form of grants to artists and scholars in very special circumstances. Grants are awarded for travel, research or for participation in other artistic or scholarly projects. Each year over 19 grants are given totaling $60,000.

AC27-
THE KLEBAN FOUNDATION, INC.
C/o Zissu, Stein & Mosher
270 Madison Avenue
New York, NY 10016
(212) 683-5320

LOAN SUPPORT: THEATER ARTS
Financial assistance is provided to support individual theatrical lyricists and librettists. Each year 2 grants are given totaling $100,000.

AC28-
KOUSSEVITZKY MUSIC FOUNDATION, INC.
200 Park Avenue
New York, NY 10166
(212) 351-3092

LOAN SUPPORT: MUSICIANS
Funds are provided in the form of commissions based on merit. Candidates must be composers of serious music, over 25 years of age,

have completed formal conservatory studies or have a B.A. from a recognized conservatory, college or university or demonstrated equivalent. Applicants must also have had music published, recorded and/or performed in public and be sponsored by a performing organization. Each year 9grants are awarded totaling $120,000.

AC29-
LIFETIME TV COMPLETION GRANT
Women in Film Foundation
6464 Sunset Boulevard, Suite 530
Los Angeles, CA 90028
(213) 463-6040

LOAN SUPPORT: VIDEO ARTS
This program offers financial assistance to fund completion of any approved video about women being produced and directed by women. Film topics are to be related to general humanitarian concern. Films must be broadcast quality and be available for exclusive 1 year or 4 year broadcast rights on Lifetime Cable. Ten awards are given each year and the dollar amount varies according to the project.

AC30-
ISRAEL MATZ FOUNDATION
14 East Fourth Street, Room 403
New York, NY 10012
(212) 673-8142

LOAN SUPPORT: WRITERS
Financial support is provided to indigent Hebrew writers, scholars, public workers and their dependents in Israel and the United States. Each year 26 grants are awarded totaling $37,000.

AC31-
MEDIA ARTS PROGRAM GRANTS
National Endowment for the Arts
Attn: Media Arts
Nancy Hanks Center

1100 Pennsylvania Avenue, NW, Room 720
Washington, DC 20506
(202) 682-5452

LOAN SUPPORT: MEDIA ARTISTS
Financial assistance is provided to encourage new work by artists of exceptional talent. Applications for institutional support should be requested from the NEA for specifics for grant monies. The amount awarded each year varies depending upon the nature of the funded project.

AC32-
MONEY FOR WOMEN FUND GRANTS
Money for Women/Barbara Deming Memorial fund, Inc.
P.O. Box 40-1043
Brooklyn, NY 11240

LOAN SUPPORT: ARTISTS
Financial assistance is provided for small support grants to aid in the completion of a feminist's unfinished artistic work. The Fund does not give loans or money for educational assistance, dissertation projects or research. Each year over 25 grants are awarded totaling $12,000.

AC33-
MUSICAL RESEARCH SOCIETY ENDOWMENT FOUNDATION, INC.
1115 Brookside Parkway
Bartlesville, OK 74006
(918) 333-6719

LOAN SUPPORT: MUSIC
Scholarship awards are granted to undergraduate and graduate students studying music at an accredited school, college or university. Candidates must also be U.S. citizens. The number of annual individual grants varies each year according to need and range from $100 to $5,000.

AC34-
MUSICIANS FOUNDATION, INC.
    200 West 55th Street, No. 41
    New York, NY 10019
    (212) 247-5332

LOAN SUPPORT: MUSICIANS
Funds are provided in the form of emergency financial assistance to professional musicians and their families. Each year over 74 grants are awarded totaling $105,000.

AC35-
NAOMI BERBER SCHOLARSHIP
    Graphic Arts Technical Foundation
    Attn: National Scholarship Trust Fund
    4615 Forbes Avenue
    Pittsburgh, PA 15213
    (412) 621-6941
    e-mail: ntsf@gatf.lm.com

LOAN SUPPORT: PUBLISHING
The purpose of this scholarship fund is to provide financial assistance to women preparing for a career in printing or publishing industries. Candidates must be high school seniors or already in college at an accredited school or university. The number of awards varies each year with individual amounts varying from $500 to $1,500. Awards are renewable for up to three years.

AC36-
NATIONAL SCULPTURE SOCIETY, INC.
    15 East 26th Street
    New York, NY 10010-1505
    (212) 889-6960

LOAN SUPPORT: SCULPTORS
Financial assistance is provided in the form of grants to encourage the creation and appreciation of sculpture throughout the U.S. Awards are

given to sculpture students. Each year over 23 awards are given totaling $13,000.

AC37-
NFPW FRESHMAN SCHOLARSHIP
>National Federation of Press Women, Inc.
>4510 West 89th Street, Suite 110
>Prairie Village, KS 66207
>(913) 341—165

LOAN SUPPORT: JOURNALISM
This scholarship program offers financial assistance to female high school students preparing to major in journalism upon entry into college. Candidates must plan to attend a college or university with a department of journalism and be planning to develop a career in the field of journalism. Each year one award is presented in the amount of no less than $500.

AC38-
VERNA ROSS ORNDORFF CAREER PERFORMANCE GRANT
>Sigma Alpha Iota Philanthropies, Inc.
>C/o Arlene Jospe Veron
>7 Hickey Drive
>Farmingham Centre, MA 01701

LOAN SUPPORT: MUSIC
This program is available to women who are members of Sigma Alpha Iota and need financial assistance to advance their study in music. Applicants may not have professional management. Several areas of music and music development are eligible to apply. An annual award of $2,000 is given.

AC39-
CISSY PATTERSON FELLOWSHIP
>American Press Institute
>Attn: Fellowship Program Coordinator

11690 Sunrise Valley Drive
Reston, VA 22091
(703) 620-3611

LOAN SUPPORT: JOURNALISM
Financial assistance is provided to women journalists wanting to attend an American Press Institute seminar. Women reporters or editors working on a newspaper with less than 25,000 circulation may apply. One award is given each year. The fellowship provides tuition, room, meals and a travel subsidy.

AC40-
POETRY SOCIETY OF AMERICA
15 Gramercy Park South
New York, NY 10003
(212) 254-9628

LOAN SUPPORT: POETS
Funds are provided in the form of awards and prizes to professional and student poets. Several awards are given for poems, prose or verse-drama. Each year 19 grants are awarded totaling $11,000.

AC41-
THE POLLOCK-KRASNER FOUNDATION, INC.
725 Park Avenue
New York, NY 10021
(212) 517-5400

LOAN SUPPORT: ARTISTS
This fund provides financial assistance to individual working artists of established ability. Painters, sculptors, graphic, mixed media and installation artists are encouraged to apply. The Foundation does not give grants to commercial artists, photographers, video artists, film makers, craft-makers, or students who are not working artists. Individual grant amounts are not known, grants to individuals total $1,000,000.

AC42-
THE POYNTER FUND
P.O. Box 625
St. Petersburg, FL 33731
(813) 893-8111

LOAN SUPPORT: JOURNALISM
Students majoring in journalism at the undergraduate or graduate level may apply to this annual scholarship/fellowship fund for financial aid. The number and amounts of awards varies according to need.

AC43-
P.T. BARNUM FESTIVAL JENNY LING COMPLETITION
P.T. Barnum Foundation, Inc.
120 Hawley Lane
Trumbull, CT 06611
(203) 381-6836

LOAN SUPPORT: MUSIC – VOCAL ARTISTS
Any female singer show has not reached professional status may apply for financial aid to this foundation. Applicants must be between the ages of 20 and 27 and be U.S. citizens. One award is given each year in the amount of $2,000.

AC44-
THE ROCKEFELLER FOUNDATION
1133 Avenue of the Americas
New York, NY 10036
(212) 869-8500

LOAN SUPPORT: ARTISTS
Funds are provided in the form of grants and fellowships to creative artists and scholars whose work strives to advance international and intercultural understanding in the United States. Each year over 424 grants are awarded totaling $7,700,000.

AC45-
R.L. GILLETTE SCHOLARSHIP
American Foundation for the Blind, Inc.
11 Penn Plaza, Suite 300
New York, NY 10001
(212) 502-7600

LOAN SUPPORT: MUSIC
The purpose of this fund is to provide financial assistance to legally blind undergraduate women studying the field of literature or music. Applicants must be U.S. citizens and enrolled in a 4 year baccalaureate program in either field. Two awards are given each year in the amount of $1,000 each.

AC46-
JULIUS RUDEL AWARD TRUST FUND
1800 West Magnolia Boulevard
Burbank, CA 91506

LOAN SUPPORT: OPERA
The purpose of this program is to provide financial assistance to students studying opera at the undergraduate or graduate level. Annual awards and individual amounts vary according to need.

AC47-
THE SHEARWATER FOUNDATION, INC.
C/o Alexander Nixon
423 West 43rd Street
New York, NY 10036

LOAN SUPPORT: HOLOGRAPHERS
Financial assistance is provided to support the advancement of the art of holography through grants to art holographers. Each year 4 grants are awarded totaling $40,000.

AC48-
SCHRIPPS HOWARD FOUNDATION

P.O. Box 5380
Cincinnati, OH 45201
(513) 977-3035

LOAN SUPPORT: JOURNALISM, BROADCASTING
This fund provides scholarships to professional print and broadcast journalists or students pursuing careers in these fields. Amounts vary each year according to need.

AC49-
JOHN F. AND ANNA LEE STACEY TESTAMENTARY TRUST
C/o Security Pacific National Bank
P.O. Box 3189, Terminal Annex
Los Angeles, CA 90051

LOAN SUPPORT: ARTISTS
Funds are available in the form of fellowships and scholarships to artists whose work is committed to classical or conservative tradition of western culture. Artists must be between the ages of 18 and 35 and be U.S. citizens.

AC50-
FRANCES SHAW FELLOWSHIP
Ragdale Foundation
1260 North Green Bay Road
Lake Forest, IL 60045
(708) 234-1063

LOAN SUPPORT: WRITERS
Funds are available to reward the writings of mature women. Candidates must be women who started their serious writing after the age of 55. The fellowship covers travel expenses and room and board at Ragdale in Lake Forest, Illinois.

AC51-
WILLIAM MATHEUS SULLIVAN MUSCIAL FOUNDATION, INC.

251 West 89th Street, Suite 10-B
New York, NY 10024
(212) 874-2372

LOAN SUPPORT: SINGERS
Funds are available to provide financial assistance to gifted professional singers. Applicants must have future engagements with a full orchestra. Over 142 grants have been awarded totaling $105,000.

AC52-
RICHARD J. & FLORENCE J. TENHOLDER TRUST
P.O. Box 332
Atchinson, KS 66002

LOAN SUPPORT: ART – THEATER
The purpose of this program is to provide scholarships for women seeking a degree in art or theater. Applicants must maintain a college GPA orf3.0 or higher to apply. Annual awards vary from $1,500 to $500.

AC53-
THANKS BE TO GRANDMOTHER WINIFRED FOUNDATION GRANTS
Thanks Be To Grandmother Winifred Foundation
P.O. Box 1449
Wainscott, NY 11975

LOAN SUPPORT: ARTISTS
Funds are provided as financial assistance to women and to encourage the creative activities of older women. Applicants must be at least 54 years of age and interested in developing and implementing projects, programs or policies that empower themselves as well as other women. The number of awards varies each year, grants range from $500 to $5,000.

AC54-
LUDWIG VOGELSTEIN FOUNDATION, INC.

P.O. Box 4924
Brooklyn, NY 11240
(718) 596-4925

LOAN SUPPORT: ARTS AND HUMANITIES
Financial assistance is available to aid individuals in the arts and humanities. No scholarships, student aid or faculty assistance is granted. Each year over 22 grants are given totaling $60,000.

AC55-
VIRGINIA VOLKWEIN MEMORIAL SCHOLARSHIP
Women Bank Directors National Association
C/o Gladys \s. Wright
345 Overlook Drive
West Lafayette, IN 47906

LOAN SUPPORT: BAND LEADER
The purpose of this scholarship program is to encourage women music majors to become band directors. Applicants must be enrolled in a college of education and working toward a degree in music education. One award is given each year in the amount of $300.

AC56-
WIFF FILM FINISHING FUND GENERAL AWARDS
Women in Film Foundation
6464 Sunset Boulevard, Suite 530
Los Angeles, CA 90028
(213) 463-6040

LOAN SUPPORT: WOMEN AND FILMS
Financial support is provided for women in the film industry who wish to complete film projects about women and make a positive statement about women. Applicants may be independent producers or nonprofit corporations and be producing an English speaking film. Grants are awarded up to $5,000. The number of awards given each year varies with the need and scope of the project.

AC57-
WOMEN'S JEWELERY ASSOCIATION SCHOLARSHIP
Women's Jewelry Association
333 B route 46 West, Suite B-201
Fairfield, NJ 07004
(201) 575-1445

LOAN SUPPORT: JEWELRY ARTIST
The purpose of this scholarship program is to provide financial assistance to women who are studying for a career in any area of the jewelry industry. Applicants must be planning to enroll in a jewelry related curriculum at an institution of higher learning in the U.S. The number of awards varies each year, with individual awards up to $1,000

OTHER RESOURCES

Financial security resulting from good job or career opportunities is one just one financial resource for women. Women also need to plan for financial security as they reach retirement age. Statistics have shown that in the past, women were limited in their education and information about retirement funds and investment funds. Being informed and actively planning for long term financial security is vital for any women to be secure during her retirement years.

The information provided in this section is meant to help each woman learn more about these beneficial resources. This is basic information of what and how you can invest your money with IRA's, mutual funds and stocks.

STRESS RESOURCE NETWORK
STOCK AND MUTUAL FUND RECOMMENDATIONS

To help you with your retirement or investment plans, The Stress Resource Network features a group of excellent stock recommendation and several very high quality mutual fund recommendations monthly on the web site.

These stocks and mutual funds are the collective choices of five leading stock analysts in the United States. If you would like to access information on these investments please go to the web site: www.stressresource.com.

Mutual Funds

Investing For Future Needs or Retirement

For millions of investors seeking an appreciation of their money (capital), the stock markets in the U.S. have for years been a primary way of attaining this appreciation. As a whole, equity securities (stocks) have generated a higher return on investments than almost any other investment alternative. Stocks represent ownership in a company. They give the owner or stockholder the right to share in both the company's profits (stock dividends) and its growth (the rising price of its stock). However, the stock market has its ups and down. Individual stocks can rise spectacularly one day and fall precipitously the next. Yet, stocks have outperformed all other types of investments including bonds, CDs and U.S. Government securities. They have outpaced inflation and have become a selected method of investment for thousands of people. Most individuals just entering the market ask the question "Can the dramatic ups and downs of individual stocks be avoided?" The answer to this question is a qualified yes. For the investor who is troubled by the gyrations in the market, mutual funds provide an excellent alternative to owning individual stocks. Mutual funds have the following advantages:

- A mutual fund by its very nature is diversified. Its assets are invested in the securities of a large number of companies. This broad ownership has a tendency to provide some stability in the ups and downs of the market.

- Investment requirements in many mutual funds are liberal: this allows even the smallest investor to get started. A small investor can, through investment in a mutual fund, participate in the growth of major corporations. Investments of this kind would otherwise be unavailable to the small investor because of their high per share prices.

- Mutual funds provide professional management for your investments.

- The fund is responsible for accounting and record keeping for your account – irrespective of its size.

The efficiency and stability of mutual funds is evidenced by the fact that over 40 million people have selected them as their investment vehicle. Today there are over three trillion dollars invested in mutual funds. The popularity of the mutual fund has increased over the past 20 years. Mutual funds make it easy and less costly for investors, particularly small investors, to meet their needs for capital growth, income and/or income preservation. A mutual fund brings the benefits of diversification and money management to the individual investor.

This provides an opportunity for financial success that was once available only to the wealthy.

The mutual fund is a simple concept. It is a fund or company that pools money from many investors to invest in a variety of different securities. Investments may be stocks, bonds, money market securities or some combination of these. Those securities are professionally managed on behalf of the shareholders. Each investor holds a pro rata share of the portfolio and is entitled to participate in the company's earnings through dividends and profits when securities are sold.

To help you select mutual funds, the authors have provided descriptions of the characteristics of various funds. These descriptions are organized by the type of securities purchased by each fund: equities, fixed income, money market instruments or some combination of these.

Because mutual funds have specific investment objectives: growth of capital, safety of principal, current income or tax-exempt income, you can select one fund or any number of different funds to help meet specific goals. Basically, mutual funds fall into three categories:

- **Equity funds** invest in shares of common stock.

- **Fixed Income Funds** invest in government or corporate securities, which offer fixed rates of return.

- **Balanced Funds** invest in a combination of both stocks and bonds.

Growth Funds

Growth funds invest in stocks for growth rather than current income. They are considered conservative in their approach because they usually invest in established companies to achieve long term growth. They are not likely to invest in smaller companies which provide short term substantial gains but present the risk of substantial declines. Growth funds invest in well established companies where the company itself and the industry in which it operates are thought to have good long term growth potential. Growth funds provide low current income, but the investor's principal is more stable than it would be in a more aggressive growth fund. While the growth potential may be less over the short term, many growth funds have superior long term performance records.

Although growth funds are conservation, they are still relatively volatile. They are suitable for growth oriented investors, but not investors unable to assume risk or who are dependent on maximizing current income from their investments.

Aggressive Growth Funds

These funds seek to provide maximum growth of capital with secondary emphasis on dividend or interest income. They invest in common stocks with a high potential for rapid growth and capital appreciation. They often invest in the stocks of small emerging growth companies. Generally they provide low current income because these companies usually reinvest their profits in their business paying small dividends or none at all. Aggressive growth funds incur higher risks that growth funds in an effort to obtain higher growth. These funds may invest in a broad range of industries or concentrate on one or more industry sectors. Some use borrowing, short-selling, options and other speculative strategies to leverage their results.

Aggressive growth funds are suitable for investors who can afford to assume the risk of potential loss in value of their investment in the hope of achieving substantial and rapid gains. They are not suitable for investors who must conserve their principal or who must maximize current income.

Growth and Income Funds

Growth and income funds seek long-term growth of capital as well as current income. The investment strategies used to reach these goals vary among funds. Some invest in a dual portfolio consisting of growth stocks and income stocks, or a combination of growth stocks, stocks paying high dividends, preferred stocks, convertible securities or fixed income securities such as corporate bonds and money market instruments. Others may invest in growth stocks and earn current income by selling covered call options on their portfolio stocks. Growth and income funds have moderate principal stability and good potential for current income and growth. They are suitable for investors who can assume some risk to achieve growth of capital, but who also want to maintain a moderate level of current income.

Fixed Income Funds

The goal of fixed income funds is to provide high current income and protect an investor's capital. Capital growth is of secondary importance. Fixed income funds invest primarily in bonds and preferred stocks. These funds invest in corporate bonds or government backed mortgage securities having a fixed rate of return

Since bond prices fluctuate with changing interest rates, there is some risk involved despite the fund's conservative nature. When interest rates rise, the market price of fixed income securities declines and so will the value of the income fund's investments. Conversely, in periods of declining interest rates, the value of fixed income funds will rise and investors will enjoy capital appreciation as well as income.

Fixed income funds offer a higher level of current income than money market funds. They have more price stability than funds that invest in stock. Within the fixed income category, there are variations in principal stability and in divided yields. High yield funds, which seek to maximize yield by investing in lower rated bonds have less principal stability than fixed income funds that invest in higher rated, but lower yielding securities. Some fixed income funds seek to minimize risk by investing exclusively in securities whose timely payment of interest and principal is backed by the full faith and credit of the U.S. Government. These include securities issued by the U.S. Treasury, the Government National Mortgage Association ("Ginnie Mae" securities), the Federal National Mortgage Association ("Fannie Maes") and Federal Home Loan Mortgage Corporation ("Freddie Macs").

Fixed income funds are suitable for investors who want to maximize current income and who can assume a degree of capital risk in order to do so. Always carefully read the fund's prospectus to learn if a fund's investment policy regarding yield and risk coincides with your own objectives.

Retirement Accounts

Increasingly over the last years, the future of the social security program has come under scrutiny by both the President and members of Congress. A current general debate is going on about what to do with surplus funds coming from the first balanced budget in many years. Included are discussions "whether to use these surplus funds to 'fix' social security." There is continuing uncertainty over the stability of social security as a retirement program. Therefore, looking at other retirement possibilities is necessary. There are a series of other private retirement programs that can be used to supplement the Social Security Retirement Benefits Program or replace it. For these reasons, the importance of Individual Retirement Accounts has been greatly accelerated over the past few years. Information provided here on private retirement accounts may assist you in evaluating the various private retirement programs options open to you.

Individual Retirement Account (IRA)

The Individual Retirement Account (IRA) was set up by the tax code 20 years ago to allow women (and men) to put away money for their retirement. To encourage this kind of savings, the code gives

IRA holders two tax breaks. First, if you qualify, you can invest up to $2,000 a year into an IRA if you are single, $4,000 a year if married. If you are married and both you and your spouse have earnings from taxable compensation, you can each invest $2,000 a year into separate IRAs. If your spouse doesn't have earnings from taxable compensation, the total you can place into your IRA and the spousal IRA is $2,250. Whether you are married or single, if your earnings from taxable compensation are less than $2,000, then your deduction is limited to the amount of your taxable compensation.

To contribute to an IRA, you have to be under age 70 ½ on December 31 of the year you make a contribution. You must have earnings from taxable compensation which includes wages, salaries, bonuses, earnings from self-employment and similar revenues. Not included is income from interest, dividends and other passive investments. You won't pay any tax on the IRA earnings until you begin taking the money out of the account.

Meeting additional qualifications, a second tax break allows you to deduct your IRA contributions from your current income, whether you itemize deductions or not. This account is called a contributory Individual Retirement Account. A contributory Individual Retirement Account is a savings arrangement set up under the tax code providing a tax shelter for the IRA income. Meeting these qualifications allows you to deduct the 'contributions from other income' on your tax return, even if you don't itemize deductions on your return. A contributory IRA is a smart investment even if you can't deduct the deductions because the IRA earnings are not taxed until they are taken out of the account. Whether you deduct your IRA contributions or not, the money in the account grows tax deferred. This means you don't have to declare the IRA income on your tax return. Since earnings are not taxed until taken from the account, your money grows faster than it would in a regular savings account.

A rollover IRA is an account containing funds coming from an employer retirement plan. It can contain the cash-out value of employer pension plans, funds from 401(k) plans, 403(b) plans and others. When you retire, it is advisable to roll the money you receive from these retirement plans over into an IRA. This procedure avoids heavy taxes on the distribution and allows you to take control over your own money. Besides retirement, other situations could result in distribution of funds from an employer retirement plan. These include changing jobs, termination of the employer plan and disability. When changing jobs, you may want to place your money in a "conduit IRA." A conduit IRA is a holding account to "rollover" funds from one employer plan to another. If you receive a distribution of this kind, you can roll over part or all of the funds into one (or more) conduit IRA(s). Funds can stay in this account until you are ready to roll over those funds into a new employer's plan. The conduit IRA must be made up of only those assets received from the first employer's plan plus gains and earnings on those assets. The funds can't be mixed with other income.

IRAs have to be set up with an IRA custodian recognized as qualified by the Treasury Department to handle IRA funds. A custodian can be a bank, a brokerage house, a mutual fund company or an insurance company. You can move your funds from one custodian to another at any time. You do not have to place money into your IRA every year for the account to be valid. In any year, you can put in nothing or less than the maximum. The value of the investment in your IRA is for long term retirement funds, so the more you can invest the better your retirement security. For income tax purposes, it is valuable to know you may be able to deduct all of your contributions, part of them, or none of them, depending on your circumstances. If you and your spouse, if married, are not covered by an employer's retirement plan, you may be able to deduct the entire amount. If you are covered by an employer's retirement plan, the amount you can deduct depends on your income level. If you are entitled to deduct your IRA contributions, you can deduct them whether or not you itemize your deductions.

You can invest funds from the IRA into just about anything: stocks, bonds, mutual funds, bank accounts, etc. Since this is money to be invested for a long time – choose an investment which will grow. The growth needs to cover annual inflation and yield a good return on your investment. Probably the best choice is a growth-type equity mutual fund that does not charge annual fees. You can get excellent investment suggestions from the IRA custodian. Except for emergencies, you have to leave the money in the IRA until you are at least 59 ½ years old. If you do decide to take out some or all of your money before that age, you will pay a 10% federal penalty plus an additional state penalty. For example, California, adds on a 2 ½ % penalty. If you contribute to an IRA for 20 years, you can accumulate about $100,000 if single, $200,000, if married. Contribute for 30 years and the numbers jump to $250,000, if single, and $500,000, if married. Get started now and stick with it!

Keogh Plans

A Keogh plan is a type of qualified retirement plan designed for the individual who is either self-employed or the sole owner of a non-incorporated business. The main difference between a Keogh plan and an IRA is the contribution limit. Although exact contribution limits depend on the type of Keogh plan, in general, a self-employed individual may contribute 25% of her self-employed income or a maximum of $30,000 to a Keogh plan each year and deduct that amount from taxable income. With a limited partnership, the partner owning more than 10% of the capital or profit sharing qualifies for a Keogh plan.

Keogh plans are intended for self-employed individuals and their employees. Self-employed means a sole proprietorship or partner in a partnership. If the self-employed individual has a Keogh plan and she has employees, the employees must be covered under the plan. If an employee works 1,000 hours or more each year and has worked for the company more that three years, the employee qualifies for the Keogh plan. Self-employment income may not include dividends, interest, or capital gains from investments. Whatever contribution the employer makes to her own account must also be made to the employee's account.

Like an IRA, the Keogh plan offers an individual a chance for savings to grow free of taxes. Taxes are not paid until the person begins withdrawing funds from the plan. Participants in Keogh plans are subject to the same restrictions on distribution as IRAs, namely distributions cannot be made without a penalty before age 59½ and distributions must begin before age 70½. Any person taking a distribution from her Keogh plan before age 59½ is subject to all taxes due and a 10% early distribution fee. At retirement, there are two options for distribution of funds. The first, a lump sum pay out allows you to income average the amount, reporting 20% of the total amount each year for five year. The second is a monthly pay out which is regarded as ordinary income for income tax purposes.

If an individual has her own self-employment income, and a full-time job elsewhere where she is an employee and is covered under the company retirement plan, she may also have her own Keogh plan. She just can't use any of the income from where she is an employee to count toward her self-employment income. If, for some reason, (such as termination, company going out of business, etc.) you received a lump sum pay out, have a Keogh plan and are not 59½, you must roll the lump sum pay out money into an IRA within 60 days or pay taxes on it. Once it is in the IRA, it is covered by all the rules regarding IRAs. If you don't roll it over fast enough into an IRA, you will be subject to the 10% premature distribution (penalty tax) charge.

There are three types of Keogh plans. All types limit the maximum contribution to $30,000 per year. Additional constraints may be imposed depending on the type of plan you choose. Setting up a Keogh plan is significantly more involved than establishing an IRA. Any competent financial firm, bank or insurance company will be able to help you set up a Keogh plan.

The Roth IRA

The Taxpayer Relief Act of 1997 created the Roth IRA. The Roth IRA has broad rules of eligibility. The most attractive feature of the Roth IRA is the potential for accumulating retirement savings not taxed upon withdrawal. Rules for penalty-free early withdrawals for certain qualified expenses other than retirement also make assets in the IRA more accessible. As a result of the new tax act, there are three different individual retirement accounts to plan and save for your future.

Some benefits of the new Roth IRA are:
- Distributions are free from federal income taxes if taken after age 59½, or in the event of death or disability, as long as the account has been funded for at least five years.
- Early withdrawals are free from both penalties and federal income taxes if the five-year rule is met and the withdrawals are used to pay for qualifying first-time house purchases (subject to a lifetime limit of $10,000).
- There are no age limitations – individuals can continue to make contributions after age 70½.
- No mandatory withdrawals are required during the account-holder's lifetime.
- Contributions to a Roth IRA are not tax-deductible; however, **the account earnings grow tax-free**.
- Withdrawals are also tax-free if the account has been funded for five years and you are at least 59½ or you qualify for an exception.
- Exceptions are allowed for first-time home purchases (with a $10,000 lifetime limit), or disability or death.

Generally, joint income tax filers who have an adjusted gross income not exceeding $150,000 per year, and single income tax filers who have an adjusted gross income not exceeding $95,000 per year, may contribute up to $2,000 of compensation annually. You can convert your current IRA to a Roth IRA if you are single or you and your spouse jointly have "modified adjusted gross income" not exceeding $100,000 in the year you two can convert. The traditional IRA must be distributed (subject to ordinary income tax) then rolled over into the Roth IRA. Even with non-qualified withdrawals, you enjoy a tax break because you withdraw the already taxed contributions first. Only if you take out more than you contributed will you be subject to ordinary income taxes. Also there may be a 10% early-withdrawal penalty tax. So, this IRA gives flexibility to withdraw funds in an emergency or for non-retirement needs.

The use of a Roth IRA may mean giving up a traditional IRA tax deduction now. In the long run it may provide significantly greater after tax retirement savings. Instead of deferring taxes, the Roth IRA can eliminate them. The higher the tax bracket in retirement, the greater the return earned on the IRA assets; the longer the money is invested, the greater the advantage of the Roth IRA. With a traditional IRA, the more your assets grow, the more taxes you will owe when you take money out. With the Roth IRA, taxes are paid at your current rate before the assets grow significantly. When you retire and start withdrawals, you will keep all the money you have earned, without paying any federal income taxes. The Roth IRA also offers a special opportunity to preserve IRA assets for your heirs. With a Roth IRA, you are not required to begin minimum distributions after age 70½, as is required with a traditional IRA. Your money can continue growing tax free as long as you live. You can also make additional contributions as long as you have earned income.

If you expect your tax bracket to be lower in retirement than it is today, you may come out ahead with a tax deductible traditional IRA. The 1997 tax law has expanded the availability of deductible IRAs in two ways:

- First, the new law is gradually raising the income limits for deductible contributions for people who participate in employer sponsored retirement plans.
- Second, individuals not participating in a retirement plan, but whose spouses do, can now deduct IRA contributions up to $2,000 a year. The ability to take these deductions phases out with adjusted gross incomes between $150,00 and $160,000 on a joint return.

If you are not eligible for either a deductible IRA or a Roth IRA, keep in mind, contributing to a nondeductible traditional IRA is still a smart move. Your money will grow tax deferred until you make withdrawals. You may have the opportunity to convert your traditional IRA to a Roth IRA so you can take advantage of tax free growth and distributions. To be eligible to convert, your adjusted gross income on either a joint or individual return must be $100,000, or less (not counting the amount you convert) in the year of conversion. If you are married, but filing separately, you are not eligible to convert. The 10%

early withdrawal penalty tax does not apply when you convert an account. But you will pay ordinary income taxes on any previously deducted IRA contributions and on all earnings.

Keep in mind, it may be better to have a Roth IRA if:
- You project earning a high rate of return on your IRA investments and/or you will be in a higher tax bracket at retirement. With the traditional IRA, the more your assets grow, the more tax you will pay when you take distributions.
- With the Roth IRA, you will pay taxes at your current rate. Your assets keep growing and you keep all of what the IRA assets have earned.
- Your adjustable gross income is sufficiently high so that you are not able to make tax deductible contributions to the traditional IRA.
- If you are age 70½ or older, still working and wish to continue setting aside retirement funds. The Roth IRA is also particularly appropriate for estate planning. Because there are no mandatory withdrawals during your lifetime and distributions may not be subject to income tax, the Roth IRA can potentially help you pass more assets to your heirs.

Simplified Employee Pension Plans

Simplified employee pension plans (SEPs) enable smaller businesses to provide retirement benefits with lower costs and less reporting requirements than other qualified retirement plans. SEPs are not qualified plans as are profit sharing and money purchase plans, yet several rules are comparable. A simplified employee pension plan is a group of individual retirement accounts maintained for employees. Under a typical SEP plan, the employer establishes IRA accounts for all participating employees. The employer contributes to the IRAs, subject to the contribution limits for SEP plans not IRAs. Employer contributions are limited to 15% of salary, up to $22,500 per year. The company's contributions are not counted as current income for the employee. SEP plans provide an effective retirement planning option for employees. It also provides the employer with an effective tax shelter.

A SEP can also be funded by employees through a pre-tax salary reduction. Under a salary reduction SEP, employees can elect to defer up to $9,500 of their salary to the plan. Employee funding further reduces costs to the employer. This salary reduction feature enables a SEP to work much like a 401(k) plan. In fact, some refer to the SAR-SEP as a mini-401(k) plan.

For employees, SEPs offer substantially higher contribution limits than regular IRAs. This enables employees to accumulate more for retirement. The benefits are fully vested as they are contributed. This makes a SEP completely portable. Departing employees can roll their SEP balances into an IRA or have them transferred to a retirement plan sponsored by their new employer.

SEPs are great for sole proprietors. You can contribute as much as 15% of your before-tax compensation or $22,500, whichever is less, to your own account every year. If you have eligible employees, you must contribute the same percentage of their pay for them. They don't contribute a nickel. A SEP probably is not the best choice if you have any part-time employees and do not wish to make a contribution for them. The definition of eligible employees is so broad, you may end up making contributions for all your workers.

Simplified Employee Pension Plans are far less costly than the more complicated retirement plans. Contributions are fully tax deductible to employers. They are flexible, inexpensive and easy to maintain. Money may be withdrawn without penalty after age 59½. Individuals must start distributions no later than April 1 of the year following the year they turn 70½. All distributions are taxed as ordinary income.

To determine the retirement plan best for you, consult a financial consultant, review your options and then make decisions based on your needs. Don't wait! Retirement age comes faster than most of us plan.

Stock Market/Bond Investments

A Stock Exchange is an organized market for buying and selling financial instruments (securities) which including stocks, options, and futures. Most stock exchanges have specific locations where commissioned intermediaries called *brokers* conduct trading, e.g., buying and selling securities. Securities are not always traded on a stock exchange. Some are traded *over the counter,* without a specific central trading location.

Major stock exchanges in the United States include the New York Stock Exchange (NYSE) and the American Stock Exchange (AMEX), both in New York City. Nine smaller regional stock exchanges also operate in Boston, Massachusetts; Cincinnati, Ohio; Chicago, Illinois; Los Angeles, California; Miami, Florida; Philadelphia, Pennsylvania; Salt Lake City, Utah; San Francisco, California; and Spokane, Washington. In addition, most of the world's industrialized nations have stock exchanges. Among the larger international exchanges are those in London, England; Paris, France; Milan, Italy; Hong Kong, China; and Tokyo, Japan.

In 1794, brokers in New York began trading stocks in a park. Two years later the traders moved indoors and in 1817 they formed the New York Stock and Exchange Board, drew up a formal constitution, and moved closer to its present Wall Street location. By 1863, when it changed its name to the New York Stock Exchange, the exchange was trading the stocks and bonds of the major industrial and railroad corporations of the day. As New York City became the financial center of the United States during the 19th century, the New York Stock and Exchange Board became one of the nations most important financial trading centers.

During the second half of the 19th century, New York City emerged as the primary financial center of the United States and the New York Stock Exchange (NYSE) became its most successful exchange. Its members concentrated on trading the securities of the largest corporations. Today, the NYSE is often referred to as the *big board* because it lists more major corporations than any other exchange in the world.

In 1908, other brokers formed an organization called the New York Curb Agency. In 1911 this exchange changed its name to the New York Curb Market Association and in 1953 the name was changed to the American Stock Exchange (AMEX Trading on the AMEX is accomplished by stock brokers placing orders with members of the exchange called specialists who generally specialize in specific stocks and who negotiate and arrive at a price for the stock.

NASDAQ, is an acronym for the National Association of Securities Dealers Automated Quotation system, one of the largest markets in the world for the trading of stocks. In 1998, over 5,500 companies were listed on NASDAQ--more than on any of the other stock exchanges in the United States, including the New York Stock Exchange (NYSE) and the American Stock Exchange (AMEX). The majority of companies listed on NASDAQ are smaller than most of those on the NYSE and AMEX. NASDAQ has become known as the home of new technology companies, particularly computer and computer-related businesses.

Trading on NASDAQ is initiated by stock brokers acting on behalf of their clients. These brokers place orders with certain NASDAQ brokers, called *market makers,* who concentrate on trading specific stocks. The broker and the market maker negotiate to reach a price for the stock.

Unlike other stock exchanges, NASDAQ has no central location where trading takes place. Instead, its market makers are located all over the country and make trades by telephone and via the Internet. Because brokers and market makers trade stocks directly instead of on the floor of a stock exchange, NASDAQ is called an *over-the-counter* market. The term over-the-counter refers to the direct nature of the trading, as in a store where goods are handed over a counter.

The National Association of Securities Dealers started the NASDAQ system in 1971 to organize the over-the-counter market. Until then, the over-the-counter market had few regulations, and traders often took unfair advantage of individual investors. Today companies who list their stock with NASDAQ must meet certain standards and the rules for trading stocks are strictly enforced.

The Importance of Stock Exchanges

Stock exchanges serve important roles in national economies. They encourage investment by providing places for buyers and sellers to trade *securities* such as stocks, bonds, and other financial instruments. Companies issue stocks and bonds to obtain capital to expand their business.

Corporations issue new securities in the primary market (as opposed to the secondary market, where securities are bought and sold), usually with the help of investment bankers. In the primary market, corporations receive the proceeds of stock sales. Thereafter, they are not involved in the trading of stocks. Owners of stocks trade them on a stock exchange in the secondary market. In the secondary market, investors, not companies, earn the profits or bear the losses resulting from their trades. Stock exchanges encourage investment by providing this secondary market. By allowing investors to sell securities, exchanges increase the safety of investing.

Stock exchanges also encourage investment in other ways. They protect investors by upholding rules and regulations that ensure buyers will be treated fairly and receive exactly what they pay for. Exchanges also support state-of-the-art technology and the business of brokering, which both help traders to buy and sell securities quickly and efficiently.

How Stocks Are Traded

Stocks are shares of ownership in companies. People who buy a company's stock are entitled to dividends, or shares of any profits. A company can list its stock on only one major stock exchange, though options on its stock may be traded on another. Each exchange establishes requirements that a company must meet to have its stock listed. The different exchanges tend to attract different kinds of companies. Smaller exchanges typically trade the stock of small, emerging businesses, such as high-tech companies.

Stock brokers must be registered with the exchange in which they trade. Most brokers belong to brokerage firms. Brokerage firms maintain staffs of many brokers, each has experience in the trading of securities of certain companies or those of particular economic sectors, high tech, utilities, or transportation businesses, for instance. Brokerage firms also tend to trade in the stocks of specific companies, and therefore keep inventories of the stocks of those companies. To become a member of an exchange, a firm must register its brokers by buying *seats* for them. A seat is simply a right to trade on an exchange. Member firms have the right to vote on exchange policy and must also arbitrate in disputes among customers. In larger exchanges, seats may sell for several hundreds of thousands of dollars.

Brokerage firms that pay high membership fees to stock exchanges have opportunities to make large profits trading in the stock of very successful businesses. They also risk losing large amounts, and therefore charge their clients higher prices than do smaller firms. In part, large companies use large brokerage firms and list on large exchanges because of the potential losses possible to those trading their securities.

Stock Specialists and The Exchange Floor

At a stock exchange, certain brokers specialize in trading certain stocks. These specialists operate on the *floor* of the exchange, the area where all trading takes place. Brokers pack the floor during trading. They often use bargaining and negotiation to execute larger trades, and they take bids for the highest prices. The process is noisy and frantic, and brokers use hand signals to communicate above the chaos.

Specialists sometimes act as dealers--instead of as intermediaries, or brokers--trading directly in the stocks of their firms' accounts. For this reason, they are also known as broker-dealers. They do this when market trends favor the trading of certain stocks and investors have not ordered enough trades to clear the market, or balance supply and demand. Floor traders always trade only in stocks owned by their brokerage firms and never act as intermediaries.

Other brokers, called floor brokers (not the same as floor traders), do not act as specialists. They instead handle large orders to buy or sell stocks of specific companies. Clients place such orders with brokerage firms, who then contact their floor brokers. After receiving orders, floor brokers take them to specialists to arrange the trades. Floor and specialist brokers negotiate trades as representatives of clients and companies. In smaller trades, orders commonly go directly to specialist brokers via computer.

Institutional brokers specialize in bulk purchases of securities, including bonds, for institutional investors. Institutional brokers generally charge their clients a lower fee per unit than do brokers who trade for individual investors.

Trading In Stocks

Stock certificates represent shares of ownership in a corporation. When individuals or organizations purchase shares in a company, they receive stock certificates indicating the number of shares they have acquired. Such certificates entitle them to shares in the profits of the company, which are paid out at intervals, in the form of dividends. Besides a claim on company profits, stockholders are entitled to share in the sale of the company if it is dissolved. They may also vote in person or by proxy for corporation officers, inspect the accounts of the company at reasonable times, vote at stockholders' meetings, and, when the company issues new stock, have priority to buy a certain number of shares before they are offered for public sale.

The price of stocks depends on the market forces of supply and demand. Because companies only issue limited numbers of shares, sellers can demand higher prices if there are more buyers of a given stock than there are sellers. Conversely, lack of demand for a stock will result in its trading for a lower price.

Stocks are generally negotiable; stockholders have the right to assign or transfer their shares to another individual. Unlike a sole proprietor or partner in a business, a stockholder is not liable for the debts of the corporation in which he or she has invested. The most the stockholder can lose if the company fails is the amount of her or his investment. According to the New York Stock Exchange, about 47 million people in the U.S. owned stocks in publicly held corporations in 1985.

Common and Preferred Stock

The rights and benefits of a stockholder vary according to the type of stock held. The two main stock categories are called common and preferred. Financial loss or gain can be greater with common stock than with preferred stock. Holders of common stock have residual equity in a corporation; that is, they have the last claim on the earnings and assets of a company, and may receive dividends only at the discretion of the company's board of directors and after all other claims on profits have been satisfied. For example, if the company is dissolved, stockholders share in what is left only after all other claims have been settled. Dividends and equity conferred by common stocks have no fixed dollar value; holders of such stock, therefore, benefit more from a company's prosperity or lose more from a company's adversity than do holders of preferred stocks.

If a stock has preferred dividends, the owner is entitled to receive a fixed dividend rate before any dividends are distributed to other stockholders; if a stock has preferred assets, the stockholder receives a share of the proceeds from the dissolution of a company before holders of non-preferred stock do. Some stocks have both preferred dividends and preferred assets. Stock with first preference in the distribution of dividends or assets is called first preferred or sometimes preferred A; the next is called second preferred or preferred B, and so on.

Although holders of preferred stock may have to forego a dividend during a period of little or no profit, this is not true for two types of preferred stock. One is cumulative preferred stock, which entitles the owner to the accumulation of past-due and unpaid dividends; the other is protected preferred. When the latter is issued, the corporation, after paying the preferred-stock dividends, places a specified portion of its earnings into a reserve, or sinking, fund in order to guarantee payment of preferred-stock dividends.

Two other stock categories are redeemable stock and convertible stock. The former is preferred stock issued with the stipulation that the corporation has the right to repurchase it. The latter stock endows the stockholder with the option of exchanging preferred stock for common stock under specific conditions, such as when the common stock reaches a certain price, or when the preferred stock has been held for a particular time.

Although most stockholders have the right to vote at their meeting, thus participating in corporate management, some stocks specifically prohibit this. Although such nonvoting stocks may be among any of those previously mentioned, at least one kind of stock issued by a corporation must be endowed with the voting privilege. Voting stock may not be changed to nonvoting stock without the stockholder's consent. So-called vetoing stock is between voting and nonvoting stock; its holders may vote only on specific questions. Before voting by proxy was permitted, independent stockholders influenced the management of a company. After it was authorized, however, company managers and directors holding a stock minority obtained enough proxies from absentee stockholders to outvote any opposition, thus perpetuating their control.

Capital Stock

The term *capital stock* denotes the equity or claims of all the stockholders and bondholders of a corporation, as an entity in the total assets of the corporation. Capital stock differs from capital in that the latter includes both the profits earned and retained by the corporation and the amounts invested by the stockholders. A corporation may be chartered with a capital stock of $10,000; if it earns profits of $5,000 and retains these earnings, its total capital is raised to $15,000.

Trading In Other Securities

Exchanges trade in all forms of securities. While the general operations of exchanges apply to all securities trading, there are some differences. In particular, trades in non-stock securities are often managed by financial intermediaries other than brokers.

Bonds

Stocks provide the means for a corporation to raise money. An alternative method is the issuing of bonds. Bonds are evidence of loans; stocks are evidence of ownership. As a financial claim against a company, *bonds take precedence over all types of stock.* Thus, they are a safer investment than stocks, especially in times of deflation. Stocks, however, are usually the better investment during inflation because they represent ownership of assets that will probably rise in value as fast as or faster than general prices. Because the dollar value of bonds is fixed, they cannot serve as a hedge against inflation as do common stocks.

Bonds provide a way for companies to borrow money. People who invest in bonds are lending money to a company in return for yearly interest payments. Bonds are traded separately from stocks on exchanges. Most bonds are bought in large quantities by *institutional investors*--large investors such as banks, pension funds, or mutual funds.

How Bonds Work

A bond's *principal,* or *face value,* represents the amount of the original loan that is to be repaid on the bond's *maturity* date. The interest that the issuer agrees to pay each year is known as the *coupon,* a term derived from the obsolete practice of attaching coupons that could be redeemed for interest payments to the bottom of the bond certificate. The interest rate, or coupon rate, multiplied by the principal of the bond provides the dollar amount of the coupon. For example, a bond with an 8 percent coupon rate and a principal of $1,000 will pay annual interest of $80. In the United States, the usual practice is for the issuer to pay the coupon in two semiannual installments.

Kinds of Bonds

A number of different kinds of bonds offer variations on this basic formula. Some types of bonds provide alternative interest structures. A *zero-coupon bond* does not make periodic interest payments. The bondholder realizes interest by buying the bond substantially below its face value. A *floating-rate bond* has an interest rate that is changed periodically according to an established formula. There also may be provisions that allow either the issuer or the bondholder to alter a bond's maturity date. A *callable bond* entitles the issuer to pay off the principal prior to the stated maturity date. Similarly, the owner of a *putable bond* can force the issuer to pay off the principal before the maturity date. A *convertible bond* gives the bondholder the right to exchange the bond for shares of the issuer's common stock at a specified date.

Issuing Bonds

Bond issuers can sell bonds directly through an auction process or the use investment banking services. The investment banker buys the bonds from the issuer and then sells them to the public.

Corporate bonds are issued by private utilities, transportation companies, industrial enterprises, or banks and finance companies. These corporate bonds can be divided into two additional categories: *mortgage bonds,* which are secured by the issuer's assets, and *debentures,* which are backed only by the issuer's credit. Most companies try to establish a financial structure based on a combination of stocks, representing distributed ownership, and bonds, representing debt obligations. A company that raises funds by issuing bonds is said to be *leveraged.* Because bondholders are paid at a set rate regardless of profits, this approach increases the potential for profit to stockholders but also increases the level of financial risk.

The U.S. government issues bonds through the Department of the Treasury. These bonds, known as *government securities,* are backed by the unlimited taxing power of the federal government. Federal agencies and government-sponsored enterprises also issue bonds of their own. Generally, all of these federal bonds are considered to be among the safest investments.

Municipal bonds are issued by state and local governments and other public entities, such as colleges and universities, hospitals, power authorities, resource recovery projects, toll roads, and gas and water utilities. Municipal bonds are often attractive to investors because the interest is exempt from federal income taxes and some local taxes. There are two types of municipal bonds: *general obligation bonds* and *revenue bonds.* Like a government security, a general obligation municipal bond is secured by the issuer's taxing power. Revenue bonds are used to finance a particular project or enterprise. Income generated by the project provides funds to pay interest to bondholders.

Investing In Bonds

From an investor's perspective, stocks offer a higher potential return if profits rise, but bonds are generally a safer investment. Stock dividends are paid out of company profits, while bond interest payments are made even if the company is losing money. If a corporation goes bankrupt, bondholders must be paid before stockholders. Nonetheless, risks are associated with investing in bonds. Because most bonds offer a fixed rate of return, a bond with a low coupon rate will be less valuable if interest rates rise to the point that the investor's money could be more profitably invested elsewhere. If the inflation rate rises in relation to the coupon rate, the value of the investor's return will be reduced.

The value of bonds also will vary due to changes in the *default risk,* or credit rating, of bond issuers. If the issuer of the bond is unable to make timely principal and interest payments, the issuer is said to be in default. Bonds issued by the U.S. government and by most federally related institutions are considered free of default risk. For other issuers, the risk of default is gauged by credit ratings assigned by four nationally recognized rating companies: Moody's Investor Service, Standard and Poor's Corporation, Duff & Phelps Credit Rating Company, and Fitch Investors Service. Bonds that these rating companies place in the highest categories are known as *investment-grade bonds.* Bonds that are not assigned an investment grade rating are called *junk bonds.* These bonds have a higher degree of credit risk but also offer a higher potential yield.

Options

Options are traded on many U.S. stock exchanges, as well as over the counter. Options writers offer investors the rights to buy or sell--at fixed prices and over fixed time periods--specified numbers of shares or amounts of financial or real assets. Writers give *call options* to people who want options to buy. A call option is the right to buy shares or amounts at a fixed price, within a fixed time span. Conversely, writers give *put options* to people who want options to sell. A put option is the right to sell shares or amounts at a fixed price, within a fixed time span. Buyers may or may not opt to buy, or sellers to sell, and they may profit or lose on their transactions, depending on how the market moves. In any case, options traders must pay premiums to writers for making contracts. Traders must also pay commissions to brokers for buying and selling stocks on exchanges. Options trading is also handled by options clearing corporations, which are owned by exchanges.

Futures

Futures contracts are also traded on certain U.S. exchanges, most of which deal in commodities such as foods or textiles. Futures trading works somewhat like options trading, but buyers and sellers instead agree to sales or purchases at fixed prices on fixed dates. After contracts are made, the choice to buy or sell is not optional. Futures contracts are then traded on the exchanges. Commodities brokers handle this trading.

Futures and options traders often judge market trends by monitoring compiled indexes and averages of stocks, usually organized by industry or market ranking. Among the most closely watched U.S. indexes are the Dow Jones averages and Standard & Poor's.

The Over The Counter Market

Thousands of companies do not list their stock on any exchange. These stocks make up the over-the-counter (OTC) market. The largest of these companies are traded on the NASDAQ stock market. NASDAQ stands for National Association of Securities Dealers Automated Quotation system. The member countries of the European Union (EU) have an equivalent market, called EASDAQ. NASDAQ is a shareholder in and provides operational advice to EASDAQ. NASDAQ and EASDAQ operate like exchanges, but instead of having central locations, their specialists are located at computer terminals all over the United States and Europe. Trades are carried out primarily online through computer networks. Companies that list their stock on NASDAQ and EASDAQ are generally smaller than those listed on centralized exchanges. However, some large high-tech corporations also trade in this market.

Regulation of Exchanges

Investors lost faith in the stock markets partly because of unfair practices and a lack of strict rules in the exchanges before and during the 1920s. Large investors were able to cheat small investors because no laws existed to forbid these practices. To remedy this, the federal government passed the Securities Act of 1933, which regulated new securities issues, and the Securities Exchange Act of 1934, which created the Securities and Exchange Commission (SEC). The SEC regulated stock exchanges and required companies to disclose information that could help potential investors evaluate its stock. The exchanges also adopted stricter rules after the crash to protect investors and prevent another crash. In 1938, the Maloney Amendment set up the National Association of Security Dealers to regulate the over-the-counter market. From the end of World War II in 1945 through the 1960s, new regulations, combined with a generally strong economy, encouraged investors to return to the stock markets.

In 1945, the U.S. Federal Reserve Board established that all borrowing to purchase securities should be covered by a margin, or percentage of the actual market price. Between 1945 and the 1980s, investors were required to make initial margin deposits ranging from 50 to 100 percent of market value of the securities in which they wished to trade. The National Association of Securities Dealers and the

NYSE subsequently established their own minimum margin maintenance requirements.

In the 1970s, the SEC, Congress, and other government and private institutions were instrumental in establishing further regulations on stock exchanges. In 1972, the SEC developed a Consolidated Tape System, which provides trading information to investors from all exchanges and the OTC market. In 1975, Congress created the National Market System, which provides that prices of stocks and bonds from all exchanges be available simultaneously at each exchange. This encourages competition among exchanges. A particular provision of this system also requires that all commissions be competitively negotiated rather than fixed. In response to this provision, many discount brokerage firms have opened. Discount brokers provide less financial advice to investors and therefore can charge lower commission fees than were available under the fixed-fee system. Ultimately, the enforced competition among exchanges has opened them to smaller investors who want to trade without paying for, or being limited by, various exclusive exchange privileges.

Recent Developments

In the 1980s and 1990s, stock exchanges have achieved new levels of market efficiency through their increased use of fast and inexpensive computers. Computer networks have also allowed exchanges to connect to each other, both within countries and internationally. Electronic exchanges have fostered the growth of an open, global securities market.

Although the overall value of the U.S. stock market has increased substantially since 1946, occasional recessions have occurred during recent decades. In 1987, the stock market experienced a brief, but major crash, marked by a more than 20 percent decline, over one day's trading, in the S & P index of stock prices.

Economists potentially linked the 1987 U.S. crash to the use by traders of new, low-margin stock index futures markets. Exchanges had opened these markets earlier in the decade in response to increased margin requirements on securities trading. Traders in the late 1980s began to sell their securities on the new futures markets when stock prices dropped. After the government released pessimistic economic forecasts in October of 1987, traders rushed to sell their stocks on the futures markets with low margin backing. After the crash, the government established new rules for higher margin requirements across markets, including futures trading. It is unknown, however, whether new regulations, or competitive deregulation, will make exchanges less volatile in the future.

Different Kinds of Accounts

A brokerage house offers clients a number of different accounts. The most common are cash accounts, margin accounts and option account. Basically, these accounts represent different levels of credit and trustworthiness of the account holder as evaluated by the brokerage house.

A *cash account* is the traditional brokerage account. If you have a cash account, you may make trades, but you have to pay in full for all purchases by the settlement date. This is becoming somewhat less common, especially in the age of internet trading; most brokers are stricter and require good funds in the account before they will accept an order to buy. Just about anyone can open a cash account, although some brokerage houses may require a significant deposit before they open the account.

A *margin account* is a type of brokerage account that allows you to take out loans against securities you own. Because the brokerage house is essentially granting you credit by giving you a margin account, you must pass their screening procedure to get one. Even if you don't plan to buy on margin, note that all short sales have to occur in a margin account. If you have a margin account, you will also have a cash account.

An *option account* is a type of brokerage account that allows you to trade stock options. To open this type of account, your broker will require you to sign a statement that you understand and acknowledge the risks associated with derivative instruments. This is actually for the broker's protection and came into place after brokers were successfully sued by clients who had large losses in options and then claimed they were unaware of the risks. It's my understanding that otherwise an option account is identical to a margin account.

Some Investment Considerations

Learn the basics before you begin. If you want to build an investment portfolio to achieve your lifetime financial goals, you should learn the basics of investing. This information is designed to help you do that. Additional information can be obtained from investment companies and securities dealers. There are large lists of these dealers in the Yellow Pages of your telephone directory and available on the Internet (search: mutual funds or securities dealers). These companies all provide excellent educational materials, in addition to information kits and stock and bond prospectuses. A call to their toll-free number puts you in touch with a person qualified to answer your questions and explain the various features of the securities they offer. You can also refer to financial publications such as magazines of newspapers that feature articles on securities.

Invest regularly. There are many advantages to maintaining a regular investment program. Keep in mind the ability to reach long-term goals depends upon a long-term plan. A discipline of regular monthly investments in quality stocks or bonds provides an easy way to grow your investments over time and take advantage of market cycles. It also ensures that your investment program stays on track toward your goals, month in and month out.

Diversify your investments. As you go along, if possible, spread your investments over several different types of stocks. This increases your chances of reaching your goals, and increases the stability of your investments.

Give your investments time to grow. Develop an understanding of performance and the patience that is necessary to reach long-term goals. Don't expect overnight results. Rely on good judgement in evaluating both the long and short-term performance of the securities you select, and then give your investment time to grow.

Learn to accept market fluctuations. Unlike bank CD's and passbook savings, stocks are not federally insured and return on your investment is not guaranteed. In fact the value of your investment fluctuates over time; it increases or decreases according to movement of the financial markets. Investors concerned over this should take heart: the movement of the markets is what produces the opportunity for investment growth.

Differences in Investments for Men and Women. In many ways men's and women's investment planning issues are the same. Both need to start early, be informed and keep up a steady pattern of investments. Both should identify the purpose of each dollar invested, i.e., emergency fund, college education, retirement, etc. and invest accordingly.

There are differences in women's life patterns, however, that suggest they should take investing for the future even more seriously than men do, especially when it comes to retirement planning. This is born out by the fact that 75% of the elderly poor are women. More than 60% of working women do not have a pension. Women who have primary childcare responsibilities lose pension benefits often because of disruption to their income while their children are growing up. In addition, women start saving later in life than men and tend to save less (1.5% of their income vs. 3.1% for men). They also make more conservative investment decisions than men.

One of the problems that women face in investing money and accumulating wealth is that there is a general "lack of knowledge" about how to pick the appropriate investments among women. Over

50% of all women fail to determine their financial goals and, to them saving becomes a priority.

There are other factors that are different for women that make good money management a necessity:

- Women live longer than men. The average life expectancy is 7 years longer for women than for men (79 years for women, 72 years for men).

- Health care needs for women are likely to be greater than for men, and they require more money to cover them.

- Elderly women outnumber elderly men 3 to 2.

- Women are more likely than men to have lifelong responsibilities for children.

Invest prudently. Don't rush to invest. If you receive a lump sum payment of any kind, don't rush to invest. Sound investing requires careful study. Consider putting your funds in a money market while you explore your options. Invest the money only when you feel ready. Otherwise, you may make bad decisions based on poor information or high-pressure sales tactics.

Understand your investment. It's important that you research thoroughly each investment you are considering. Don't take your broker's word that a particular investment fits your financial needs. Ask to receive information about the investment product in writing. Make sure you understand the information you are given. Compare that information with your own financial goals. This will help you decide if the investment is right for you.

The most detailed source of information on an investment product is a document called a "prospectus." Unfortunately, most prospectuses are too long and technical to understand easily. Don't feel you have to read every word of the prospectus. Pick out the information that will help you decide if the product is right for you.

Review the new account agreement carefully. Most brokerage firms require customers to sign a new account agreement. Review this document carefully. It may affect your legal rights. Do not sign the new account agreement unless you understand it and agree with its terms and conditions.

Read your account statement. Review your account statement to make sure it contains only those investments that you have authorized. If you don't recognize an investment listed on your statement, raise the problem immediately with your broker. Ask questions about the meaning of unfamiliar terms and abbreviations that appear on your account statement. Notice how your investments have performed since you received your last statement. Keep track of how much your investments are costing you in commissions and fees. If you don't find this information on your account statement, ask your financial professional to give you these figures in writing. Do not work with a financial professional who is unwilling or who claims to be unable to provide this information.

Broker/Investment Advisor Considerations

Investigate your investment professional. Take care when choosing the person who will be handling your investment. Meet with more than one potential broker. Ask each broker about his or her investment experience, professional background and education. Check out your investment professional with the securities division of your state's government. This will tell you if he or she has an established record of disciplinary actions, negative arbitration decisions, or civil litigation judgements. For the telephone number of the securities division in your state, contact the North American Securities Administrators Association (NASAA) at 202-737-0900. Or, call the toll-free hotline operated by the National Association of Securities Dealers (NASD) at (800) 289-9999. If you are working with an investment advisor, ask to see both parts of his or her Form ADV. Part One provides you with the advisor's disciplinary history. Part Two presents his or her method of compensation, education, areas of expertise, investment strategies, and business methods.

Make sure the broker/advisor you select trades those securities if you regularly trade options or bonds or mutual funds. Even if the broker trades them, they may not be traded over the Internet and may incur a higher than desirable commission. Be sure and check those commissions.

Ask questions. You control your money, even if you hire an expert to help you manage it. You have every right to ask a financial professional why he or she is making a certain recommendation. If you are uncertain about a security, cost or commission, ask questions until you fully understand. Remember the following points:

- It may seem impolite but you have the right to full disclosure of all information regarding a security; all costs of any investment, including all commissions, markups, and fees. Ask your broker about commission rates, annual fees, transaction costs, and any other expenses. No fee should show up on any confirmation slip or account statement that you haven't been told about in advance.

- Your broker/advisor may encourage you to buy certain stocks, bonds, mutual funds, or other investments that bring extra income to him or her through higher commissions, bonuses, or points toward a vacation or other contest prize. When a product is sold as part of a contest or because it earns additional compensation, you run the risk that the broker/advisor's interest in the contest or extra compensation may be placed ahead of your interest in getting the best investment. Understanding that makes you a smarter investor. So don't be afraid to ask your broker if he or she is participating in any sales contests, or receiving any other form of special compensation for the products he or she recommends.

- Keep a running tally of the commissions and fees you have paid for your investments. If transactions appear on your account statement that you did not authorize, or if there appears to be excessive trading, contact a supervisor immediately to have the situation corrected. Don't wait to see how the investments perform, as waiting may be viewed as giving approval to the unauthorized trades. Therefore, be on guard if you notice an excessive number of transactions in your account. This activity may generate additional commissions without giving you any benefit.

- Some brokerage firms offer accounts with no commissions. Instead, the investor pays an annual fee based on a fixed percentage of assets in return for which he or she gets a certain number of trades each year. Such a fee arrangement presumably removes the broker's incentive to sell high-commission products or to increase the frequency of trades in order to earn commissions. Under a fee arrangement, brokers get paid regardless of what you buy, and their income rises only if your assets do. So ask your broker whether it makes sense for you to pay by the transaction or whether a flat-fee arrangement may be appropriate. If you do choose a commission arrangement, try negotiating for lower percentages. After all, the lower the fee you negotiate, the less you have to earn before you start making a profit on your investments.

- If you have a problem with a broker/investment advisor, talk to his or her boss. Put your complaint in writing. Keep written records of all conversations. Ask for written explanations.

Begin your investment program as soon as possible. Begin small if necessary JUST begin. Continue your investments regularly, even if they are small. You will be amazed at how small investments become larger than larger again. So begin today!

Economic And Financial Glossary

A - B

Acquisition: The purchase of one company by another.

Arbitrage: A form of hedged investment to capture slight differences in the prices of two related securities--for example, buying gold in London and selling it at a higher price in New York.

Balanced budget: A budget is balanced when receipts equal current expenditures.

Balance of payments: The difference between all payments, for some categories of transactions, made to and from foreign countries over a set period of time. A *favorable* balance exists when more payments are coming in than going out; an *unfavorable* balance, when the reverse is true. Payments may include gold, the cost of merchandise and services, interest and dividend payments, money spent by travelers, and repayment of principal on loans.

Balance of trade (trade gap): The difference between exports and imports, in both actual funds and credit. A nation's balance of trade is *favorable* when exports exceed imports and *unfavorable* when the reverse is true.

Bear market: A market in which prices are falling.

Bearer bond: A bond issued in bearer form rather than being registered in a specific owner's name. Ownership is determined by possession.

Bond: A written promise or IOU by the issuer to repay a fixed amount of borrowed money on a specified date and generally to make payments of interest at regular intervals in the interim.

Bull market: A market in which prices are on the rise.

C

Capital gain (loss): An increase (decrease) in the market value of an asset above (below) the price originally paid, at the time the asset is sold.

Commercial paper: An extremely short-term corporate IOU, generally due in 270 days or less. Available in face amounts of $100,000, $250,000, $500,000, $1,000,000 and combinations thereof.

Convertible bond: A corporate bond (see below) that may be converted into a stated number of shares of common stock. Its price tends to fluctuate along with fluctuations in the price of the stock and with changes in interest rates.

Corporate bond: A bond issued by a corporation. The bond normally has a stated life and pays a fixed rate of interest. Considered safer than the common or preferred stock of the same company.

Cost of living: The cost of maintaining a standard of living measured in terms of purchased goods and services. Inflation typically measures changes in the cost of living.

Cost-of-living benefits: Benefit payments whose sum in current dollars is regularly adjusted for changes in the cost of living.

Credit crunch (liquidity crisis): A situation in which cash for lending is in short supply.

D

Debenture: An unsecured bond backed only by the general credit of the issuing corporation.

Deficit spending: Government spending in excess of revenues, generally financed with the sale of bonds.

Depression: A long period of economic decline when prices are low, unemployment is high, and there are many business failures.

Derivatives: Financial contracts whose values are based on, or *derived* from, the price of an underlying financial asset or price--for example, a stock or an interest rate.

Devaluation: The official lowering of a nation's currency, decreasing its value in relation to foreign currencies.

Discount rate: The rate of interest set by the Federal Reserve that member banks are charged when borrowing through the Federal Reserve System.

Disposable income: Income after taxes that is available to persons for spending and saving.

Dividend: Discretionary payment by a corporation to its shareholders, usually in the form of cash, stock shares, or other property.

Dow Jones Industrial Average: An index of stock market prices, based on the prices of 30 leading companies on the New York Stock Exchange.

E - F

Econometrics: The use of statistical methods to study economic and financial data.

Federal Deposit Insurance Corporation (FDIC): A U.S. government-sponsored corporation that insures accounts in national banks and other qualified institutions.

Federal Reserve System: The entire banking system of the U.S., incorporating 12 Federal Reserve banks (one in each of 12 Federal Reserve districts), 24 Federal Reserve branch banks, all national banks, and state-chartered commercial banks and trust companies that have been admitted to its membership. The governors of the system greatly influence the nation's monetary and credit policies.

Full employment: The economy is said to be at full employment when everyone who wishes to work at the going wage-rate for his or her type of labor is employed. This excludes only the small amount of unemployment due to the time it takes to switch from one job to another.

G

Golden parachute: Provisions in the employment contracts of executives guaranteeing substantial severance benefits if they lose their position in a corporate takeover.

Government bond: A bond issued by the U.S. Treasury considered the safest security in the investment world. Government bonds are divided into 2 categories--those that are not marketable and those that are. *Savings Bonds* cannot be bought and sold once the original purchase is made. These include the familiar Series EE bonds. You buy them at 50 percent of their face value, and when they mature 12 years later, they can be cashed in for 100 percent of face value. Another type, Series H, are not discounted, but issued in amounts of $500, $1,000, $5,000, and $10,000 and pay their interest in semiannual checks. Marketable bonds fall into several categories. *Treasury Bills* are short-term U.S. obligations, maturing in 3, 6, or 12 months. They are sold at a discount of the face value, and the minimum denomination is $10,000. *Treasury Notes* mature in up to 10 years. Denominations currently range from $500 to $10,000 and up. *Treasury Bonds* mature in 10 to 30 years. The minimum investment is $1,000.

Greenmail: A company buying back its own shares for more than the going market price to avoid a threatened hostile takeover.

Gross Domestic Product (GDP): The market value of all goods and services that have been bought for final use during a year. It became the official measure of the size of the U.S. economy in 1991, replacing the *Gross National Product (GNP),* which had been in use since 1941. GDP covers workers and capital employed within the nation's borders. GNP covers production by American residents, regardless of where it takes place. The switch aligned the U.S. with most other industrialized countries, making exact comparisons easier.

H - L

Hedge fund: A flexible investment fund for a limited number of large investors (the minimum investment is typically $1 million). Hedge funds use almost all investment techniques, including those forbidden to mutual funds, such as short-selling and heavy leveraging.

Hedging: Taking 2 positions whose gains and losses will offset each other if prices change, in order to limit financial risk.

Individual Retirement Account (IRA): A self-funded retirement plan that allows employed individuals to contribute up to a maximum yearly sum toward their retirement while deferring tax on the interest until retirement.

Inflation: An increase in the level of prices.

Insider information: Important facts about the condition or plans of a corporation that have not been released to the general public.

Interest: The cost of borrowing money.

Investment bank: A financial institution that arranges the initial issuance of stocks and bonds and offers companies advice about acquisitions and divestitures.

Junk bonds: Bonds issued by companies with low credit ratings. They typically pay relatively high interest rates because of the fear of default.

Leading indicators: A series of 11 indicators from different segments of the economy used by the Commerce Department to predict when changes in the level of economic activity will occur.

Leverage: The extent to which a purchase was paid for with borrowed money. Amplifies the potential gain or loss for the purchaser.

Leveraged buy-out: An acquisition of a company in which much of the purchase price is borrowed, with the debt to be repaid from future profits or by subsequently selling off company assets. Typically carried out by a small group of investors, often including incumbent management.

Liquid assets: Assets that include cash or those items that are easily converted into cash.

M

Margin account: A brokerage account that allows a person to trade securities on credit. A **margin call** is a demand for more collateral on the account.

Money supply: The currency held by the public, plus checking accounts in commercial banks and savings institutions.

Mortgage-backed securities: Created when a bank, builder, or government agency gathers together a group of mortgages and then sells bonds to other institutions and the public. The investors receive their proportionate share of the interest payments on the loans as well as the principal payments. Usually, the mortgages in question are guaranteed by the government.

Municipal bond: Issued by government units such as states, cities, local taxing authorities, and other agencies. Interest is exempt from U.S.--and sometimes state and local--income tax. *Municipal Bond Unit Investment Trusts* offer a portfolio of many different municipal bonds chosen by professionals. The income is exempt from federal income taxes.

Mutual fund: A portfolio of professionally bought and managed financial assets in which you pool your money along with thousands of other people. A share price is based on net asset value, or the value of all the investments owned by the funds, less any debt, and divided by the total number of shares. The major advantage, relative to investing individually only in a small number of stocks, is less risk--the holdings are spread out over many assets and if one or two do badly the remainder may shield you from the losses. *Bond Funds* are mutual funds that deal in the bond market exclusively. *Money Market Mutual Funds* buy in so-called "Money Market"--institutions that need to borrow large sums of money for short terms. Usually the individual investor cannot afford the denominations required in the "Money Market" (e.g., treasury bills, commercial paper, certificates of deposit), but through a money market mutual fund he or she can take advantage of these instruments when interest rates are high as well as get the diversification advantages. These funds often offer special checking account advantages.

N - R

National debt: The debt of the national government as distinguished from the debts of the political subdivisions of the nation and private business and individuals.

National debt ceiling: Total borrowing limit set by Congress beyond which the national debt cannot rise. This limit is periodically raised by congressional vote.

Option: A type of contractual agreement between a buyer and a seller to buy or sell shares of a security. A **Call** option contract gives the right to purchase shares of a specific stock at stated price within a given period to time. A **Put** option contract gives the buyer the right to sell shares of a specific stock at stated price within a given period of time.

Per capita income: The nation's total income divided by the number of people in the nation.

Prime interest rate: The rate charged by banks on short-term loans to large commercial customers with the highest credit rating.

Producer price index: A statistical measure of the change in the price of wholesale goods. It is reported for 3 different stages of the production chain: crude, intermediate, and finished goods.

Program trading: A term for trading techniques involving large numbers and large blocks of stocks, usually used in conjunction with computer programs. Techniques include *Index Arbitrage*, in which traders profit from price differences between stocks and futures contracts on stock indexes, and *Portfolio Insurance*, which is the use of stock-index futures to protect stock investors from large losses when the market drops.

Public debt: The total of the nation's debts owed by state, local and national government. Increases in this sum, reflected in public-sector deficits, indicate how much of the nation's spending is financed by borrowing rather than by taxation.

Recession: A mild decrease in economic activity marked by a decline in real GDP, employment, and trade, usually lasting 6 months to a year, marked by widespread decline in many sectors of the economy.

Risk arbitrage: The purchase and/or selling of the securities of companies expected to be involved in takeover situations, in order to realize a profit.

S

Savings Association Insurance Fund (SAIF): Created in 1989 to insure accounts in savings and loan associations up to $100,000.

Seasonal adjustment: Statistical changes made to compensate for regular fluctuations in data that are so great they tend to distort the statistics and make comparisons meaningless. For instance, seasonal adjustments are made in midwinter for a slowdown in housing construction and for the rise in farm income in the fall after the summer crops are harvested.

Short-selling: Borrowing shares of stock from a brokerage firm and selling them, hoping to buy the shares back at a lower price, return them, and realize a profit from the decline in prices.

Stagnation: Economic slowdown in which there is little growth in GDP, capital investment, and real income.

Stock: *Common Stocks* are shares of ownership in a corporation; they are the most direct way to participate in the fortunes of a company. There can be wide swings in the prices of this kind of stock. *Preferred Stock* is a type of stock on which a fixed dividend must be paid before holders of common stock are issued their share of the issuing corporation's earnings. Prices are higher and yields lower than comparable bonds. However, preferred stock is attractive to corporate investors because 85% of preferred dividends are tax exempt to corporations. *Convertible Preferred Stock* can be converted into the common stock of the company that issued the preferred. This stock has the advantage of producing a higher yield than common stock, it also has appreciation potential. *Over-the-Counter Stocks* are not traded on the major or regional exchanges, but rather through dealers from whom you buy directly. *Blue Chip* stocks are so called because they have been leading stocks for a long time. *Growth* stocks are those whose earnings are expected to grow over several years.

Stock-index futures: A futures contract is an agreement to buy or sell a specific amount of a commodity or financial instrument at a particular price at a set date in the future. Futures based on a stock index (such as the Dow Jones Industrial Average) are bets on the future price of that group of stocks.

Supply-side economics: A school of thinking about economic policy holding that lowering income tax rates will inevitably lead to enhanced economic growth and general revitalization of the economy.

T - Z

Takeover: Acquisition of one company by another company or group by sale or merger. A friendly takeover occurs when the acquired company's management is agreeable to the merger: when management is opposed to the merger, it is an unfriendly takeover.

Tender offer: A public offer to buy a company's stock: usually priced at a premium above the market.

Zero coupon bond: A corporate or government bond that is issued at a deep discount from the maturity value and pays no interest during the life of the bond. It is redeemable at face value.

Request For Funding Application

Please fill in the information below and use the appropriate section for the type of financial aid you are requesting. **Only one section (Education, Business, Arts and Culture, General Welfare or Other) may be filled out with each application.**

Name _____

Address _____

City/State/Zip _____

Telephone Number _____

Occupation _____

Employer _____

Many loan opportunities are available based on personal background. The following request for information will help search for funds specific to your needs. For example, funds are available through several ethnic groups. American Indian, Jewish, Latina, and Italian are a few of the groups supporting women. If you are interested in searching through ethnic supported funding, please describe your background. Please describe any special features about yourself you believe will assist in this search.

Age _____ Single _____ Married _____ Widowed _____

Student: Full time _____ Part time _____ Military Service : Which branch _____

If either parent was in the military, please provide information on area of service.

___

Application For Educational Support

Please state the degree level and educational field for which you are seeking funds. Indicate the state in which you intend to study.

___

If this request is for research, travel, etc., please state the type of research, any affiliating institutions, purpose of research, travel, etc.

___

Application For Business Support

Describer the business and its purpose. Indicate if this is a new or existing business.

___

Where will the business be located? State, county, city, home based or office based.

_____
_____
_____
_____

Application For Arts and Culture Support

In what profession or craft do you seek financial support? What is the purpose of the support? (Project, showing, travel, education, etc.)

_____
_____
_____
_____
_____
_____

Application For General Welfare Support

Describe the need for financial support. Is the money needed for short term or long term support, please describe.

_____
_____
_____
_____
_____
_____
_____

Mail your application with the processing fee of $39.95 to:

Stress Resource Network
699 Peters Avenue
Pleasanton, CA 94566

Please make checks payable to STRESS RESOURCE NETWORK

Or use the convenient form below to charge the Request for Funding. Please allow three weeks for processing your request.

Charge Information

Name _____

Card Number _____

MC _____ Visa _____ Expiration Date _____

Signature Approval _____

INDEX

The index is arranged in alphabetical order by subject matter, program interest or student classification. Each entry is subdivided by type of entry; i.e. Arts & Culture, Awards, Business, Fellowships, Grants, General Welfare, Loans, Scholarships. Within each entry type the numbers cited refer to an entry within the category, not a page number. I.E. **Grants:** 1, 23, 89 refers to Grant #1, #23, #89.

Accounting: **Grants,** 65, **Scholarships,** 16, 24-25, 34, 58, 187
Accounting career: **Fellowships,** 11, 36, 54
Aeronautics: **Grants,** 114
Aerospace: **Fellowships,** 92
Agricultural colleges: **Scholarships,** 36
American Legion Auxiliary: **Loans,** 22, **Scholarships,** 14
Animal science: **Scholarships,** 15
Architecture: **Fellowships,** 78
Armenian students: **Scholarships,** 74
Artist, book : **Arts & Culture,** 5, **Grants,** 15
Artist, visual: **Arts & Culture,** 2, 11
Artists: **Arts & Culture,** 2-3, 8, 11, 21-22, 25-26, 41, 44, 49, 53-54, **General Welfare,** 36, **Awards,** 6
Arts: **Awards,** 14
Arts & Humanities: **Awards,** 14, **Grants,** 75
Astronomy: **Grants,** 14, **Fellowships,** 14. 65, 67
Atmospheric research: **Grants,** 115
Atmospheric sciences: **Scholarships,** 19-20, 121, 151, **Fellowships,** 12, 65
Aviation: **Scholarships,** 10, 61, 183

Band leader: **Arts & Culture,** 55
Banking: **Fellowships,** 28
Beauty, recognition: **Awards,** 23
Behavioral research: **Loans,** 19
Behavioral sciences: **Grants,** 139, **Fellowships,** 21, 23, 29, 37, 50, 67, 81
Biochemistry: **Scholarships,** 88
Biology: **Fellowships,** 31-32, 47-48, 72, 73
Biomedical research: **Loans,** 19, 21

Biomedical sciences: **Grants,** 25, 84, 100, 120, 137, 139, 147
Blind students: **Scholarships,** 22, 99, **Fellowships,** 13
Blue Star Mothers: **General Welfare,** 9
Bond Investments: *Page* 401+
Book artists: **Arts & Culture,** 5, **Grants,** 15
Bowlers: **Awards,** 5
Boxers, professional: **General Welfare,** 75
Broadcast industry: **General Welfare,** 10, 16
Broadcasters: **Arts & Culture,** 10, 48
Burial funds: **General Welfare,** 29, 39, 58
Business: **Awards,** 14, **Loans,** 9, 15-16, 24, 27-28, **Scholarships,** 24, 25, 38, 113, 154
Business careers: **Fellowships,** 7, 20, 34, 45, 53, 80
Business loans: **Business,** 1-34
Business loans, general: **Business,** 2, 7, 9, 11-15, 18-21, 24-25, 29, 31-34
Businesses, disadvantaged: **Business,** 16, 22-23
Businesses, health care: **Business,** 30

Cancer patients: **General Welfare,** 69
Cancer research: **Grants,** 7-8, 148
Cardiovascular research: **Grants,** 11
Catholic students: **Loans,** 13, **Scholarships,** 123
Catholic teachings: **Grants,** 103
Chemistry: **Scholarships,** 19, 88, 176, **Fellowships,** 12, 31-32, 65, 67, **Awards,** 4
Child development: **Grants,** 29, 141
Child welfare: **General Welfare,** 24
China studies: **Grants,** 34
Chinese students: **Grants,** 34, **Scholarships,** 40
Chiropractic medicine: **Scholarships,** 78, 92
Christian women: **General Welfare,** 60
Coal miners: **General Welfare,** 15
Communications: **Scholarships,** 145, **Fellowships,** 52, 74
Composers: **Arts & Culture,** 8
Computer science: **Fellowships,** 12, 26, 31-32, 61, 65, 67, 78, 89, **Grants,** 35, 52, **Scholarships,** 2, 19, 33, 41, 130
Construction: **Scholarships,** 140

Deaf students: **Fellowships,** 49
Dental sciences: **Grants,** 119
Dentistry: **Loans,** 12, 17-19, **Scholarships,** 33, 46, **Fellowships,** 2, 26
Diabetes research: **Grants,** 48-49
Directors, film: **Arts & Culture,** 13, 28, 56
Disabilities: **Grants,** 80
Disadvantaged businesses: **Business,** 16, 22-23
Disaster funds: **Business,** 10
Doctoral dissertations: **Awards,** 18

Eagle: **General Welfare,** 20
Earth sciences: **Grants,** 101
Economic justice: **Grants,** 58, **Business,** 1
Economic/social: **Business,** 4
Economic studies: **Grants,** 32, 142
Economics: **Scholarships,** 93, 154
Education: **Grants,** 1-3, 21, 37, 39, 54, 60, 71, 83, 102, 131, 147, 156, **Loans,** 1, 3, 8, 13, 23, 25, **Scholarships,** 1, 4, 6, 8-9, 12, 17-18, 26, 32-33, 35-37, 40, 42-43, 45, 47-52, 57, 64, 67-68, 70, 72, 83, 91, 110, 127-128, 131-132, 134-136, 140, 152-153, 155, 159. 161-162, 166-168, 174, 184, 186, 191, **Fellowships,** 1, 5, 13, 26-27, 39, 49, 52-53, 63, 66, 70, 75, 77, 83-85, 91
Emergency funds: **General Welfare,** 41
Energy research: **Fellowships,** 35, 52
Engineering: **Grants,** 9, 30, 35, 43, 51-53, 63, 146, **Awards,** 4, **Loans,** 7, **Scholarships,** 2, 19, 21, 38-39, 41, 62, 84-85, 100, 104-106, 111, 118, 124, 130, 148-150, 172, 177, 181-182, **Fellowships,** 12, 18, 21, 26, 31-32, 41, 51-52, 56, 61, 67-69, 73, 76, 78, 89, 92
Environmental sciences: **Grants,** 52-53, **Scholarships,** 19, **Fellowships,** 12, 21, 42, 47, 67, 76, 79
Exchange programs: **Grants,** 41

Faculty, training: **Awards,** 3
Federal service families, **Scholarships,** 76
Film & television: **Grants,** 50, 104, **Awards,** 20-21
Finance: **Grants,** 65, **Scholarships,** 38
Fire fighters: **General Welfare,** 20, **Scholarships,** 125
Food service: **Grants,** 59, **Scholarships,** 69, 170
Future Homemakers of America: **Awards,** 11

General welfare: **General Welfare,** 11, 23, 26, 30, 35, 41-42, 55, 62, 64-65, 70
Geographic education: **Fellowships,** 90
Geological research: **Grants,** 26, 78, **Fellowships,** 3, 65
Geology: **Scholarships,** 23, 188
Girl Scouts: **Scholarships,** 86
Girls, Inc.: **Scholarships,** 87
Government studies: **Grants,** 82, **Fellowships,** 33
Greek students: **Scholarships,** 51, 173

Hawaiian students: **Scholarships,** 103
Health care: **General Welfare,** 14, **Loans,** 17, **Scholarships,** 144
Health care businesses, **Business,** 30
Health care law: **Fellowships,** 40
Health information management: **Scholarships,** 28, **Fellowships,** 22
Health physics: **Fellowships,** 15, 68
Health science: **Scholarships,** 165
Hearing impaired: **General Welfare,** 1, 27
Heart disease research: **Grants,** 12
Hispanic models: **Awards,** 25
Hispanic students: **Scholarships,** 141
Holographers: **Arts & Culture,** 47
Home economics: **Awards,** 10, **Scholarships,** 82
Homeopathic medicine: **Grants,** 159
Home purchase: **Loans,** 26
Hotel management: **Scholarships,** 170
Hydrology: **Scholarships,** 19-20, 151, **Fellowships,** 12

Italian families: **General Welfare,** 30
Italian students: **Scholarships,** 83, 146

Jewelry artists: **Arts & Culture,** 57
Jewish students: **Scholarships,** 71, 80
Jockeys: **General Welfare,** 31, 67
Journalism: **Scholarships,** 59, 81, 98, 112, **Arts & Culture,** 14, 16, 17, 37, 39, 42, 48

Knights of Columbus: **Loans,** 13, **Scholarships,** 116, **Fellowships,** 24
Korean culture: **Grants,** 91
Korean students, **Scholarships,** 115

Landscape architecture: **Scholarships,** 96
Latina students: **Scholarships,** 120, 156, 158
Law enforcement: **Grants,** 77, **Fellowships,** 45, 62
Law, health care: **Fellowships,** 40
Lawyers: **Grants,** 148
Librarians: **General Welfare,** 33, **Grants,** 42
Life sciences: **Loans,** 21, **Scholarships,** 147
Literacy programs, **Grants,** 67

Manufacturing: **Scholarships,** 185
Maritime workers: **General Welfare,** 34
Marketing: **Scholarships,** 24
Mathematics: **Grants,** 43, 52-53, **Awards,** 26, **Scholarships,** 19, 29, 142, **Fellowships,** 12, 21, 31-32, 56-58, 65, 67, 73, 78
Mechanical engineers: **Grants,** 51, **Fellowships,** 16, 18, 46
Medical: **Grants,** 40, 99, 138, **Loans,** 14, 17, 19
Medical care: **General Welfare,** 28, 38, 53, 73
Medical information systems: **Grants,** 121
Medical profession, families: **General Welfare,** 43
Medical research: **Fellowships,** 9-10, 19, 43, 50, 55, 59-60, 81, 87-88
Medical students: **Awards,** 16
Medicine: **Fellowships,** 4, 26, 30, 45, 55, 81, 88, **Grants,** 36, **Scholarships,** 3, 7, 31, 44, 46, 137, 164-165
Meteorology: **Scholarships,** 20, 102, 121, 151
Methodist colleges: **Scholarships,** 31
Micrographics: **Grants,** 57, **Scholarships,** 66
Middle East research: **Grants,** 14
Midwifery: **Scholarships,** 13, 97, **Fellowships,** 8
Military families: **General Welfare,** 2, 9, 18, 25, 29, 39-41, 45-49, 59, 63, 71-72, **Loans,** 2, 4-6, 10, 20, 26, **Scholarships,** 32, 45, 52, 73, 79, 117, 122, 143, 160, 178-179
Ministry: **Grants,** 28, 54
Music: **Grants,** 19, **Awards,** 7, 34, **Scholarships,** 30, 89-90, 109

Music education: **Arts & Culture,** 19
Musicians: **Arts & Culture,** 7, 9, 11, 18, 24-25, 28, 33-34, 38, 43, 45, **General Welfare,** 6, 36-37, 56
Musicians, retired: **Arts & Culture,** 6
Muslims: **General Welfare,** 17, **Scholarships,** 49
Mutual Funds: *Page* 383+

National Association of Women Business Advocates: *Page 277+*
National Score Women's Business Ownership Coordinators: *Page 283+*
Native American Indian students: **Scholarships,** 26, 75, 133
Navajo Indians: **Loans,** 120
Navajo veterans: **General Welfare,** 39, 40
Negro students: **Scholarships,** 139
NFL players/family: **General Welfare,** 13, 44
Norwegians: **General Welfare,** 19
Nuclear sciences: **Scholarships,** 56, 108, **Fellowships,** 51, 68
Nurses: **General Welfare,** 51
Nursing: **Grants,** 36, 122, **Scholarships,** 31, 46, 97, 109, **Fellowships,** 20
Nutrition: **Grants,** 72, 128, 135, **Scholarships,** 15, 53, 77, **Fellowships,** 44

Occupational therapy: **Loans,** 11, **Scholarships,** 46
Oceanography: **Scholarships,** 19-20, 151, **Fellowships,** 12, 47
Opera: **Arts & Culture,** 46
Optometry: **Scholarships,** 63
Otosclerosis, **Grants,** 130

Painters: **Arts & Culture,** 7, 20
Paralegal: **Scholarships,** 33
Parapsychology research: **Grants,** 124
Periodical industry: **Grants,** 22
Personal achievement: **Awards,** 23-24, 32
Physical education: **Fellowships,** 38, 63-64
Physical sciences: **Grants,** 52-53, 125, **Fellowships,** 56
Physical therapy: **Scholarships,** 46

Physics: **Grants,** 97, **Scholarships,** 19, **Fellowships,** 12, 31-32, 65, 67
Physicists: **Awards,** 22
Poets: **Arts & Culture,** 40
Political science: **Scholarships,** 94, 101
Postal service families: **Scholarships,** 76
Printmakers: **Arts & Culture,** 20
Professional achievement: **Awards,** 1, 13, 33
Professional career: **Fellowships,** 6, 25
Psychology: **Grants,** 31, 88, **Loans,** 17-19, **Fellowships,** 30
Public power systems: **Scholarships,** 55
Publication: **Arts & Culture,** 4, 35, **Grants,** 103
Publishing industry: **General Welfare,** 7, 36, 74
Pulmonary research: **Grants,** 73

Rabbi training: **Grants,** 33
Railroad employees/families: **General Welfare:** 32, 57
Religious studies: **General Welfare,** 8, 42, **Grants,** 20, 45, 70, 105, **Scholarships,** 11, 27, 54, 60, 95, 107, 114, 126, 138, 164, 175, 192
Research: **Grants,** 4-7, 10, 13, 16, 29-30, 47, 55-56, 62, 64, 66, 68, 72, 90, 92, 94-96, 98, 100-101, 106, 108-109, 114-116, 118-119, 127-128, 130, 132-134, 136, 144, 146-148, 150, 154, 157, **Awards,** 10, **Loans,** 17-18, **Fellowships,** 17, 71, 79, 81, 87
See also Medical research, Research, medical
Research, Atmospheric: **Grants,** 115
Research, cancer: **Grants,** 7-8, 148, *See also Medical research, Research, Research, medical*
Research, cardiovascular: **Grants,** 11, *See also Medical research, Research, Research, medical*
Research, diabetes: **Grants,** 48-49, *See also Medical research, Research, Research, medical*
Research, geological: **Grants,** 26, 78
Research, heart disease: **Grants,** 12, *See also Medical research, Research, Research, medical*
Research, medical: **Grants,** 7-8, 10-11, 20, 23-24, 46, 48-49, 55-56, 69, 74, 81, 107, 110-111, 137-138, 145, 148, 151-152, 158, *See also Medical Research, Research*
Research, Middle East: **Grants,** 13
Research, parapsychology: **Grants,** 124
Research, pulmonary: **Grants,** 73, *See also Medical research, Research, Research, medical*

Research, unemployment: **Grants,** 143
Research & Development: **Business,** 8, 17, 26-27
Retirement Accounts: *Page* 389+
Rural area students: **Scholarships,** 35

Sabbatical support: **Grants,** 31
SBA Demonstration Programs: *Page* 269+
SBA Office of Women's Business Ownership: *Page* 293+
Scholarly achievements: **Awards,** 1-2, 8-9
Science: **Scholarships,** 33, 56, 65
Sciences: **Grants,** 9, 30, 43, 64, 79, 83, 85, 89, 117, 134, 146
Scottish descent: **General Welfare,** 61
Sculptors: **Arts & Culture,** 20, 36, **General Welfare,** 3
Small Business Development Centers: *Page 313+*
Social improvement: **Grants,** 76
Sociology: **Scholarships,** 164, **Fellowships,** 30- 82
Sports: **Grants,** 17, 68, 123, 128, 145, 155, **Scholarships,** 5, 72, 119, 157, 169, 171, 180, 190, **Fellowships,** 38, 64, 86
Sports management: **Fellowships,** 38, 64
Sport psychology: **Fellowships,** 38
Sports trainers: **Grants,** 27
Stock Market/Bond Investments: *Page* 401+

Tax relief, veterans: **General Welfare,** 46, 48-50, 68
Teachers: **Grants,** 87, **General Welfare,** 56, **Awards,** 13
Teaching education: **Grants,** 38, 61, 146, **Scholarships,** 116, 163-164, **Fellowships,** 24-25, 41
Technical career: **Fellowships,** 6
Television/film: **Grants,** 50, 104
Theater: **Arts & Culture,** 27, 52, **Grants,** 44, **Awards,** 27, 31
Transportation field: **Scholarships,** 189

UFCW union member families: **Scholarships,** 129
Unemployment research: **Grants,** 143

Vascular surgery: **Grants,** 95
Venture capital: **Business,** 28

Venture capital clubs/Venture capital funders/SBA: *Page 287+*
Veterans, tax relief: **General Welfare,** 46, 48-50, 68
Veterinary medicine: **Loans,** 17, 19, **Scholarships,** 59
Vision care: **General Welfare,** 53
Vision & sports: **Grants,** 18
Visual artists: **Arts & Culture,** 2, 11, **General Welfare,** 5, 36
Vocal artists: **Arts & Culture,** 43, 46, 51

Writers: **Arts & Culture,** 1, 8, 11-12, 15, 23, 31-32, 50, **General Welfare,** 4, 12, 36, **Awards,** 12, 15, 17, 19, 28-31
Women, Christian: **General Welfare,** 60
Women, discrimination: **General Welfare,** 35
Women, mature: **General Welfare,** 22, 52, **Awards,** 24
Women's projects: **Business,** 3
Women's rights: **General Welfare,** 21, **Grants,** 129
Women's studies: **Grants,** 86, 93, 112-113, 126, 140, 142, 147, 149-154, 156-158

Bibliography

Annual Register of Grant Support: A Directory of Funding Sources. 26th ed. New York: R.R. Bowker Co., 1997

Brunner, Helen, M, ed. *Money to Work II: Funding for Visual Artists.* Washington: Art Resources International, Annual

Carlotta R. Mills, ed. Foundation Grants to Individuals. 8th ed. New York: The Foundation Center, 1997

Catalog of Federal Domestic Assistance. U.S. Office of Management and Budget. Washington: Government Printing Office, Annual

Christensen, Warren. *National Directory of Arts Internships.* Valencia, Ca: California Institute of the Arts, Irregular

Coalition For Women's Economic Development. 1ed. Los Angeles, CA.1994

Directory of Biomedical and Health Care Grants. 8th ed. Phoenix, AZ: Oryx Press, Annual

Directory of Research Grants. Phoenix, AZ, Oryx Press, Annual

Directory of U.S. Micro-enterprise Programs. The Aspen Institute, Washington D.C. Irregular

Federal Register, Part IX, Department of Commerce, Economic Development Administration

Financial Aid: A Partial List of Resources for Women. Washington: Project of the Status and Education of Woman, Association of American Colleges, Irregular

Glossary of Terms Source: *World Almanac and Book of Facts 1997,* K-III Reference Corporation

Stock Market Source: *Microsoft Encarta Encyclopedia 99*

Mutual Funds Source: *Adapted from Mutual Funds – Basics* http://invest-faq.com

Mutual Funds Source: *Adapted from "Norman G. Fosback"* ng-f@MFMAG.COM

The National Directory of Grants and Aid to Individuals in the Arts. International. Des Moines, IA: Arts Letter, 1996

National Endowment for the Arts. International Office. *Guide to Funding Opportunities.* Washington: National Endowment for the Arts, Annual

National Science Foundation. *Research Opportunities for Women.* Washington: National Science Foundation, 1987

Patricia Ayres, *Thanks, But No Banks!,* Women's Economic Development Corporation of California, Los Angeles, CA. 1994

Richards, Gillian, and Peter Burton, eds. *Dramatists Sourcebook: Complete Opportunities for Playwrights, Translators, Composers, Lyricists and Librettists.* New York: Theatre Communications Group, 1994

Schlachter, Gail Ann. *Directory of Financial Aids for Women.* El Dorado Hills, CA: Reference Service Press, 1997-1999

Schlachter, Gail Ann. *How to Find Out about Financial Aid: A Guide to over 700 Directories Listing Scholarships, Fellowships. Loans, Grants, Awards, and Internships.* El Dorado Hills, CA: Reference Service Press, Biennial

Schlachter, Gail Ann, and R. David Weber. *College Student's Guide to Merit and Other No-Need Funding.* El Dorado Hills, CA, Reference Service Press, Biennial

Singson, Karen P., ed. *The Awards Almanac: An International Guide to Career, Research, and Education Funds.* Chicago: St. James Press, 1992

SBA's Micro-loan Demonstration Program. U.S. Small Business Administration, Washington, D.C. Annual

The Small Business Financial Resource Guide Braddock Communications, Inc. Reston, VA, Biennial

The Women's Business Resource Guide, The Resource Group, Eugene, Oregon, Irregular

BOOK DISCLAIMER

The Stress Resource Network, LLC herein provides information on certain resources, references and services. The information contained in this book is for references only. It has been obtained from sources believed to be reliable, but Stress Resource Network, LLC cannot guarantee its total accuracy or completeness.

The information contained herein is provided for informational purposes. Use of subject information is at the risk of the reader without responsibility on the part of the Stress Resource Network, LLC.

ORDER FORM

FAX ORDERS: 925-484-3112
TELEPHONE ORDERS: 925-484-2330
ON-LINE ORDERS: www.stressresource.com
POSTAL ORDERS: Stress Resource Network
699 Peters Avenue
Pleasanton, CA 94566 USA

To order additional copies of *Financial Freedom for Women* complete the information below.

Ship to:

Name: _____

Company Name: _____

Address: _____

City: _____

Telephone: (___) _____

_____ copies @ $19.95 each $ _____
Shipping add $4.00/book, $2.00 each additional book $ _____
California residents add 8.25% tax $ _____

Payment: Check: Make checks payable to: ***Stress Resource Network***
Credit Card: MasterCard _____ Visa _____

Card Number: _____

Name on Card: _____

Expiration Date: _____

Signature of Cardholder: _____